Elizabeth Bowen

Elizabeth Bowen

The Shadow Across the Page

Maud Ellmann

Edinburgh University Press

Frontispiece: Elizabeth Bowen reading. Photography Collection, Harry Ransom Humanities Research Center, The University of Texas at Austin.

© Maud Ellmann, 2003

This paperback edition 2004

Edinburgh University Press Ltd
22 George Square, Edinburgh

Typeset in New Baskerville
by Hewer Text Ltd, Edinburgh, and
printed and bound in Great Britain by
MPG Books Ltd, Bodmin

A CIP record for this book is
available from the British Library

ISBN 0 7486 1703 5 (paperback)

The right of Maud Ellmann
to be identified as author of this work
has been asserted in accordance with
the Copyright, Designs and Patents Act 1988.

Contents

In memory of Mary Ellmann

Acknowledgements

Many friends, colleagues, and students have contributed to the making of this book. In particular I thank Nicholas Royle and Andrew Bennett for introducing me to Bowen and for their inspiring readings of her work. I also thank Isobel Armstrong for proposing that I write this monograph, Ruth Morse and Stefan Collini for their kind encouragement at critical moments, and Anita Sokolsky for her invaluable criticism in the later stages of revision. Deirdre Toomey was generous enough to share with me the fruits of her own original research on Bowen for the *Dictionary of National Biography*. I am also grateful to Jackie Jones at Edinburgh University Press for her assistance throughout the project. A Knopf Fellowship from the Harry Ransom Humanities Research Center at the University of Texas at Austin enabled me to study Bowen's unedited writings. My research on literary modernism, of which this monograph forms a part, has been supported by fellowships from the Guggenheim Foundation and the American Council of Learned Societies, and a research grant from the Arts and Humanities Research Board of the British Academy. I have also benefited from discussing Bowen's writing with Ronald Bush, Derek Attridge, David Trotter, Stephen Tifft, Manuel Barbeito, Christine Froula, Anne Janowitz, Jacqueline Rose, Josephine McDonagh, Gillian Beer, John Kerrigan, Heather Glen, Hermione Lee, Luke Gibbons, Ian Patterson, Jeri Johnson, and Neil Reeve. Most of all I thank my husband John Wilkinson for his astute criticism and tireless encouragement.

Abbreviations

A   *Afterthought: Pieces about Writing* (London: Longmans, Green, 1962).

BC   *Bowen's Court* (1942; reissued in 1964 with revised Afterword); in *Bowen's Court and Seven Winters*, ed. Hermione Lee (London: Virago, 1984).

CI   *Collected Impressions* (London: Longmans, Green, 1950).

CS   *The Collected Stories of Elizabeth Bowen*, intro. Angus Wilson (Harmondsworth: Penguin, 1983).

DH   *The Death of the Heart* (1938; Harmondsworth: Penguin, 1962).

ET   *Eva Trout, or Changing Scenes* (1968; Harmondsworth: Penguin, 1982).

FR   *Friends and Relations* (1931; Harmondsworth: Penguin, 1943).

H   *The Hotel* (1927; Harmondsworth: Penguin, 1943).

HD   *The Heat of the Day* (1949; Harmondsworth: Penguin, 1962).

HP   *The House in Paris*, intro. A. S. Byatt (1935; Harmondsworth: Penguin, 1976).

HRHRC   Harry Ransom Humanities Research Center, University of Texas at Austin.

LG   *The Little Girls* (1964; Harmondsworth: Penguin, 1982).

LS   *The Last September* (1929; Harmondsworth: Penguin, 1942).

MT   *The Mulberry Tree: Writings of Elizabeth Bowen*, ed. Hermione Lee (London: Virago, 1986).

N   *To the North* (1932; Harmondsworth: Penguin, 1945).

PC   *Pictures and Conversations* (London: Allen Lane, 1975).

SE   *The Complete Psychological Works of Sigmund Freud,* Standard Edition, trans. James Strachey, 24 vols (London: Hogarth, 1953–74).

SW   *Seven Winters: Memories of a Dublin Childhood* (1942), in *Bowen's Court and Seven Winters,* ed. Hermione Lee (London: Virago, 1984).

WL   *A World of Love* (1955; Harmondsworth: Penguin, 1983).

Preface

Elizabeth Bowen is one of the finest writers of fiction in English in the twentieth century. She is also one of the strangest. Born in 1899, she was the same age as her century and confronted its major upheavals in her prose. Her historical vision extends from the Irish Troubles of the 1920s, to the growth of international travel between the wars, to the bombardment of London in World War II, to the technological revolution of the postwar years. Generically, her work blends popular and highbrow literary forms, exploiting the resources of the thriller, drawing-room comedy, melodrama, Gothic romance, ghost story, pastiche, prose-poem, and novel of ideas, yet filtering all these through her unmistakable sensibility. Her fiction is always entertaining – funny, moving, and suspenseful – but it is also profoundly disconcerting. While her novels negotiate their public and intimate affairs, they are characterised by an arresting oddness, marked in a prose-style whose reflexivity and material intrusiveness associates her work with the modernist tradition.

In the last ten years or so, Bowen's works have enjoyed an overdue revival, owing to a larger reconsideration of the place of women writers in the map of modern literature. The dominance of Joycean modernism in critical accounts of twentieth-century fiction has overshadowed the achievements of writers such as Bowen, Rebecca West, and Ivy Compton-Burnett, whose writing hovers on the borderline between classic realism and modernist experimentalism. 'Revolutionary in a manner impossible to pin down' (as Bowen said of E. M. Forster), these writers show that literary innovation in the period cannot be confined to the largely masculine story of 'high modernism.'

Thanks to the development of feminist criticism, Irish studies, and reassessments of the cultural impact of World War II, much has recently been gained from re-evaluating Bowen as a woman writer, an Anglo-Irish writer, and a war writer. But her novels and short stories far exceed these classifications. As an anatomist of consciousness she rivals Henry James; as an observer of social mores she rivals E. M. Forster; as a journalist of the sensations she rivals Joyce; as a lyricist of obsession she rivals Patrick Hamilton. Her narratives are as compelling as Graham Greene's, her satires as sharp as Evelyn Waugh's, her sentences as multivalent as Virginia Woolf's. Yet Bowen is stranger than her rivals: ethically, psychologically, stylistically, her fiction constantly takes our categories by surprise.

Elizabeth Bowen: The Shadow Across the Page teases out Bowen's strangeness through close readings informed by psychoanalytic and deconstructive methods of interpretation. Bowen's writing is contextualised in the Irish and modernist traditions to reveal unexpected affinities to Joyce and Beckett, as well as intertextual skirmishes with Woolf, James, Forster, Flaubert, and Proust. Investigated are the motives and methods of Bowen's work; the interplay between her life and her writing; her conflicts and complicities with other Irish, British, and European writers; her negotiations with contemporary history, and with the long decline of the Anglo-Irish Protestant ascendancy; her peculiar take on gender and sexuality; her hallucinatory treatment of objects, particularly furniture and telephones; and the surprising ways in which her writing pre-empts and in some cases confounds the literary theories brought to bear upon it. Most important, this study strives to do justice to a remarkable body of fiction.

Chronology

1899   Elizabeth Dorothea Cole Bowen – only child of Henry Charles Cole Bowen, a barrister of Bowen's Court, Kildorrery, Co. Cork, and Florence Isabella Pomeroy Colley Bowen, daughter of Henry Fitz-George Colley of Mount Temple, Dublin – born in Dublin on 7 June.

1905   Father succumbs to mental illness, diagnosed as 'anaemia of the brain'. Elizabeth develops a marked stammer.

1906   Florence and Elizabeth Bowen move to the Kent coast.

1912   Mother dies of cancer. Elizabeth sent to school at Harpenden Hall, Hertfordshire, where she takes part in the burying ritual recreated in *The Little Girls*.

1914   Elizabeth sent to school at Downe House near Orpington in Kent, formerly the home of Charles Darwin.

1917   Finishes schooling at Downe House.

1918   Works in hospital for shell-shocked veterans of World War I.

1919   Attends the LCC School of Art in Southampton Row, London, for two terms. Begins to write stories.

1921   Henry Bowen marries Mary Gwynn. Elizabeth Bowen briefly engaged to Lieutenant John Anderson, a British officer. Travels to Italy, staying with an aunt in a hotel in Bordighera that inspired the novel *The Hotel.*

1923   Publishes first collection of short stories, *Encounters*. Marries Alan Charles Cameron, then Assistant Secretary for Education for Northamptonshire. Born in 1893, Cameron had been badly gassed during his military service in World War I and had been awarded the MC.

1925   Bowen and Cameron move to Waldencote, Old Headington, Cameron having been appointed Secretary for Education for the city of Oxford.

1926   *Ann Lee's and Other Stories*

1927   *The Hotel* (novel)

1929   *The Last September* (novel); *Joining Charles and Other Stories*

1930   Father dies; Bowen inherits Bowen's Court.

1931   *Friends and Relations* (novel). Meets Goronwy Rees.

1932   *To the North* (novel)

1933   Embarks on affair with Humphry House, who marries Madeline Church.

1934   *The Cat Jumps and Other Stories*

1935   *The House in Paris* (novel). Cameron appointed Secretary to the Central Council for Schools Broadcasting; Cameron and Bowen move to 2 Clarence Terrace, Regent's Park, London, where they remain until the house is bombed around them in 1944.

1936   Humphry House moves with his family to Calcutta. Goronwy Rees, thought to be the model for Eddie in *The Death of the Heart*, falls in love with Rosamond Lehmann at a summer house-party at Bowen's Court.

1937   Embarks on affair with Sean O'Faolain, and brief affair with May Sarton.

1938   *The Death of the Heart* (novel)

1940   Bowen volunteers her services to the Ministry of Information and is commissioned to write confidential reports on neutral Ireland.

1941   *Look at All Those Roses* (short stories). Begins affair with Charles Ritchie, a Canadian diplomat, which develops into life-long friendship.

1942   *Bowen's Court* (family history); *Seven Winters* (autobiography); *English Novelists* (literary criticism)

1945   *The Demon Lover and Other Stories*; published in the United States as *Ivy Gripped the Steps and Other Stories*.

1948   Awarded the CBE.

1949   *The Heat of the Day* (novel). Awarded the honorary degree of Doctor of Letters from Trinity College Dublin. Appointed a member of the Royal Commission on Capital Punishment, which reported in 1953 in favour of abolition. Bowen successfully argued the case that verbal provocation, in addition to physical provocation, should be regarded as grounds for turning murder into manslaughter.

1950   *Collected Impressions* (essays)

1951   *The Shelbourne* (history of the Dublin hotel); published in the United States as *The Shelbourne Hotel.*

1952   Alan Cameron dies on 26 August

1955   *A World of Love* (novel)

1956   Receives honorary degree of Doctor of Letters from Oxford University.

1959   Sells Bowen's Court to a neighbour, Cornelius O'Keefe.

1960   *A Time in Rome* (travel memoir). Bowen's Court demolished.

1962   *Afterthought: Pieces About Writing*

1964   *The Little Girls* (novel)

1965   *A Day in the Dark and Other Stories*; *The Good Tiger* (children's book). Made Companion of Literature by the Royal Society of Literature. Purchases modest house in Hythe and names it Carbery after her mother's ancestral estate.

1968   *Eva Trout, or Changing Scenes* (novel); first British edition 1969.

1973   Dies of lung cancer in University College Hospital, London. Buried in St Colman's churchyard, Farahy, Co. Cork.

1975   *Pictures and Conversations* (autobiography, essays, fragment of a novel called *The Move-In*) published posthumously.

1

Shadowing Elizabeth Bowen

Nothing

Edward and Lou are rushing in an open car through empty country-side, locked in antagonistic silence. The outing from London has not been amusing, and the drive has now begun to last too long: they feel bound up in the tired impotence of a dream. Suddenly a gabled house, sheathed in dazzling roses, flashes past their speeding car. A few minutes later, a ghastly knocking in the car's vitals forces Edward, who is always in a hurry, to a halt. Stranded on the empty road, the lovers walk back to the rose-blistered dwelling in the hope of tele-phoning a garage. As they approach, the house seems to be waiting for them, a trap baited with beauty, its flowers burning bright in the spellbound afternoon. A shabby amazon of a woman answers the door, showing no surprise at their arrival. Since she has neither telephone nor bicycle to lend them, she advises Edward to walk three miles to the nearest village. 'Leave your wife here,' she says.

Lou, who is not his wife and lives in constant dread of losing him, walks deeper into the house. In contrast to the violent gaiety of the rose-garden, the interior looks whitened and gutted, as if by a fire. In a sepulchral parlour Lou feels herself being looked at by a girl of thirteen lying in a wicker invalid carriage. The child, Josephine, explains that her back was injured by her father, Mr Mather, who went away six years ago. Now mother and daughter live in deathly stillness interrupted only by the visits of a mentally defective servant. 'Then aren't you rather . . . alone? – I mean, if anything happened,' Lou wonders. 'Nothing more can happen,' Mrs Mather replies. For a

1

moment, Lou indulges the astounding fancy that Mr Mather lies buried at the roses' roots.

Tea is served, but Lou declines the food: 'She thinks if she eats she may have to stay here for ever,' Josephine comments. Accepting the offer of some roses to take home to London, Lou goes out to cut them, and Josephine is wheeled out in her wicker carriage. On both sides of the garden path hundreds of standard roses bloom, over-charged with colour, as though this were their one hour. To Lou they look like forced roses, magnetised into being: crimson, coral, blue-pink, lemon, and cold white, they disturb with fragrance the dead air. 'Lie down and let's pretend we're both asleep,' Josephine instructs her guest. So Lou lies down beside the invalid carriage, and lets go inch by inch of the life that she has always clutched so desperately. Her obsession about keeping Edward drifts away, and she sinks into an ecstasy of indifference, wanting nothing more than to gaze at the white circle distending underneath her eyelids. Josephine wakes her when a taxi drives up to the house, and Edward jumps out, more hurried than ever. He hustles Lou into the vehicle, her roses abandoned on the garden path, for he has heard alarming rumours in the village about the abrupt disappearance of Mr Mather.

'The apparent choices of art are nothing but addictions, pre-disposi-tions,' Elizabeth Bowen wrote in 1946. 'The aesthetic is nothing but a return to images that will allow nothing to take their place; the aesthetic is nothing but an attempt to disguise and glorify the enforced return.'[1] With the incantatory repetition of the term 'nothing,' this statement performs the 'enforced return' that it describes – for nothing is precisely what returns in Bowen's fiction. In the story summarised above, 'Look at All Those Roses' (1941), nothing takes the form of the deserted landscape, the stupefying stretches of horizon, and the white circle luring the sleeper into living death.[2] Lou is faced with a choice between two nothings: between the ennui of her futureless affair with Edward, and the burning stillness of the Mathers in their pyre of roses. To some extent this is a choice between two sexualities: Bowen's female characters tend to be bewitched by members of their own sex, while officially attached to members of the other. The stiller the siren, the stronger the enchantment: Mrs Kerr in *The Hotel*, Madame Fisher in *The House in Paris*, and Mrs Piggott in *The Little Girls* owe their attraction to their immobility, to 'the magnetism they all exercised by their being static' (*LS* 166). Of 'burning Jose-phine,' Lou thinks: 'People who stay still generate power' (*CS* 519).

This story also demonstrates the way that Bowen's writing leads the reader up the garden path by inviting yet exceeding psychoanalytic scrutiny – for her fictions refuse to be contained within a single frame of reference. From a psychoanalytic perspective, the sorceresses in 'Look at All Those Roses' could be said to represent the lure of the pre-Oedipal attachment to the mother, which in this case has been re-established after the violent intrusion and elimination of the father. It is notable how many fathers are absent, dead, or simply unaccounted for in Bowen's fiction, Mr Mather being one of the unluckiest. Mrs Mather (one vowel away from 'mother') entices Lou away from the patriarchal world of hurry back into the timeless world of the unconscious, where the paralytic Josephine embodies the arrested impulses of infancy. This is a silent world beyond the reach of telephones: 'We are accustomed to quiet,' Mrs Mather says. Edward, on the other hand, represents 'the typewriter, the cocktail-shaker, the telephone . . . the car.' These accoutrements, both phallic and communicational, connect him to a world of other people – in Edward's opinion, 'life without people was absolutely impossible.' Edward, like his author, is a writer, and in the end the writer wins the day, snatching the sleeping princess out of the 'trap baited with beauty' – the trap of symbiosis with the mother (*CS* 512–18). But the story intimates how hard it must have been for Bowen to wrench herself away from the Mathers' maternal world of silence into the world of typewriters and telephones. It is tempting to interpret her lifelong stammer as a symptom of an everlasting struggle between speech and muteness, speed and stasis, words and roses . . .[3]

The pages that follow attempt to shadow some of Bowen's most significant addictions through the cunning passageways of her imagination. Many of these addictions assert themselves in 'Look at All These Roses': the car careering through deserted countryside; the stylish couple going nowhere in a hurry; the womb-like, tomb-like house strangled in voracious vegetation; the absent father; the motionless enchantress; the demonic child; the irresistible attraction of the death drive – these are familiar leitmotifs of Bowen's fiction. The story also typifies its author's penchant for florid clashes between literary forms. The bored couple of the opening scene could be refugees from Evelyn Waugh or Ford Madox Ford, while the mother and daughter of the rose-house are the stuff of fairy tales; when Lou crosses the threshold, in a Pinteresque transition, she steps from modern satire into ancient fable. Other literary echoes resonate: echoes of Christina Rossetti (*Goblin Market*, where those who eat must stay forever, as in the myth of Persephone); echoes of Dickens (the Mathers are reminiscent of Miss Havisham and Estella in *Great Expectations*, cooped up in a sepulchral house and sworn to eternal vengeance against men; while Josephine also resembles Jenny Wren, the crippled doll's dressmaker in *Our Mutual Friend*, who invites visitors to 'come back and be dead'); echoes of Henry James (the house 'burning' with roses harks back to the burning house of Poynton, or to the flowery palazzo in *The Aspern Papers* where the widow and daughter of a famous writer have retreated into suffocating intimacy); echoes of Edith Wharton (the crippled cottagers of *Ethan Frome*, frozen in inter-destructive love); echoes of D. H. Lawrence (the fiery flowers, the vampiric women, the emasculated father).[4] On the Irish side, Sheridan Le Fanu's lesbian vampire story *Carmilla* (1871–2) also lurks behind this story, along with the whole legacy of Irish Gothic.

What is unusual about Bowen's fiction is not so much its richness of association as its frictional disjunctions between modes of writing. Instead of trying to homogenise literary echoes in a seamless whole, Bowen shakes them up like a kaleidoscope (asked on *Desert Island Discs* which object she would take into the wilderness, Bowen chose a kaleidoscope).[5] In 'Look at All Those Roses,' there is no attempt to reconcile the urbanity of social comedy with the dreamscape of the fairy tale: rather, the collision between genres dramatises the resurgence of the infantile impulses of the unconscious in the midst of the complacencies of adult life. In the most quoted passage of her fiction, Bowen writes: 'I swear that each of us keeps, battened down inside himself, a sort of lunatic giant – impossible socially, but full-scale – and that it's the knockings and batterings we sometimes hear in each other that keeps our intercourse from utter banality' (*DH* 310).

This book attempts to listen to these knockings and batterings in Bowen's works, when the lunatic giant lays siege to the edifice of social realism. Yet this is a risky enterprise, for Bowen's fiction is 'a trap baited with beauty,' which constantly outsmarts the interpretative methods brought to bear on it. Bowen's lover Charles Ritchie reports in his diary of 1941 that Bowen was consulting a psychoanalyst about her lifelong stammer. 'So far it seems to me that she has told him nothing while he has told her the story of his life. This hardly surprises me,' Ritchie comments.[6] This anecdote should warn us that in prying into Bowen's secrets we are likely to betray our own. Her fiction interprets its interpreters, shaking our assumptions, undermining our defences, and penetrating deep into the haunted chambers of the mind.

So enticing are these chambers that we are tempted to remain forever, neglecting the outer world of Bowen's fiction in favour of its forays into the interior. But the fact that Edward wins the contest for Lou's soul in 'Look at All Those Roses' should warn us that Bowen ultimately sides with the waking world of realism, as opposed to the hypnotic world of dreams. In a review of Virginia Woolf's *A Writer's Diary* in 1954, Bowen quotes Woolf's exasperation with the 'the narrative business of the realist: getting from lunch to dinner: it is false, unreal, merely conventional. Why admit anything to literature that is not poetry – by which I mean saturated?' (*MT* 179). The difference between Bowen and Woolf is that Bowen relishes the narrative business of the realist, insofar as it releases her from the stifling rose-house of inner life into the world of cars and cocktail-shakers, typewriters and telephones – in short, into the modern world, which claims her attention just as much as the archaic phantoms of the mind. Fascinated by the gadgetry of modernity, Bowen's writing documents the changes to personal and social life wrought by innovations in technology throughout the century. Always mindful of the furniture of life, the objects that hold the subject in position, her imagination also extends beyond such objects to encompass the cataclysms of her times. She once expressed the wish that 'the English kept history in mind more, and that the Irish kept it in mind less,' but Bowen herself was cursed – or blessed – with an Irish sensitivity to history.[7] Her fiction examines how world-historical events penetrate the shadows of private life, transforming the ways that people talk, shop, move, dress, work, love, and kill. Yet in spite of her delight in innovations in high-tech, fashion, commerce, architecture, cinema, sexual arrangements, modes of speech, and tele-communications, Bowen remains aware of the primeval impulses battering at the bastions of modernity. In the context of the twenty-first century, when atavistic fundamentalists are crashing hijacked aeroplanes into skyscrapers, Bowen's sense of the irruption of the primitive within the futuristic shows unnerving prescience.

In Woolf's novels, objects serve as springboards for flights of consciousness – a technique that emphasises the superiority of mind to matter. To put it another way, Woolf treats the object as a grain of sand to be surrounded in a pearl of thought. In Bowen, on the contrary, things behave like thoughts and thoughts like things, thus impugning the supremacy of consciousness. Thoughts are outsiders within, rattling in the empty chambers of the mind, while things are insiders without, phantasmal fugitives from consciousness. Bowen's addiction to personification creates the sense that every object has a psyche; in fact, her objects even have neuroses – every house, for instance, has a watchful face; every car a gamut of anxieties. In 'Look at All Those Roses,' the house '[stares] with no expression,' the roses '[glare] at the strangers,' while the ghastly knocking in the car's vitals seems to 'come from everywhere, and at the same time to be a special attack' on its resented occupants (*CS* 512–14). In a paranoid exaggeration of Merleau-Ponty's theory that the world reciprocates the gaze of the spectator, Bowen's objects scrutinise their own beholders, usually with an evil eye.[8] In T. S. Eliot's 'Burnt Norton,' 'the roses/ Had the look of flowers that are looked at'; but Bowen's roses have the look of flowers that look back in anger at whoever should obey the anonymous imperative to look at them – 'look at all those roses!' In other words, the look is a vortex turning inside-out incessantly. (Incidentally, the Anglo-Irish playwright Sheridan was reputed to have asked his guests into the garden to let his roses have a look at them.)[9]

In a 1949 Preface to a re-edition of her first collection of short stories, *Encounters,* originally published in 1923, Bowen remembers how the room where she worked: 'the convulsive and anxious grating of my chair on the board floor were hyper-significant for me: here were sensuous witnesses to my crossing the margin of a hallucinatory world' (*MT* 118). The objects in her fiction could also be described as substantial witnesses to the crossing of reality into hallucination; often it is unclear whether these objects belong to fact or fantasy. In 'Look at All Those Roses,' are the roses real? Or are they the figments of a dream? If so, this is a dream without a dreamer, for it cannot be imputed to a single consciousness. Unlike dreams, the roses are visible to all – the visitors, the spooky inmates, presumably the village gossips – everyone can 'see' the incandescent vision, but is 'seeing' in this case a matter of absorption or projection, of taking in or casting out? Josephine, 'the nerve and core of the house,' seems to represent the source of the hallucination, the mind that dreams the roses into life: 'they looked like forced roses, magnetized into being. Magnetized, buds uncurled and petals dropped' (*CS* 515–16). Yet if it is the child who forces them to bloom, the other characters are also swept into her nightmare, and it is hard to tell the difference between self and other, mind and matter, perceiver and perceived.

It is this 'perceptual instability,' in Jacqueline Rose's words, that distinguishes Bowen's world from Woolf's, in which the object functions as a passport to the heights of thought.[10] Such sublimation is impossible in Bowen, because the object is too 'over-charged' to be transcended; it hovers on the threshold of hallucination, 'frighteningly bright,' confounding reality with fantasy. In Bowen's fiction, the inner world of consciousness is 'whitened and gutted,' like the inside of the Mathers' house, in order to provide the outer world of objects with its frightening vitality. It is as if the mind succumbs to death-in-life in order to endow the thing with life-in-death. While the object is 'magnetised into being,' it also vampirises being from the magnet; Josephine may force the roses into blooming, but the roses also drain her of her force. Lying 'flat as a board' in the 'long, low and narrow parlour,' she is presented as a corpse in a coffin, her animation having bled into the blossoming shroud (*CS* 514–17). In Woolf, consciousness exists in opposition to the object; in Bowen, consciousness escapes into the object, leaving human beings as vacant as the landscapes that threaten to devour them. While Woolf uses fiction to flesh out her ideas, which could be translated into other idioms, Bowen *thinks in fiction*: her ideas are inseparable from her objects, settings, plots, and characters, and from the oddities of her unnerving syntax. This means that Bowen is a greater novelist than Woolf, though Woolf is arguably a finer prose-poet. It also implies that Bowen's works require close analysis of plot, for their meaning cannot be abstracted from the actions by which it is performed, or from the objects in which it is encrypted. Her stories rarely unfold chronologically, but tend to psychoanalyse themselves, tracing present crises to past causes. Meanwhile her syntax – with its double negatives, inversions, and obliquities; its attribution of the passive mood to human agents, and of the active mood to lifeless objects – constantly ambushes our ontological security.

'Nothing can happen nowhere,' Bowen declares: a resounding double negative that undercuts its own assertion.[11] Her fiction fends off nothing and nowhere with an anxious solicitude for place, hallucinatory in its intensity of focus: 'the Place is *frightfully* important,' she insists. Her characters are products of place, engendered by their habitats like autochthonous births. 'Take *The Death of the Heart*, for instance,' she told an interviewer. 'I saw and knew the Place long before the characters came into my mind.'[12] Action is also determined by its setting – by the houses, furnishings, and knickknacks described with such exactitude that persons, by comparison, seem ill-defined. Roland Barthes has argued that the clutter typical of realist novels, their minute attention to details of décor, serves the purpose of creating a 'reality-effect.'[13] Bowen's objects, however, loom too large for the exigencies of realism – like 'all those roses,' they order us to look at them. If such detail serves to set the scene, it also seems to harbour the capacity to overthrow the stage, as in Guy de Maupassant's story 'Qui Sait?' (1890), in which the furniture stampedes out of the house in the middle of the night, trampling over its flabbergasted owner. Ezra Pound deplored Henry James's 'damn'd fuss about furniture,' but Bowen fusses even more obsessively than James.[14] Yet there is something elegiac in her treatment of objects and appurtenances – this verbal caressing of the stuff of life. Things, in Bowen, offer none of the expected comforts of solidity; they stand, like Freudian fetishes, as monuments to lack and loss. Nothing, by contrast, bears down on her imagined world with a weight more oppressive than materiality.

There are many different kinds of nothingness in Bowen's work, ranging from the ruins of the Irish countryside to the silence of the inarticulate imagination. The next part of this introduction traces Bowen's sense of nothingness back to the self-destruction of her class, the Anglo-Irish Protestant ascendancy – a debacle encapsulated in the short story 'The Back Drawing-Room' (1926). A further section, 'Company,' contrasts Bowen's ideas of nothingness with those of her modernist contemporaries, Eliot, Joyce, and Beckett, showing how her fiction wavers on the boundary between classic realism and modernist experimentalism. Love is the theme of most of Bowen's fiction, but she demystifies the tender passion as remorselessly as Freud. While love between women is presented as dyadic, symbiotic, and wombish to the point of claustrophobia, heterosexual lovers are always haunted by an absent third: 'love's necessary missing part,' as Stella puts it in *The Heat of the Day* (*HD* 320). The third is the nothing that brings couples together but also tears them ruthlessly apart.

After a discussion of Bowen's algebra of love, this introduction ends with a brief account of the author's life, showing how her fiction literally houses her experience. In a course on the short story given at Vassar in 1960, Bowen compares a story to a house: each 'has a structure.'[15] And within the structures of her fiction, house after house rises up on her imaginary landscape, rampant as those housing-estates which Bowen, from her privileged vantage-point, regarded as an eyesore on the British countryside. Her interiors (in the words of her short story 'Human Habitation' (1926)) are 'little guarded squares of light walled in carefully against the hungry darkness, the ultimately all-devouring darkness.'[16] Because of such recurrent images, it has been argued that Bowen's fiction is repetitious, but the present study shows that all her works invoke a different nothingness and build a different kind of dwelling-place to shut it out – or hold it in. What is remarkable is the infinite variety of stories that Bowen fashions out of the limited repertoire of her addictions, much as Beethoven elicits symphonies out of a single phrase, or the Freudian unconscious conjures up a world of dreams out of a few psychic scars. Bowen's moving tribute to Virginia Woolf captures the courage of her own imagination: 'she recognised her own virtue – the untouched ice, the savage intractability of the spirit that must experiment . . . Never once did she do the same thing over again' (*MT* 179).

Back

In *The House in Paris*, Bowen describes relations between the Irish and the English as 'a mixture of showing off and suspicion, nearly as bad as sex' (*HP* 92). This implies that national identity is a performance, rather than a birthright or a native attribute. While Simone de Beauvoir famously observed that a woman is not born but made, Bowen implies that a country is not born but overacted.[17] The Irish and the English – intimate as lovers, bound up for centuries in one another's fate – can disentangle their identities only by playing up their national stereotypes. What goes for country also goes for country matters: Bowen's witticism hints that there is always an element of trumpery in sex, of masquerade in masculinity and femininity.

Bowen's background gave her ample cause for scepticism about national identity. Born in Dublin in 1899 into the Anglo-Irish Protestant ascendancy, she lived in Ireland for only seven years before she was transplanted with her mother to Kent, her father having suffered a nervous breakdown. From this point onwards Bowen was to travel back and forth throughout her life from England to Ireland, both in fact and in her fictional imagination. Her novels and short stories zigzag between the islands, stopping off at all her favourite haunts: at County Cork, where generations of her family lived at Bowen's Court; at the Kent coast, where she spent the latter portion of her childhood; and at London, where she lived at Regent's Park through World War II, finding inspiration for some of her greatest fiction in the 'extraordinary battle in the sky' (*HD* 96).

9

Sean O'Faolain, Bowen's sometime lover and perhaps her shrewdest critic, described her as 'heart-cloven and split-minded' with regard to her two nations. Another friend remembered her as 'Irish in England and English in Ireland.'[18] When challenged, Bowen insisted on her standing as an Irish writer, yet she credited England with making her a novelist, the Irish genius having flourished in the theatre.[19] Her loyalty to England strengthened during the war years, when she worked as an Air Raid Precautions (ARP) warden in London and revelled in the fellow-feeling of a city under siege, so different from the 'cut-off' life of the Protestant ascendancy in Ireland (*BC* 126). Yet in the same period she defended the Irish policy of neutrality as ardently as she supported the British war effort. Victoria Glendinning, Bowen's biographer, notes that 'Elizabeth contradicted herself continually,' and it is evident that Bowen's contradictory relationship to her two nations was never resolved. In old age, she is reported to have snapped, with a vehemence that startled her friends: 'I *hate* Ireland.'[20]

Ireland has also shown split-mindedness towards Elizabeth Bowen. The Aubane Historical Society's *North Cork Anthology* (1993) features in its table of contents the full name Elizabeth Dorothea Cole Bowen CBE, but crosses it out, with the explanation that Bowen was an English writer illegitimately lodged in County Cork: 'We include her in this anthology, in deleted form, in order to explain why she does not belong to it.'[21] Maniacal though it is, this editorial manoeuvre demonstrates the paradoxical position of the Anglo-Irish, ensconced in a country to which they could never belong. In this sense the Anglo-Irish could be said to exist 'under erasure,' which is Derrida's term for the uncanny afterlife of that which is crossed out. The sense of homelessness so prevalent in Bowen's fiction derives at least in part from the predicament of the Anglo-Irish, an alien enclave marooned in its own home. Eva Trout could be speaking for the Anglo-Irish when she says, 'Anywhere would seem strange to me that did not' (*ET* 59).

Although generalisations about national temperament are always risky, Bowen's dividedness finds numerous precedents among the Anglo-Irish people. Historian of Anglo-Irish civilisation J. C. Beckett claims that the 'most pervasive Anglo-Irish quality is a kind of ambivalence, or ambiguity of outlook, arising from the need to be at once Irish and English, and leading sometimes to detachment, sometimes to a fierce aggressiveness that may, on occasion, mark an underlying sense of insecurity.'[22] Whatever its origins, ambivalence ignited Bowen's creativity, producing her art 'out of dualities.'[23] Like Yeats, another Anglo-Irish Protestant, who claimed that 'conscious-ness is conflict' and attributed his art to the struggle between self and anti-self, Bowen believed that conflict galvanised her fiction.[24] In an open letter to Graham Greene, published in 1948, Bowen wrote: 'I do think conflict essential – conflict in the self (a never quite dislodge-able something to push against), and an if anything hyper-acute sense of every kind of conflict, and every phase of any kind of conflict, in society' (*MT* 228). Bowen's novels and short stories stage conflicts between the Irish and the English, the innocent and the experienced, the silent and the eloquent, the living and the dead. Her characters are torn between the torpor of domestic life and the death-dealing power of desire.

Behind these personal conflicts loom the global struggles of her war-torn lifetime. Like Stella Rodney in *The Heat of the Day*, Bowen was the same age as her century and participated in its 'clear-sightedly helpless progress towards disaster' (*HD* 134). She lived through two World Wars, as well as through the Civil War in Ireland, and died in 1973, during the ignominious finale of the war in Vietnam. (Bowen, a staunch conservative who regarded the United States as a great nation, hated to see its pundits 'whining' about Vietnam.)[25] In view of her experience, it is not surprising that Bowen regarded war 'more as a territory than as a page of history,' a condition of existence rather than a singular event.[26] 'I can't imagine myself without a war,' declares the narrator of her unpublished radio play of 1949.[27] Gertrude Stein, her near contemporary, commented with chilling faux-naivety: 'there is always war, and sometimes a nice war, and sometimes an interesting war.'[28] From Bowen's point of view, the most interesting war took place in 1939–45; she later wrote: 'I would not have missed being in London throughout the war for anything: it was the most interesting period of my life.'[29] But the persistent warfare of her native Ireland also left its imprint on her imagination. In her family history *Bowen's Court*, itself composed in London during World War II, Bowen comments: 'perhaps one does not say of Ireland that war began again, but that war resumed' (*BC* 437).

But conflict is more than just a theme in Bowen's fiction: it insinuates itself into the very structure of her sentences, which often seem to be contending with an unseen obstacle, 'a never quite dislodgeable something to push against.' The resulting contortions have been criticised even by Bowen's admirers, and prompted Virginia Woolf to quip: 'I feel you're like somebody trying to throw a lasso with a knotted rope.'[30] Frequently accused of imitating Henry James, whose syntax she admitted to finding infectious – 'like a rash' – Bowen achieves a knottedness distinct from his, a style that dramatises, in her own peculiar way, the intolerable wrestle with words and meanings.[31] Her contemporary Samuel Beckett, also Anglo-Irish by descent, described the modern artist's plight as one of having 'nothing with which to express, nothing from which to express, no power to express, no desire to express, together with the obligation to express.'[32] Bowen also seems to feel obliged to express the resistance of nothing to expression. Yet to express nothing is to coerce it into language, and Bowen's twisted sentences (like the stammer she developed in reaction to her father's breakdown) suggest a sense of guilt about the act of writing as a violation of the inarticulate. In 'Look at All Those Roses,' this conflict takes the form of a tug-of-war for Lou's allegiance, battled out between the writer and the women of the silent rose-house. Nothingness beckons from without and from within: outside lies the empty landscape, which seems to have devoured its inhabitants ('there was nobody on the roads; perhaps there was nobody anywhere . . .'); inside lies the 'white circle,' sucking memory and thought out of the mind ('she was looking at nothing – then knew nothing . . .') (*CS* 513, 519).

To the stranded travellers in Bowen's fiction, houses seem to offer refuge from nothingness, but these houses often turn out to be mausoleums. Take the early short story 'The Back Drawing-Room' (1926), which opens with a gathering, reminiscent of the Dublin Hermetic Society, where the guests are debating the question of survival after death. Is survival a matter of 'fitness' or 'tenacity'?

Underneath their pompous talk, the men are competing for the admiration of their hostess, Mrs Henneker, whose charisma unites the fractious company: 'She swept a glance round them smilingly, to glean up any wandering attention.' We view the scene from the perspective of Mrs Henneker's most ardent admirer, a girl called Lois who, like many of her sisters in Bowen's fiction (including her namesake Lois Farquar of *The Last September*), is infatuated with an older woman. In a remarkably suggestive gesture, Lois secretly fingers a fold of Mrs Henneker's dress. All of a sudden, a little man whom no one seems to know, 'propped up . . . like an umbrella that an absent-minded caller has brought into the drawing-room,' interrupts the high-minded discussion to spin a yarn about his own encounter with a ghost.

He tells the company that he was cycling in Ireland when he

punctured his back tyre and found himself stranded in deserted countryside. 'To increase my embarrassment, the sky was growing perceptibly darker, and I had that uncomfortable feeling of being overtaken and closed in upon': a feeling shared by most of Bowen's homeless wanderers, and often by her readers too. After walking some distance, the little man reached the boundary of a 'gentleman's demesne,' whose gates stood wide open 'with an expression of real Irish hospitality.' Passing a barred and shuttered lodge, he approached an Anglo-Irish Big House, encircled in dense trees. Its front door stood ajar, and only the faint 'ping pong' of tennis balls disturbed the silence. No one replied to his knock, but at the end of the dim hall a door swung open, revealing the silhouette of a pretty woman. Without speaking, she turned and walked deeper into the house, leaving the door open behind her. The story-teller followed her into a back drawing-room – 'really quite an intimate room' – where he heard her sobbing piteously on the sofa. When he tried to speak some words of comfort, she lifted her unseeing eyes with the desperate expression of a drowning soul. Aghast, the little man rushed down the steps, 'simply not caring if they did think I was a burglar or a Republican, and fired at me from the bushes.' Hurrying back to his anxious relatives, he recounted his adventures to his cousin, who insisted that the house in question had been burned down by rebels two years previously. Although speaking of the former owners as if they were dead, his cousin's wife unexpectedly revealed that they had merely moved away. 'Well, how can one feel they're alive?' she explained. 'How can they be, any more than plants one's pulled up? They've nothing to grow in, or hold on to' (*CS* 199–210).

In Toni Morrison's *Beloved*, Sethe the heroine reflects:

> If a house burns down, it's gone, but the place – the picture of it – stays, and not just in my rememory, but out there, in the world . . . Someday you be walking down the road and you hear something or see something going on. So clear. And you think it's you thinking it up. A thought picture. But no. It's when you bump into a rememory that belongs to somebody else . . . The picture is still there and what's more, if you go there – you who never was there – if you go there and stand in the place where it was, it will happen again; it will be there for you, waiting for you.[33]

In 'The Back Drawing-Room,' the story-teller also bumps into a rememory that belongs to someone else. Seduced into the spectral mansion, he finds himself dreaming someone else's dream, rehearsing someone else's unpropitiated memory. For the tearful ghost does not belong to his unconscious, nor has she risen from the grave – the woman that she shadows forth is still alive. It is characteristic of Bowen's fiction that the narration zeroes in on liminal spaces: as the stranger approaches the house, one door opens after another, and as he penetrates each aperture he also crosses boundaries between self and other, hallucination and reality, the living and the dead. At the same time the boundary blurs between the telling and the tale, for this is a story-within-a-story, but like the play-within-the-play in *Hamlet*, it sets a mousetrap for the audience in that they find themselves recast into its roles. This is most striking when the little man concludes his narrative and Mrs Henneker remains in silence, 'petulantly blind' to the gesticulating story-teller, her blindness mirroring the sightless phantom weeping in the burnt-out house (*CS* 210).

In both the inner and the outer story, the story-teller takes the part of the intruder, barging into the esoteric conversation with a vulgar ghost story, much as he invaded the stately mansion in his dusty knickerbockers. The odd man out, he is odd in the sense of being strange (though this is mitigated by his constant recourse to cliché, especially his egregiously conventional remarks about the unconventionality of Irish people), but also in the sense of being singular, extraneous, and supplementary, like an odd shoe or an odd woman. In his case, survival is a matter of unfitness or not-fitting-in: one gets the feeling he could pop up wherever he is out of place. In an open letter to V. S. Pritchett, Bowen reflects that 'one emotional reason why one may write is the need to work off, out of the system, the sense of being solitary and farouche . . . My writing, I am prepared to think, may be a substitute for something I have been born without – a so-called normal relation to society. My books *are* my relation to society.'[34] Similarly solitary and farouche, the nameless raconteur in 'The Back Drawing-Room' creates a brief relation to society by telling stories. When he interrupts the seminar with the words 'Ah, ghosts!' everyone turns round in surprise, 'as though the umbrella had spoken.' In this portrait of the artist as a misplaced umbrella, Bowen suggests that the fiction-maker is an outsider within, an odd number queering the seating-plan of the community. For an umbrella also brings the outside into the interior, while promising protection from the 'heavy rain' that threatens to wipe out Bowen's world (*CS* 202–5). Is Bowen hinting that a story serves as an umbrella in a storm? If so, it offers little shelter from the deluge.

Like umbrellas, houses promise shelter from the 'hungry darkness, the ultimately all-devouring darkness.' But Bowen's houses often

incarcerate a darkness more malignant than the shadows that obliterate the outer world. Once across their thresholds, travellers are
lured into a catacomb, where every room leads into a deeper
dungeon, like Poe's crypts within crypts. In the innermost chamber
waits an undead woman. In 'The Back Drawing-Room,' it is important
that this woman belongs to the obsolescent Protestant ascendancy,
for Bowen regarded the Anglo-Irish as living ghosts. Endorsing a
common conservative position, she argued that the Anglo-Irish
signed their own death-warrant with the Act of Union of 1800: this
was the sell-out that condemned her people to their irresistible
'descendancy.' In this sense the Anglo-Irish died before their mansions were burnt down, haunting their ancestors' crumbling de-
mesnes, their culture frozen in the state that Yeats describes as
'death-in-life and life-in-death.'[35] Their civilisation now defunct,
the Anglo-Irish have nothing left to do but tell their story, and
Bowen's writings rank among the finest achievements of that voluble
afterlife. The final words of Beckett's *The Unnamable* could be understood as an epitaph to the ascendancy: 'I can't go on, I'll go on.'[36]

Company

Bowen's preoccupation with nothingness suggests an affinity to
modernists like Eliot, with his nightmare of the urban waste land;
or Beckett, with his vision of the long declension into nullity; or Joyce,
with his image of the world suspended in the void.[37] But Bowen's
waste land differs from those imagined by her modernist contemporaries. It originates in the Anglo-Irish landscape of her childhood,
where 'emptiness' was the prevailing impression of the countryside
surrounding her ancestral mansion Bowen's Court. Here 'history
evaporates': in this 'country of ruins,' abandoned dwellings, grappled
by ivy and corroded by storms, vanish rapidly into the earth, their
human stories blotted out.[38] In modernist writing, nothingness
usually implies the death of God, but Bowen remained a church-
going conservative throughout her life, who honoured the traditions
of her withering class. As she said of the landed aristocracy in
Chekhov's work, hers was a 'class which fosters its own annihilation,
and which revolution cannot obliterate.'[39] Even her lordly unconventionality in matters of the heart (*The Guardian* recently sensatio-
nalised her as a 'serial adulteress') testifies to her aristocratic
heritage.

The major modernists of Bowen's era were reactionaries of a

different order. Eliot became a Royalist in politics, an Anglo-Catholic in religion, and a Classicist in art to rebel against his family's liberalism in these matters. Joyce, Pound, and Beckett also asserted their modernity by severing their links with family, nation, and religion, while repudiating their Victorian precursors. Bowen, on the contrary, never ceased to identify herself with the history of her family and their so-called 'race.' Her conservatism, like her Christianity, stemmed from deeper sources than the modernists' and required no fanfare to sustain itself; it was immune to fanaticism of all kinds, including the siren-song of fascism. As Bowen grew older, the godlessness of younger people disconcerted her – she found atheism 'claustrophobic' – but her own religion, rooted in the central humanist tradition of European culture, was a matter of civility rather than evangelism.[40] Recalling the pieties of Catholic neighbours in her childhood, she remarked that a 'predisposition to frequent prayer bespoke, to me, some incontinence of the soul' (*SW* 48). Her lifelong allegiance to the Tory party she attributed to her early reading of *The Scarlet Pimpernel*, her 'first view of a reign of terror,' which confirmed her abhorrence of the French Revolution and its legacy.[41] This charming aetiology is scarcely credible – in reality, her conservatism reflected the historical class-interests of the doomed ascendancy.

As a writer Bowen avoided movements and manifestos. Although her work reveals the influence of her contemporaries, notably Iris Murdoch, Ford Madox Ford, Henry Green, E. M. Forster, Graham Greene, Virginia Woolf, Ivy Compton-Burnett, and Rosamond Lehmann, many of whom she counted among her friends, Bowen never boarded any bandwagons. For this reason, her fiction has tended to elude the standard taxonomies of modern writing. Too conservative for modernism, too idiosyncratic for traditionalism, her novels, as she said of E. M. Forster's, are 'revolutionary in a manner impossible to pin down.'[42] Nor can her peculiarities be attributed merely to her Anglo-Irishness: her models, by her own account, were Austen, Flaubert, James, and Proust. Asked on the radio programme *Desert Island Discs* which book she could not do without, Bowen chose *Emma*.[43] Only two of her ten novels are set in Ireland. This is not to deny that Irish writers, such as Sheridan Le Fanu and Somerville and Ross, also made their mark on her imagination. To be schematic, her English models steered her towards the front drawing-room, while her Irish models lured her towards the back. 'Back' for Bowen (as for Henry Green in his 1946 novel *Back* about a mutilated veteran's return from World War II) has both a spatial and a temporal dimension. In 'The Back Drawing-Room,' to go back into the inner-most recesses of the house is to go back into the depths of time, where the spectres of the past come back to haunt the living. It is also to go back to Ireland and Irish Gothic. Yet the Irish literary revival completely passed Bowen by, although her family lived for seven winters in spitting distance of the Abbey Theatre. Elizabeth heard of the revival only in 1916, when she was a teenager at school in England.

It is partly because Bowen's fiction resists categorisation that it has been neglected in academic criticism, although the recent publication of some major critical studies, along with the reissue of her works in paperback, indicates the tide has turned. The most important influence on the present study is Andrew Bennett and Nicholas Royle's *Elizabeth Bowen and the Dissolution of the Novel* (1995), with its skilful deployment of the psychoanalytic theories of Nicolas Abraham and Maria Torok, its emphasis on refused or impossible mourning, unspeakable secrets, and transgenerational haunting, and its audacious interpretations of Bowen's works.[44] Apart from Bennett and Royle, few critics have made use of the psychoanalytic and deconstructive methods that her writing so uncannily premeditates, although there are notable exceptions, especially the groundbreaking work of feminist critics such as Harriet Chessman and Patricia Coughlan, and John Hildebidle's masterly anatomy of Bowen's fictional obsessions.[45] The most fecund area of Bowen scholarship at present focuses on her writings of World War II, and belongs to a wider reconsideration of the cultural implications of the Blitz: here Heather Bryant Jordan, Adam Piette, Roy Foster, Gill Plain, and Karen Schneider have made particularly valuable contributions.[46] Foster, along with critics such as W. J. McCormack, Seamus Deane, Declan Kiberd, and Claire Connolly, has attempted to reintegrate Bowen's writings into a distinctively Irish tradition, counteracting the parochial attempts of the Aubane Historical Society to cross her out.[47] Meanwhile John Coates's insistence on the ethical dimension of Bowen's work represents a powerful reproof against the growing tendency to treat her writings as poststructuralist *avant la lettre*.[48]

Writers' reputations thrive on such controversies. In Bowen's case, however, critical debate has only recently revived after decades of neglect when she was relegated to the ghostly ranks of unread women writers. In the 1940s Bowen was regarded as a rival to Virginia Woolf, but by the 1980s she was virtually forgotten, especially in academia where her works were sidelined, rarely featuring in syllabi of modern literature. Outside the universities, her books have remained in print, but their popularity has only helped to ensure their exclusion from English departments, where they have often been dismissed (astoundingly!) as middlebrow. Unlike Joyce, Bowen declared no ambition to keep the professors busy for centuries unearthing the recondite allusions in her works. On the contrary she said it would be 'sad to regard as lecture-room subjects books that were meant to be part of life.'[49] Yet in addition to nine novels and dozens of short stories, many of them masterpieces of their respective forms, Bowen produced books, essays, prefaces, introductions, reviews, and broadcasts on a wide range of subjects, including literary criticism, Anglo-Irish cultural history, autobiography, social commentary, and travel. It is largely thanks to feminist scholarship, with its determination to recover lost and undervalued women writers, that Bowen's works are now enjoying an overdue revival. As a mark of this sea-change, Hermione Lee's foundational work, *Elizabeth Bowen: An Estimation*, first published in 1981, goes to considerable efforts in the introduction to justify a single-author study of a writer generally consigned to the passé. By contrast the second edition, published by Vintage in 1999, opens with the resounding declaration: 'Elizabeth Bowen is one of the greatest writers of fiction in this language and in this century.'[50]

Bowen herself, it should be noted, was no feminist. In 1936 she declared that while 'a good deal remains to be righted . . . broadly, the woman's movement has accomplished itself': a view that now seems comically short-sighted, particularly given its insensitivity to ethnic and economic inequalities. A female office-cleaner battling for equal pay might be less convinced than Bowen, heiress to a large (if penurious) estate in County Cork, that feminism had fulfilled its historic mission. Yet Bowen reiterated in 1961: 'I am not, and shall never be, a feminist.'[51] Virginia Woolf's feminism mystified her. From whence came this obsession, Bowen wondered, 'that women were being martyrized humanly, inhibited creatively, by the stupidities of a man-made world? . . . it was a bleak quality, an aggressive streak, which cannot but irritate, disconcert, the adorer of Virginia Woolf the artist.' On the contrary, it is judgements like these that irritate and disconcert the adorer of Elizabeth Bowen. However, Bowen went on to modify this pronouncement with a canny insight into Woolf's self-contradictions: 'Frustrated intellectual women took up, in person, little of [Woolf's] time: in person . . . they would have afflicted, bored her. Yet, she burned for their sorrows without rest.'[52] Since Bowen contradicted herself as readily as Woolf, the fact that she owes her growing fame to the feminist movement she pronounced defunct might have appealed to her consummate sense of irony.

Bowen's style also resists categorisation. In *The Death of the Heart* the novelist St Quentin remarks, 'Style is the thing that's always a bit phony, and at the same time you cannot write without style' (*DH* 11). Self-conscious stylist though she is, Bowen rarely allows style to upstage plot or character, as Joyce does with his polyphonic styles in *Ulysses*. Instead she disciplines the style to the story, but the tension thus created lends a special fascination to her prose, producing those electric passages where style breaks free from the constraints of action and revels in its fleeting independence. As Mary Ellmann says of Bowen's syntax, 'At moments, the intussusception of multiple phrases and clauses has an almost pathological effect. One loses hope of the sentence's recovery – how can it ever possibly, in this condition, deliver its content to a period?'[53] Yet even at these intussusceptive moments, Bowen's writing seldom baffles us, as Joyce's does, by forcing us to question who is speaking when or where. In spite of flashbacks and other disruptions of chronology, her novels and short stories resolve themselves into coherent narratives, often concerned with the vintage theme of the harsh awakenings of youth. Many of her heroines are adolescent girls, benighted and misjudged, embarking on adulthood untutored in its protocols, yet toxic in their very innocence. As Graham Greene writes in *The Quiet American*, 'Innocence always calls mutely for protection, when we would be so much wiser to guard ourselves against it; innocence is like a dumb leper who has lost his bell, wandering the world meaning no harm.'[54] The innocent and the experienced speak two different languages in Bowen's work, each prone to violent misinterpretations of the other.

Bowen's innocents are often orphans, like the protagonists of many nineteenth-century novels, but even her mature heroines tend to be divorced or otherwise detached from family life. Isolated and disoriented in a world of 'broken surfaces, perceptions, accidents,' they nonetheless avoid the depths of alienation envisaged in the works of Bowen's modernist contemporaries. There is no place in Bowen's world for a character like the Unnamable – if Beckett's limbless, urn-imprisoned talking head can seriously be called a 'character' at all.[55] At least until her final novel, *Eva Trout*, Bowen's characters conform to the principles of realism: if anything, their eccentricities reveal the strangeness of the ordinary, the unpredictability of the familiar. Had she been given to programmatic statements, Bowen might have concurred with Gertrude Stein that the abnormal is too obvious, whereas 'the *normal* is so much more simply complicated and interesting.'[56]

Bowen also differs from the modernists in that she resurrects the omniscient narrator of the classic realist tradition. In most of her novels, she tacitly rejects the notion that the novelist should show, not tell. On the contrary, her voice-over – witty, trenchant, uncannily clairvoyant – is sometimes the most memorable aspect of her fiction. Although she admired Flaubert's ideal 'book about nothing that should stay itself on itself by the inner force of its style,' her own fiction has an ethical, not merely an aesthetic, message to convey.[57] That message is encapsulated in *The Death of the Heart*: 'Not only is there no question of solitude, but in the long run we may not choose our company' (*DH* 170). Responsibility for the other is the law of our existence; whether we embrace this law or not, our lives are shaped by its imperative. Nor do we choose the objects of our care; they are cast upon us by the flood of life. Bowen deplored the 'dire period of Personal Life,' originating in the Enlightenment, which entrenched itself in the nineteenth century and still retains its stranglehold on modern consciousness (*BC* 259). Her own morality is stringently impersonal – nothing could be more repugnant to it than the vogue for self-discovery today. Bowen's characters do not 'find themselves': if they discover anything, it is that they cannot live without company, and that they cannot choose the company they keep. As it happens, *Company* is the title of a prose-work by Beckett, first published in Britain in 1980, in which an unidentified being lying in the dark hears an unlocatable voice summoning him to identify as his own the life he is being told about. In subtler ways, the existence of Bowen's characters depends upon a call or solicitation from the other.

However, much of what has just been said applies only to the first half of Bowen's career, which culminated with *The Death of the Heart* (1938), regarded by many as her masterpiece. This is the last great novel based on the struggle of 'the kid and the cad' – in Sean O'Faolain's catchy formula – the fatal passion of the child-woman for the bounder.[58] In this novel Bowen also perfected her voice-over; never again would her narrator be all-seeing or all-knowing. In her next full-length novel, *The Heat of the Day*, published in 1949 and set in war-torn London, the narrative perspective is emphatically partial rather than omniscient. At this point in history, 'there were too many theatres of war' for the world to be apprehended as a whole (*HD* 308). Bowen's two subsequent novels return to the vistas of her childhood, *A World of Love* to County Cork and *The Little Girls* to the Kentish coast. Their theme is mourning, and one of the things they are in mourning for is the kind of novel Bowen will never write again: the novel with an outside and an inside, with an external narrator and an internal psychology of character. In her final and perhaps her greatest novel Bowen veers off in a new direction: *Eva Trout* is concerned with the perils and responsibilities of fiction-making. With its disjointed narrative and playful self-reflexiveness, this novel both anticipates postmodernism and diagnoses its deficiencies. Eva Trout, a fish out of water in the social world, cannot find a home in language and retreats into a world of moving pictures, embracing the postmodernist belief that reality is nothing but a play of surfaces. In the end, however, a gunshot penetrates this celluloid mirage, affirming the existence of interiority at the very moment of destroying it.

Loving

'Elizabeth has been telling me how she goes about writing a novel,' Charles Ritchie records in a diary entry of 4 December 1941. The work in question was *The Death of the Heart*: Ritchie speculates that the two heroines of this novel represent 'the two halves of Elizabeth. – Portia has the naïveté of childhood – or genius. She is the hidden Elizabeth. The other woman is Elizabeth as an outside hostile person might see her. But all this is my own surmise and not what she told me.'[59] This acute insight extends to other paired heroines in Bowen's work, where the younger tends to be unformed and inarticulate, the older stylish and eloquent.[60] The relation between Lois and Mrs Henneker in 'The Back Drawing-Room' prefigures this polarity, which is fully fleshed out in the forms of Eva and Iseult in *Eva Trout*, Emmeline and Cecilia in *To the North*, Portia and Anna in *The Death of the Heart*, and Louie and Stella in *The Heat of the Day*. In these intense relations between women, men often recede from view, either disappearing in a puff of mystery, like Mr Mather; or limping to their own destruction, like Robert Kelway in *The Heat of the Day*; or sneaking off with a Scandinavian au pair, like Eric Arble in *Eva Trout*. In most of Bowen's fiction, the 'hated love' that binds paired women to each other is stronger than their formal attachment to the other sex: in 'Look at All Those Roses,' for example, we have the feeling that Lou would never leave the house of women if Edward did not drag her out.[61]

When men and women fall in love, as they do momentously in *To the North* and *The House in Paris*, the results are generally catastrophic. Sean O'Faolain remarks that Bowen, 'like the singer who was supposed to be able to break a champagne glass by singing at it, exposes the brittleness of romance by soliciting it ruthlessly . . .'[62] In her critical work *English Novelists*, Bowen argues that the principle of love as a 'rational passion,' compatible with domestic happiness, has constricted the English novel since the eighteenth century. Only the European novelists have faced up to 'love's inherent principles of disorder and pain.'[63] If this is so, then Bowen's own artistic sympathies are distinctly European, for she conceives of love as 'a very high kind of overruling disorder' (*FR* 104). While her lovers often meet by chance, they love by fate. Some discover they have always been in love but failed to recognise the object of desire (as Jane Austen's Emma is surprised by the sudden realisation of her lifelong love for Mr Knightley). Others are waiting for a love-object to 'bomb' the ice out of their hearts, so that they can immolate themselves in fire.[64] In *Friends and Relations* and *The House in Paris*, lovers are ambushed by their own long-standing passion; in *To the North*, a fortuitous encounter with an *homme fatal* awakens Emmeline's apocalyptic passion. Yet whether lovers are acquaintances or strangers, desire always 'precedes its object,' erupting après coup like lava from a smouldering volcano.[65] Love has no beginning, but it has an indeflectible compulsion for the end.

While passion between women tends to be associated with the claustrophobia of the interior, love between men and women has nowhere to go, either literally or metaphorically – their love is associated with the agoraphobia of the exterior. Often driving, always driven, Bowen's heterosexual lovers are 'perpetually in transit,' searching without rest for a place to be alone together (*MT* 286). In the famous wartime story, 'Mysterious Kôr' (1944), named after the great ruined city of Rider Haggard's *She*, the lovers wander through the moonscape of London – 'shallow, cratered, extinct' – in order to delay the hour when they have to sleep in separate rooms (*CS* 728). Similarly, Edward and Janet, the would-be adulterers in *Friends and Relations*, come to the shattering realisation that 'their love was homeless' (*FR* 145). It is the presence of a third, or even a fourth person, that drives these lovers out into the cold.

There is a Japanese folk-tale in which a young man, travelling through a forest, catches sight of a beautiful young woman gazing at her image in a pool. When he calls to her, she turns her head but her face is white and smooth and featureless as the shell of an egg. There is something correspondingly uncanny about Bowen's lovers: when we solicit them, we find they have no faces, no singularities to rescue them from their hypnotic subservience to fate. With her antipathy to 'Personal Life,' Bowen has little interest in delineating quirks of personality. Her men and women resemble Ivy Compton-Burnett's, or those of the later works of Henry James, in that their fate depends on the 'emotional set-up,' as opposed to their intrinsic attributes. She creates men and women 'without qualities' who operate as constellations rather than as independent agents. Bowen told an interviewer in 1942: 'The idea for a book usually comes to me in the shape of an abstract pattern. Then the job is to construct characters to fit the situation.'[66]

This 'abstract pattern,' usually a triangle or quadrangle, generates the force-field that Bowen's men and women experience as love. While love between women tends to be depicted as dyadic, like the Mathers in their rosy sepulchre, love between men and women is envisaged as triangular, quadrangular, pentangular, hexangular, and even – in one memorable instance – septangular. This means that heterosexual love involves at least three people, or more precisely, three positions – to call them 'people' is to misrepresent the inhuman logistics of desire in these texts, whereby persons are reduced to place-holders or algebraic variables. In Bowen's computations, it takes three to make two: the heterosexual couple is both united and divided by a secret sharer. One of Bowen's earliest short stories, 'The Shadowy Third' (1923), discussed in detail in Chapter 3, concerns the haunting of a married couple by the man's dead wife, who asserts her presence in the fissures opened up by her successor's alterations to the furniture.[67] Shadowy thirds, fourths, and fifths pop up repeatedly in Bowen's writing. 'The Confidante' (1923) presents a quadrangular relationship, comparable to the double couples in James's *The Golden Bowl*.[68] In Bowen's story, Veronica is officially engaged to Victor, but secretly involved in an affair with Maurice. Penelope, the confidante of both Veronica and Maurice, suddenly casts off the role of sexless intermediary (like the telegraph operator in James's novella 'In the Cage' (1898)), and reveals that she has been enjoying an affair with the aptly-named Victor all along. The flabbergasted cheaters, instead of rejoicing in their new-found freedom, discover that they cannot thrive without the shadow of the injured third. The abrupt departure of their confidante leaves 'a gap . . . unbridgeable for both . . . She had upset their bowl and left the two poor goldfish gasping in an inclement air' (*CS* 39). Deprived of a third presence, the couple falls apart: thirdness is the oxygen of passion. In 'Requiescat' (1923), Stuart explains to his dead friend's widow that he avoided her during her marriage because 'A third is never really wanted' (*CS* 45). But the story itself belies this principle: a third is always 'wanted,' in the sense that it is lacking, desired, and required.

'No, there is no such thing as being alone together,' Bowen writes in *The Heat of the Day*:

> Daylight moves round the walls; night rings the changes of its intensity; everything is on its way to somewhere else – there is the presence of movement, that third presence, however still, however unheeding in their trance two may try to stay. Unceasingly something is at its work.
>
> (*HD* 195)

Thirdness takes many forms in Bowen's fiction, ranging from the comic to the phobic, and it would be misleading to attempt to pin it down. It is enough to say that there is always one too many, an uninvited guest at every table, or, as Lacan would have it, an 'inmixing of an otherness' in every structure.[69] This otherness often takes the form of a seductive older woman, such as Mrs Kerr in *The Hotel* or Madame Fisher in *The House in Paris*. Matchmakers and match-breakers at once, these women both evoke and obstruct the passions of the rising generation; they also tend to captivate young women, deflecting their erotic interest away from suitable young men. Bowen's critics associate these older women, rightly I believe, with Bowen's mother, Florence Colley Bowen, who died of cancer when her daughter was only thirteen. Afterwards Elizabeth 'could not remember her, think of her, speak of her or suffer to hear her spoken of' (*MT* 290). Elizabeth's famous stammer, which emerged during her father's mental illness, consistently balked on the word 'mother.'[70] But the bereavement that scarred her speech also galvanised her writing, for the dead mother stalks her fiction in many guises and personae.

In Bowen's early fiction, the shadowy third functions as an obstacle yet also as a catalyst to love. In *The Heat of the Day*, however, the third is associated with responsibility for the other. The philosopher Emmanuel Levinas has a theory of the 'third term' that sheds some light on this mysterious intruder. According to Levinas, the third term is the force that separates the self from other selves. As soon as the third appears, it 'shatters the dual intimacy between myself and my neighbour.' Without this third presence, the other cannot be firmly differentiated from myself: she or he is nothing but my double, my mirror, my *semblable*. It is only with the intervention of the third that the other becomes plural, thus engendering the possibility of sociality: 'I do not exist solely with my neighbouring other, but with a multiplicity of others.'[71] In *The Heat of the Day*, the 'third presence' performs much the same function as Levinas's third term, for it shatters the 'dual intimacy' of the lovers and reminds them of the 'multiplicity of others' demanding their concern. 'Their time sat at the third place at their table,' Bowen writes, 'their time' referring to the world at war and its inexorable call to consciousness. Similarly, Levinas insists that 'consciousness is born as the presence of a third party.'[72] By ignoring the presence of the third, Bowen's lovers strive to forestall the awakening of consciousness; their love is presented as a state of sleep bordering on entropy. Yet 'however still, however unheeding in their trance two may try to stay,' the third presence has already stormed their sanctuary. The third is the company they cannot choose but keep.

The following chapters pursue these shadowy presences as they flit in and out of Bowen's fiction. For reasons of space it has been necessary to focus on Bowen's novels, while restricting close analysis of the short stories to a small selection of her masterpieces. But Bowen's central themes of loss and mourning, the necessity of company, responsibility for the other, and the third presence at the heart of love find fullest expression in the longer fiction. The novel's unhurried pace enables her to interweave these solemn themes with sparkling passages of social comedy: her satire of the English seaside in *The Death of the Heart*, for instance, or the farcical exchanges of the English and the Anglo-Irish in *The Last September*. Bowen could be very funny, and many readers have regretted that her humour is often overshadowed by her taste for melodrama. Yet the 'ambushing oddness' of her novels (as Hermione Lee describes it) owes much to the short story, a form that limits the development of character and lends itself to the apocalyptic.[73] It is telling that Bowen thought the Irish imagination better suited to brevity than length: the novel is 'too life-like, humdrum' to do the Irish justice, but 'we do not do badly with the short story, "that, in a spleen, unfolds both heaven and earth" – or should' (*MT* 276). Although she criticised her most successful novel, *The Death of the Heart*, as a short story that got out of hand, her longer fiction thrives precisely on the tension between the epiphanic concentration of the story and the leisurely expansion of the novel. Bowen writes: 'Narrative of any length involves continuity, sometimes a forced continuity; it is here that the novel too often becomes invalid. But action, which must in the novel be complex and motivated, in the short story regains heroic simplicity.'[74] In Bowen's novels, the short story injects an alien, convulsive temporality into the patient accretion of the narrative, disrupting the continuities of plot and character with 'encounters, impressions, impacts, shocks.'[75]

The present study is organised both chronologically and thematically. The first chapter places Bowen in her Anglo-Irish context, examining her family history *Bowen's Court* and her greatest novel on the fall of the ascendancy, *The Last September*. In this spellbound world, buildings and furniture mark spots of intensity in which the past irrupts into the paralysed present. The aftermath of World War I, closely followed by the Civil War in Ireland, mobilises paralysis into hectic decline. Bowen's interwar novels invoke a world of simultaneous speed and stasis. They are fascinated by state-of-the-art technologies of travel and communication: technologies that by extending physical and mental powers leave enabled individuals in constant threat of greater helplessness. World War II brought forth Bowen's most celebrated writing, *The Death of the Heart, The Heat of the Day*, and many of her finest stories. In these works, the destruction of buildings and furniture severs the link between present and past. Treason and espionage infect interpersonal relationships, while telephones render messages and their origins more cryptic. In the same period, Bowen's wartime espionage in Ireland on behalf of the British government complicates her conception of the shadowy third.

Bowen's postwar novels return to the scenes of her childhood, *A World of Love* to Ireland, *The Little Girls* to the Kentish coast where Bowen spent 'the most amusing years' of her childhood in sisterly intimacy with her mother.[76] These novels strive to exorcise the ghosts not only of her past life, but also of her former fiction, clearing the way for the sublime folly of *Eva Trout*. In this final work, the omniscient perspective of the realist novel gives way to what Bowen described as 'the convulsive shaking of a kaleidoscope.'[77] Out of this maelstrom rises the figure of the lunatic giant Eva Trout, blessed or cursed with 'a passion for the fictitious for its own sake,' who stands for the unformed imagination in all its savage majesty (*ET* 242). Although she materialises only in this final tour de force, this giant casts her shadow across every page of Bowen's work.

Living

Bowen's early life taught her much about kaleidoscopic changes of perspective. In her memoir of her childhood, *Seven Winters*, she writes: 'On the whole, it is things and places rather than people that detach themselves from the stuff of my dream.' She traces her attachment to things and places back to the successive dislocations of her early life, when she was shunted back and forth from Cork to Dublin; then to England when her father had a nervous breakdown; then to boarding school; and finally to a consortium of aunts after her mother's early death from cancer. Even when her family was still united, her parents' incommunicativeness, their retreat into their independent 'private kingdoms,' created an atmosphere of 'vagueness' in which their daughter learned to cling to things (*SW* 9–10).

Elizabeth Bowen was born in Herbert Place, Dublin, on 7 June 1899, nine years after her parents' marriage. Until the age of seven, 'Bitha' (she could not get her tongue around Elizabeth) enjoyed a sheltered Protestant childhood, spending winters in Dublin and summers in Bowen's Court. Meeting few Catholics, she developed 'an almost sexual shyness' with regard to their religion (*SW* 48). Her relationship with her mother, Florence Colley Bowen, was intense. Florence was so pained if anything went wrong between them that she appointed a governess to scold the child, but then planned ways of eluding this hired 'buffer' so that she and Elizabeth could meet and be alone together. Florence held strong and slightly dotty opinions about child-rearing: she was concerned that Elizabeth drink sufficient milk to avoid being 'runty' and 'bandy-legged,' and she deplored shyness in children, urging her daughter not to be a 'muff.' Elizabeth, far from muffish, grew up to be an indefatigable hostess and party-goer. Dottiest of all, Florence prevented her daughter from learning how to read until the age of seven, on the grounds that Bowens overworked their brains, leaving them vulnerable to hereditary instability.

Henry Bowen must have confirmed Florence's fears when he suffered a mental breakdown in 1906, diagnosed as 'anaemia of the brain,' and voluntarily committed himself to an asylum (*BC* 409). Florence, advised by doctors to leave her husband for his own sake, took Elizabeth to England, where they gravitated towards Folkestone, with its light-hearted seaside architecture, so different from the classical austerity of Bowen's Court. Bowen later recalled that 'Repetitive eighteenth-century interiors with their rational proportions and faultless mouldings, evenly daylit, without shadow, curiousness or cranny . . . said nothing to my imagination . . . I found them "sad", associating them perhaps with my father's illness' (*MT* 279). Alone together in exile, mother and daughter moved from one 'delirious' seaside villa to another, living in a state of rapturous intimacy that Bowen never talked about but must have been trying to recapture when she decided to return to Kent in her old age. During their long holiday from Ireland, Florence and Elizabeth enjoyed a game of visiting any empty house that took their fancy. Part of the fun was to obtain the key but to get rid of the house agent so that mother and daughter could explore the house alone. Occasionally Elizabeth, 'adept as a Fagin pupil,' would squeeze through a back window, unbolting the front door to let her mother in.

> The deserted rooms, downstairs in summer often embowered in shadows of the syringa embowering the bewildered gardens, of which the lawns had grown high in hay, smelled intoxicatingly of wallpaper, sunshine, mustiness. With the first echo of our steps on the stripped floors, or of our voices excitedly hushed by these new acoustics, another dream-future sprang into being. We took over wherever we were, at the first glance. Yes, what a supposititious existence ours came to be, in these one-after-another fantasy buildings, pavilions of love. In the last of the villas in which it came about that we did actually live, she died.
>
> (*MT* 279–80)

Bowen continued to play this game in her fiction by creating fantasy houses one after another: her stories typically open by entering a house, often by illicit means, where a dream-future springs into being. (The detail of the syringa reappears in *Eva Trout*, casting a green shade over the derelict conservatory in Cathay, the coastal villa where Eva takes possession after ejecting the unctuous house agent.)

Stories like 'Look at All Those Roses' portray the sinister dimension of Bowen's intimacy with her mother, but other works offer glimpses of its bliss. In the central flashback of *The Little Girls*, Dinah lives alone with her mother, confident in the illusion of her undivided love. However, in the early story 'Coming Home' (1923), Rosalind returns from school, elated by a triumph in the classroom, only to find her mother unaccountably and unforgivably away. Within a few minutes the child slides through the whole chromatics of bereavement, reacting first with anger, then with terror, and finally with agonising guilt that her resentment may have caused her mother's death. The fact that the mother eventually reappears does not assuage her daughter's new awareness of mortality.

Elizabeth lost her mother at the age of thirteen, which she later told a friend was the worst event of her life. In the meantime Henry Bowen had recovered and the family had been briefly reunited before Florence, looking forward to heaven with macabre glee, died of cancer. Elizabeth, still in a state of shock, was sent back to school at Harpenden Hall in Hertfordshire, where she arrived at mid-term with the 'sense of disfigurement, mortification, disgrace' that goes with 'total bereavement' (*MT* 289). In the grounds of this school, she participated in the curious ritual remembered in *The Little Girls*, in which three schoolgirls bury a casket full of precious objects underneath a thicket. Elizabeth may have been attempting to perform the rites of burial by proxy, having been banished by well-meaning adults from her mother's deathbed and funeral, as well as from the interment at Saltwood churchyard. At Harpenden Hall Elizabeth also persuaded her schoolfriends into 'harkening for "hollownesses"' and 'excavating for secret passages' in the school buildings. One of these passages was rumoured to run to 'the doubtless bone-strewn vaults of the parish church' (*MT* 293). St Leonard's Church in Hythe, which Bowen attended in her childhood and overlooked from the house she bought in her old age, still boasts a crypt piled high with human skulls. In her fiction, Elizabeth's childish pranks transform themselves into a fascination with the hollownesses of domestic architecture, as well as with the secret passageways of narrative, the catacombs and oubliettes of sentence-structure. Meanwhile her fictional houses, with their decaying interiors and stifling creepers, provide a means of re-imagining the mother's decomposition in the grave.

After an initial period of 'stupidity' at school, possibly 'due to denied sorrow,' Elizabeth vented her bereavement in high spirits (*MT* 292). In the summer of 1914, she was back in Bowen's Court, going to dances and tea-parties, and having such a good time that when news came of the outbreak of war, she exclaimed, 'Then can't we go to the garden party?'[78] During the war years Elizabeth boarded at another school, Downe House, formerly the home of Charles Darwin. Here the girls grew up 'under the intolerable obligation of being fought for, and could not fall short in character' without remembering that men were dying for them. The world seemed bound up in such a 'tragic attack of adolescence' that there was no reason to grow up, since moderation in behaviour had become impossible. It was difficult to eat one's fill without feeling like a 'food-hog,' in the words of a reproachful headline in the *Daily Mail;*

yet the girls were forced to finish up everything on their plates, a rule that Bowen blamed for blunting her palate for life.[79] It is notable that Bowen's fiction rarely mentions food; unlike her mentor Flaubert, who revels in elaborate descriptions of elaborate dishes, Bowen is the kind of novelist Virginia Woolf ticks off for never telling us what people ate at dinner parties.[80] Nonetheless Downe House taught Bowen how not to write – a lesson she often chose to ignore – and how not to exhibit feeling – a lesson she usually chose to obey, preferring 'life with the lid on' to incontinent emotion (*MT* 20–1).

Bowen's formal schooling ended in 1917, and she never regretted its brevity: 'Education is not so important as people think' (*BC* 124). She returned to Bowen's Court, her father having remarried, where she fell in love briefly with a British soldier, an episode memorialised in Lois's short-lived engagement to a British subaltern in *The Last September*. Until the age of twenty Bowen was planning to become a painter, and to this end enrolled in art school in London. But she gave it up after two terms: 'It suddenly dawned on me that, as an artist, I was finished. It was about this time that I became a secret writer.'[81] On the top floor of a house in Harpenden, between the ages of twenty and twenty-two, she wrote her first book of short stories, *Encounters*, published in 1923. At this time in literary history, the choice of the short story, for a young person who was 'a poet *manqué*,' was by no means obvious, and Bowen claims to have encountered almost none of the masters of the form. She had yet to read the short stories of James, Chekhov, Hardy, Maupassant, and Katherine Mansfield; she also seems to have entitled her first book *Encounters* without intending to allude to 'An Encounter,' Joyce's story of perversion in *Dubliners* (*MT* 119–20).

In the same year that *Encounters* was published, Elizabeth Bowen married Alan Cameron, who had been wounded and gassed during the Great War. At thirty, Cameron was living a comfortable bachelor's existence with his mother and a clergyman, regarded by one commentator as the prototype of Father Tony Clavering-Haight in *Eva Trout*.[82] There is a strong likelihood that Bowen's marriage was never consummated, possibly owing to Cameron's injuries. Anne M. Wyatt-Brown speculates that Cameron was homosexual, which would explain the resentful treatment of gay men in *Eva Trout*, where Eva has been neglected by her father for his manipulative lover Constantine. But Bowen, like most young women of her class and generation, intended to be married early, and not to be 'L.O.P.H. (Left On Pa's Hands)' (*MT* 17). At the time of his marriage, Cameron was Assistant

Secretary for Education in Northampton; two years later he was appointed Secretary of Education for the city of Oxford, where the couple moved in 1925. In Oxford Bowen enjoyed great social and professional success. Her first novel, *The Hotel*, was published soon after the move, to considerable acclaim. She also established long-standing friendships among the 'dons,' including Maurice Bowra, Isaiah Berlin, and David Cecil, her wit and charm having overcome the customary distrust of academics for creative artists.

In 1935 Alan Cameron took up a senior position in education for the BBC, and the couple moved to London, renting a house in Clarence Terrace, Regent's Park, where they remained until the building was bombed around them in 1944. Bowen published no novels during the war years, but wrote some of her greatest short stories, finding their brevity appropriate to the intensity of the experience. She also wrote her family history *Bowen's Court* in an effort to preserve the past. London under siege, with its shocks and dislocations, its 'inscrutable canyons' and 'glissades of ruin,' its wanderers and ghosts, resembled the world that Bowen had already dreamed into existence in her fiction (*MT* 99, 23). Her sense of the incalculable nature of reality, its resistance to interpretation and negotiation, became the norm for Londoners at war. 'Between bomb and bomb,' oppositions overturned: inside and outside, life and death, radiance and ruin. In her essay 'London, 1940,' Bowen describes how the 'whole length of Oxford Street . . . looks polished like a ballroom, glitters with smashed glass.' Here the living emerge from underground shelters after the Armageddon of the night before, looking like 'the risen dead in the doors of tombs' (*MT* 21–3).

Bowen participated enthusiastically in the British war effort, especially after Churchill was elected in 1940. She worked as an ARP warden, enforcing blackout restrictions and shepherding people into shelters. She also volunteered her services to the British Ministry of Information, and was commissioned to perform some undercover work in Eire (as it now was), specifically to find out whether the Irish were wavering in their neutrality. At first she agreed with Eamon de Valera that 'it would be more than hardship, it would be sheer disaster for this country, in its present growing stages and with its uncertain morale, to be involved in war.'[83] Yet as the war progressed she grew increasingly impatient with Irish isolationism, its 'craggy dangerous miniature world.' 'Ireland can be dementing, if one's Irish,' she admitted to Virginia Woolf.[84] When the war ended in 1945, however, Bowen was so dismayed by the victory of the Labour government that she contemplated a permanent return to Ireland. She wrote to William Plomer:

> I've been coming gradually unstuck from England for a long time. I have adored England since 1940 because of the stylishness Mr Churchill gave it, but I've always felt "when Mr Churchill goes, I go." I can't stick all those little middle-class Labour wets with their Old London School of Economics ties and their women. Scratch any of these cuties and you find the governess.[85]

'Governessy,' along with 'muffish,' 'whining,' and 'claggy,' were the most damning epithets in Bowen's arsenal.

In point of fact Bowen never lived full-time in Ireland after her marriage, but there were long holidays and lively house-parties at Bowen's Court. Her literary friends often wondered at her choice of husband. May Sarton, with whom Bowen had a brief affair in May 1937, recollected that Alan Cameron was kind and sensitive, but he was also 'quite stout, had a rather blimpish look, a red face and a walrus moustache, and spoke in a high voice, near falsetto.' When his wife was away, he would take Sarton out walking to the zoo in Regent's Park, where 'before the abstracted gaze of a tiger or panther Alan invariably exclaimed, "Elizabeth!"' (Bowen later wrote a children's story called *The Good Tiger* (1965).) There is an apocryphal story about a party at Bowen's Court in which a guest, blundering off in search of a toilet, opened a door to find Alan Cameron alone in a small room eating his supper off a tray.[86] Bowen had lovers: if her husband knew about them he must have decided to put up with them; perhaps she also decided to put up with his. Like Edith Wharton, who discovered passion after many years of sexless marriage, Bowen reached her mid-thirties before she embarked on her first love affair, with a young Oxford don named Humphry House, who was dumbfounded to discover she was still a virgin. When House met Bowen in 1933 he was already engaged to be married, and critics have speculated that Naomi Fisher in *The House in Paris* is a vengeful portrait of his wife. Deirdre Toomey has suggested that House's name is enshrined in the title of the novel (his wife's maiden name was Church).[87] After House's marriage Bowen felt that Madeline House made unreasonable demands on her husband, such as calling him back from a visit to Bowen's Court because the roof of their marital home had been demolished in a storm.[88] Bowen remained intensely involved with House until 1936, when he moved with his family to Calcutta.

The most important lover of Bowen's life was Charles Ritchie, a Canadian diplomat she met in London in 1941, and to whom she dedicated *The Heat of the Day* and *Eva Trout*. 'The first time I saw Elizabeth Bowen,' Ritchie recorded in his diary in September that year, 'I thought she looked more like a bridge-player than a poet. Yet without having read a word of her writing would one not have felt that something mysterious, passionate and poetic was behind that worldly exterior?' By June 1942, the bridge-player had disappeared. Ritchie writes:

> At first I was wary of her. Her uncanny intuitions, her flashes of insight like summer lightning at once fascinated and disturbed me. Now day by day I have been discovering more and more of her generous nature, her wit and funniness, the stammering flow of her enthralling talk, the idiosyncrasies, vagaries of her temperament. I know now that this attachment is nothing transient but will bind me as long as I live.[89]

Despite her love for Ritchie, Bowen always spoke of Alan Cameron with affection and respect, and never left him. In some ways Alan took the role of a parent, organising her finances and her wardrobe (her dress sense at the time of her marriage was atrocious). But soon after his retirement, ravaged by the long-term effects of gas-poisoning and heavy drinking, Alan died in 1952 at Bowen's Court, and was buried with Elizabeth's ancestors in St Colman's churchyard at Farahy. Widowhood, even for a woman as lionised as Elizabeth Bowen, was not easy: 'I felt maimed when Alan died.'[90] Mourning for Alan reawakened her pain about her mother's death, which provides the impetus for her last novels. Charles Ritchie had married his cousin a year before Alan's death, and although he remained devoted to Elizabeth they never lived together. The lavish entertainment still offered at Bowen's Court depleted her finances, and Bowen was forced to sell the house in 1959. After the sale her friend Eddie Sackville-West told Molly Keane that Bowen looked like someone who had attended her own execution.[91] Bowen had hoped that the purchaser, a neighbouring farmer, would fill the house with his children, but instead he demolished the 'great stone box' (as Virginia Woolf described it), and cut down much of the timber in the demesne.[92] 'It was a clean end,' Bowen concluded. 'Bowen's Court never lived to be a ruin' (*BC* 459).

Like her globe-trotting heroine Eva Trout, Bowen flew to America, where she had spent part of every year since 1950, working as a lecturer or writer-in-residence in many universities. New York she loved 'with passion,' but she never took up permanent residence there.[93] Instead she returned to Oxford, but felt left out, her old friends, such as Isaiah Berlin, being too much in demand to spend much time with her. In the end she decided to return to the scenes of her childhood in Kent, buying a modest, rather ugly house at the summit of Hythe, which enjoys a lovely view of St Leonard's Church, with its garden full of flowering trees, and glimpses of the sea below. Now ruined by bungaloid developments, Hythe was still 'a nice little town – reassuring and right-and-tight and sound' when Bowen bought her house, which she named Carbery after her mother's family estate in County Kildare. It is moving to discover that the nameplate on the house survives, along with a civic plaque commemorating Bowen's residence.

In a letter to Ritchie Bowen wrote, 'I suppose I like Hythe out of a back-to-the-wombishness, having been there as a child in the most amusing years of one's childhood – eight to thirteen.'[94] It was in Hythe that she wrote her last completed novel, *Eva Trout*, first published in the United States in 1968, which won the James Tait Black award. By now she was suffering from lung cancer, after a lifetime of chain-smoking. During her last months her voice diminished to a whisper, but she finally lost her speech-impediment. The day before she died, Spencer Curtis Brown, her literary executor, asked her if she wanted her unfinished autobiography to be published. 'I want it published,' she replied – not once but twice, without a stammer.[95] When he brought it out as *Pictures and Conversations*, Curtis Brown also included the first chapter of the novel Bowen was working on when she was dying. Called *The Move-In*, it concerns a group of youngsters who arrive by car at an Irish country house with the disturbing intention of taking occupation, despite the polite resistance of the middle-aged inhabitants. This Pinteresque fragment might have developed into Bowen's strangest variation on the theme that we do not choose our own company. Yet she did choose the company in which she died: the last person to attend her bedside was Charles Ritchie. Elizabeth Bowen died in Ireland on 22 February 1973, and was buried close to her husband and her father in Farahy churchyard, near the site of the demolished Bowen's Court.

Notes

1. Elizabeth Bowen, 'Out of a Book,' *MT* 53.
2. First published in the collection *Look at All Those Roses* (London: Gollancz, 1941); *CS* 512–20.

3. It is worth noting that Leopold Bloom uses 'roses' as a term for menstruation in the 'Lotus-Eaters' episode of *Ulysses* (1922; Harmondsworth: Penguin, 1986), ch. 5, p. 64, line 285.
4. Charles Dickens, *Our Mutual Friend* (1864–5; Harmondsworth: Penguin, 1971), p. 334. Sophia Wellbeloved drew my attention to the allusion to Persephone.
5. Interview for BBC's *Desert Island Discs*, 11 March 1957; cited by R. F. Foster in 'The Irishness of Elizabeth Bowen,' *Paddy and Mr Punch: Connections in Irish and English History*, p. 103.
6. Charles Ritchie, *The Siren Years: Undiplomatic Diaries 1937–1945*, p. 142 (entry of 24 May 1942).
7. Bowen, 'Notes on Eire,' Report to the Secretary of State for Foreign Affairs, 9 November 1940, FO 800/310, p. 255. An ill-edited version of this report can be found in '*Notes on Eire*': *Espionage Reports to Winston Churchill, 1940–2*, ed. Jack Lane and Brendan Clifford (Aubane: Aubane Historical Society, 1999). This edition, which includes a vitriolic attack on Bowen's supposed disloyalty to Ireland, is full of errata. The mysterious Aubane Historical Society, with its address in Mill Street, County Cork, allegedly has a membership in single figures: see R. F. Foster, *The Irish Story: Telling Tales and Making It Up in Ireland*, p. 257, n.1. Bowen's secret reports on Eire, prepared for the British Dominions office during World War II, are discussed in Chapter 5.
8. Maurice Merleau-Ponty, *The Visible and the Invisible*, p. 139.
9. Victoria Glendinning, *Elizabeth Bowen: Portrait of a Writer*, p. 13.
10. Jacqueline Rose, 'Bizarre Objects: Mary Butts and Elizabeth Bowen,' p. 78.
11. Bowen, 'Notes on Writing a Novel' (1945), *MT* 39.
12. 'Meet Elizabeth Bowen,' by The Bellman, in *The Bell* 4: 6 (September 1942) p. 424.
13. See Roland Barthes, *Writing Degree Zero*.
14. *Literary Essays of Ezra Pound*, ed. T. S. Eliot (1954; London: Faber, 1960), p. 304.
15. Bowen, Vassar College notebooks [Notes for lectures at Vassar College on the short story], n.d., HRHRC.
16. *CS* 157. See John Hildebidle, 'Elizabeth Bowen: Squares of Light in the Hungry Darkness,' in *Five Irish Writers: The Errand of Keeping Alive*, pp. 88–128.
17. In H. M. Parshley's translation, 'One is not born, but rather becomes, a woman. No biological, psychological, or economic fate determines the figure that the human female presents in society; it is civilisation as a whole that produces this creature, intermediate between male and eunuch, which is described as feminine' (Simone de Beauvoir, *The Second Sex*, p. 295).

18. Sean O'Faolain, 'A Reading and Remembrance of Elizabeth Bowen,' *London Review of Books*, 4–17 March 1982, pp. 15–16, cited in Foster, *Paddy and Mr Punch*, p. 122; Howard Moss, 'Interior Children,' *New Yorker* (5 February 1979) p. 128, cited in Heather Bryant Jordan, *How Will the Heart Endure: Elizabeth Bowen and the Landscape of War*, p. xii. Bowen's affair with O'Faolain began in 1937 and was brought to an end by the outbreak of war.
19. Elizabeth Bowen, *Pictures and Conversations* (1975), reprinted in *MT* 276.
20. Glendinning, *Elizabeth Bowen*, p. 31; Foster, *Paddy and Mr Punch*, p. 122.
21. Cited in R. F. Foster, 'Prints on the Scene: Elizabeth Bowen and the Landscape of Childhood,' in *The Irish Story: Telling Tales and Making It Up in Ireland*, p. 148.
22. J. C. Beckett, *The Anglo-Irish Tradition*, p. 144.
23. Bowen says that 'Gustave Flaubert's temperament bred his art out of dualities, with their attendant conflicts, more marked, more extreme, than has been often known,' in her Preface to *The Flaubert Omnibus*, *CI* 20. Apparently *The Flaubert Omnibus* was never published.
24. Cited in Richard Ellmann, *The Identity of Yeats* (New York: Oxford University Press, 1964), p. 153.
25. Glendinning, *Elizabeth Bowen*, p. 231.
26. Bowen, Postscript to the first American edition of *The Demon Lover* (1945), *MT* 95.
27. Bowen, *A Year I Remember – 1918*, broadcast on BBC Third Programme, 10 March 1949, HRHRC; quoted in Jordan, *How Will the Heart Endure*, p. 13.
28. Gertrude Stein, *Wars I Have Seen* (1945; London: Brilliance Books, 1984) p. 7.
29. Glendinning, *Elizabeth Bowen*, p. 127.
30. Ibid., p. 82.
31. Bowen, Interview with Charles Monaghan, 'Portrait of a Woman Reading: Elizabeth Bowen,' *Chicago Tribune Book World* (10 November 1968) p. 6; quoted in Jordan, *How Will the Heart Endure*, p. xv.
32. Samuel Beckett, 'Three Dialogues,' in *Disjecta: Miscellaneous Writings and a Dramatic Fragment*, ed. Ruby Cohn (New York: Grove, 1984), p. 139.
33. Toni Morrison, *Beloved* (New York: Penguin, 1987), p. 36.
34. Bowen, *Why Do I Write? An Exchange of Views Between Elizabeth Bowen, Graham Greene and V. S. Pritchett* (1948), *MT* 223.
35. W. B. Yeats, 'Byzantium' (1930/1932).
36. Samuel Beckett, *The Unnamable* (1959; London: Calder, 1994), p. 418. Julian Moynahan draws this connection between Beckett and the fall of the Anglo-Irish in 'Elizabeth Bowen: Anglo-Irish Postmortem,' *Raritan* 9: 2 (1989) pp. 68–97.
37. See Seamus Deane, *A Short History of Irish Literature*, p. 208; see also James Joyce, *Ulysses*, ch. 9, p. 170, lines 841–2, where Stephen Dedalus says that

the Roman Catholic Church is founded 'like the world, macro and microcosm, upon the void. Upon incertitude, upon unlikelihood.'
38. *BC* 3, 78, 15.
39. Elizabeth Bowen, Preface to *The Faber Book of Modern Short Stories* (1936), *CI* 39.
40. Cited in Glendinning, *Elizabeth Bowen*, pp. 102, 236.
41. Bowen, interview with Charles Monaghan, quoted in Jordan, *How Will the Heart Endure*, p. 2; letter to J. B. Priestley, 31 October 1938, HRHRC.
42. Elizabeth Bowen, 'A Passage to E. M. Forster,' in John Arlott, Elizabeth Bowen et al, *Aspects of E. M. Forster: Essays and Recollections Written for his Ninetieth Birthday* (London: Edward Arnold, 1969), p. 3.
43. See *MT* 233.
44. Andrew Bennett and Nicholas Royle, *Elizabeth Bowen and the Dissolution of the Novel: Still Lives.*
45. Harriet S. Chessman, 'Women and Language in the Fiction of Elizabeth Bowen'; Patricia Coughlan, 'Women and Desire in the Work of Elizabeth Bowen'; John Hildebidle, *Five Irish Writers.* Another adventurous feminist analysis, taking a Deleuzian perspective on the later novels, is Clare Hanson, 'Little Girls and Large Women: Representations of the Female Body in Bowen's Later Fiction'. Renée C. Hoogland, in *Elizabeth Bowen: A Reputation in Writing*, rather overdoes her excavation of lesbian motifs in Bowen; Patricia Juliana Smith takes a similar approach with a much lighter touch in *Lesbian Panic: Homoeroticism in Modern British Women's Fiction*, especially in ch. 2.
46. Jordan, *How Will the Heart Endure*; Adam Piette, *Imagination at War: British Fiction and Poetry 1939–1945*, pp. 161–72; R. F. Foster, 'The Irishness of Elizabeth Bowen,' in *Paddy and Mr Punch*, pp. 102–22; and 'Prints on the Scene: Elizabeth Bowen and the Landscape of Childhood,' in *The Irish Story*, pp. 148–63; Gill Plain, *Women's Fiction of the Second World War: Gender, Power and Resistance*, ch. 9, pp. 166–88; Karen Schneider, *Loving Arms: British Women Writing the Second World War*, ch. 3, pp. 74–108.
47. See *inter alia* Seamus Deane, *A Short History of Irish Literature*, pp. 205–7, and *Celtic Revivals: Essays in Modern Irish Literature 1880–1980*, pp. 31–2; W. J. McCormack, 'Elizabeth Bowen and *The Heat of the Day*,' in *Dissolute Characters: Irish Literary History through Balzac, Sheridan Le Fanu, Yeats and Bowen*, pp. 207–40; Declan Kiberd, 'Elizabeth Bowen – The Dandy in Revolt,' in *Inventing Ireland: The Literature of the Modern Nation*, ch. 20, pp. 364–79; Claire Connolly, '(Be)longing – The Strange Place of Elizabeth Bowen's *Eva Trout*,' pp. 135–43.
48. John Coates, 'The Misfortunes of Eva Trout,' pp. 59–79.
49. Elizabeth Bowen, *English Novelists*, p. 7.
50. Hermione Lee, *Elizabeth Bowen: An Estimation*; *Elizabeth Bowen*, revised edition.
51. Quoted in Jordan, *How Will the Heart Endure*, p. xvi.

52. Elizabeth Bowen, 'The Achievement of Virginia Woolf' (1949), *CI* 81.
53. Mary Ellmann, 'Words, Words,' review of *Eva Trout*, p. 126. 'Intussusception' means the reception of one part within another, or invagination; it is used in medicine to refer to the slipping of one part of the intestine into an adjacent part, particularly the small intestine into the large.
54. Graham Greene, *The Quiet American* (1955); cited in Glendinning, *Elizabeth Bowen*, p. 86.
55. See Deane, *A Short History of Irish Literature*, pp. 206, 190.
56. Gertrude Stein, *The Autobiography of Alice B. Toklas* (1933; New York: Random House, 1961), p. 83.
57. Bowen uses variations of this phrase in many contexts: this version is from '*The Shadow Across the Page* (1937), *CI* 136.
58. Quoted in Patricia Craig, *Elizabeth Bowen*, p. 59.
59. Ritchie, *The Siren Years*, p. 127.
60. This polarity is brilliantly analysed by Harriet Chessman in 'Women and Language in the Fiction of Elizabeth Bowen.'
61. The term 'hated love' comes from *Eva Trout* (*ET* 92).
62. O'Faolain, 'Elizabeth Bowen, or Romance Does Not Pay,' in *The Vanishing Hero: Studies in Novelists of the Twenties*, p. 171.
63. Bowen, *English Novelists*, p. 18.
64. Of Emmeline Summers in *To the North*, Bowen writes: 'A splinter of ice in the heart is bombed out rather than thawed out' (*N* 47).
65. Hildebidle, *Five Irish Writers*, p. 106.
66. 'Meet Elizabeth Bowen,' *The Bell*, pp. 423–4.
67. I have also discussed this story in 'Elizabeth Bowen: The Shadowy Fifth,' in Rod Mengham and N. H. Reeve (eds), *The Fiction of the 1940s: Stories of Survival*, pp. 1–25; and in 'Elizabeth Bowen: The Missing Corner,' in Manuel Barbeito (ed.), *Feminism, Aesthetics and Subjectivity: Women and Culture in Early Twentieth Century British Literature*, pp. 65–98.
68. The connection between 'The Confidante' and *The Golden Bowl* is suggested by Phyllis Lassner in *Elizabeth Bowen: A Study of the Short Fiction*, p. 26.
69. Jacques Lacan, 'Of Structure as an Inmixing of an Otherness Prerequisite to Any Subject Whatever.'
70. Glendinning, *Elizabeth Bowen*, p. 28.
71. Emmanuel Levinas, *Entre Nous/on thinking-of-the-other*, p. 202.
72. Emmanuel Levinas, *Otherwise than Being or Beyond Essence*, p. 160.
73. Lee, *Elizabeth Bowen* (1999), p. 12.
74. Preface to *The Faber Book of Modern Short Stories*, *CI* 38.
75. Preface to *The Last September* (1952), *MT* 123.
76. Letter to Charles Ritchie, cited in Glendinning, *Elizabeth Bowen*, p. 222.
77. This was Bowen's description of *The Heat of the Day* in an interview with Jocelyn Brooke, broadcast on 3 October 1950, HRHRC.
78. Glendinning, *Elizabeth Bowen*, p. 30.

79. Elizabeth Bowen, 'The Mulberry Tree' (1950), *MT* 16–20.
80. Virginia Woolf, *A Room of One's Own* (1929), in *A Room of One's Own and Three Guineas*, ed. Morag Shiach (Oxford: Oxford University Press, 1992), pp. 12–13.
81. 'Meet Elizabeth Bowen,' *The Bell*, p. 423.
82. Anne M. Wyatt-Brown, 'The Liberation of Mourning in Elizabeth Bowen's *The Little Girls* and *Eva Trout*,' p. 170.
83. Bowen, 'Notes on Eire,' FO 800/310, pp. 253–4.
84. Bowen, letter to Virginia Woolf, 1 July [1940], *MT* 218; letter to Virginia Woolf, 5 January [1941], *MT* 216.
85. Cited in Glendinning, *Elizabeth Bowen*, p. 166.
86. Ibid., pp. 104–5; according to Deirdre Toomey (entry on 'Elizabeth Dorothea Cole Bowen,' *Dictionary of National Biography*, forthcoming in 2004), Bowen confided in Sarton that she had had a previous affair with a woman; she took her affair with Sarton 'lightly,' whereas Sarton took it histrionically.
87. Toomey, ibid.
88. See Chris Hopkins, 'Elizabeth Bowen,' p. 120.
89. Ritchie, *The Siren Years*, pp. 115–16, 143.
90. Glendinning, *Elizabeth Bowen*, p. 201.
91. Ibid., p. 216.
92. Cited in Hermione Lee, Introduction to *Bowen's Court and Seven Winters*, *BC* xiv.
93. Glendinning, *Elizabeth Bowen*, p. 207.
94. Cited in Glendinning, *Elizabeth Bowen*, p. 222.
95. Spencer Curtis Brown, Foreword to *Pictures and Conversations*, *PC* viii.

2

Fall: Bowen's Court *and* The Last September

All is 'hidden when we would backward see from what region of remoteness the whatness of our whoness hath fetched his whence-ness,' Joyce writes in the 'Oxen of the Sun' episode of *Ulysses.*[1] If Joyce sees whoness and whatness as impenetrable mysteries, Bowen was convinced that her whoness fetched its whenceness from centuries before her birth, and that her life-story could be understood only as the closing chapter of the house of Bowen. To relate her biography from birth to death, as I have just attempted in the introduction, is to disregard the ghosts who made her what she was. 'Of course I count the ghosts,' Fleda Vetch exclaims in James's *The Spoils of Poynton.* 'It seems to me the ghosts count double – for what they were and for what they are.'[2] The ghosts count double for Bowen too; and yet the dead who presided over Bowen's Court had none of the impalpability attributed to ghosts. Rather than revisiting the house, they occupied its every nook and cranny. Bowen explains:

> What runs on most through a family living in one place is a continuous, semi-physical dream. Above this dream-level successive lives show their tips, their little conscious formations of will and thought. With the end of each generation, the lives that submerged here were absorbed again. With each death, the air of the place had thickened: it had been added to. The dead do not need to visit Bowen's Court rooms – as I said, we had no ghosts in that house – because they already permeated them . . . The land outside Bowen's Court windows left prints on my ancestors' eyes that looked out: perhaps their eyes left, also, prints on the scene? If so, those prints were part of the scene to me.
>
> (*BC* 451)

Extending Bowen's metaphor, the scenes that she perceived from Bowen's Court were palimpsests, each generation having reinscribed its eye-prints on the traces of the last.

This chapter explores the theme of the Big House in Bowen's work, showing how its architecture shapes the mentality of its inhabitants, determining the way that they perceive the world. Built in the eighteenth century at the height of Anglo-Irish civilisation, these houses embodied the soaring aspirations of their founders, but also burdened their successors with crippling expenses and an acute awareness of their own belatedness. In the wartime story 'The Happy Autumn Fields' (1944), the heroine discovers in the wreckage of her bombed-out house a box of documents belonging to a Big House family, whose vanished lives seem much more vivid than her own. 'How are we to live without natures?' she cries. 'The source, the sap must have dried up, or the pulse must have stopped, before you and I were conceived. So much flowed through people; so little flows through us. All we can do is imitate love or sorrow' (*CS* 683–4). In *Bowen's Court*, also written during World War II, Bowen excavates her family papers from the attic to reconstruct ten generations of their history, tracing her whoness to their whenceness, her lateness to their rash precocity. Her novel *The Last September*, published thirteen years before *Bowen's Court*, portrays an Anglo-Irish family clinging to its way of life in the midst of the Troubles of 1920, and ends with the 'execution' of the Big House by rebel arsonists. It is worth noting that in previous Anglo-Irish novels, the term 'execution' had been used to mean the seizure of the property of bankrupt landowners, ruined not by revolution but by the costs of their man-eating estates.[3]

In the settled world of Jane Austen's novels, a powerful influence on Bowen's work, political and social history forms the backdrop of the action, rarely impinging on the lives of the protagonists. But Bowen's world is too precarious for history to recede into the wings. Both *Bowen's Court* and *The Last September* show how human lives are controlled by forces set in motion long before their birth. In *The Hotel* (1927), Sydney Warren speaks of people 'living under the compulsion of their furniture,' and wonders if the human race were created 'for beds and dinner-tables and washstands, just to discharge the obligations all those have created' (*H* 119). Similarly, Bowen argues that the Anglo-Irish lived under the compulsion of the Big House, their whoness created by the whenceness embedded in its form and furniture. In her writing, architecture takes the place of psychology: character is shaped by rooms and corridors, doors and windows, arches and columns, rather than by individual experience. Palimpsested with the 'prints' of the dead generations, the Big House represents a prior script determining the plot of present lives. In *The Last September*, it is the clash between the past embalmed in the Big House, and the future imagined by the rebels, that causes the present to erupt in flames.

'On the whole, it is things and places rather than people that detach themselves from the stuff of my dream' (*SW* 10). Given this preference for things and places over people, it is logical that Bowen, when writing the history of her family, should have chosen their house in County Cork as her title and her main protagonist. Her chronicle, *Bowen's Court*, tells the story of an Anglo-Irish family in County Cork from the Cromwellian settlement until 1914, tracing the links between the fall of the house of Bowen and the self-destruction of the Anglo-Irish Protestant ascendancy. Thomas Henn, brought up like Bowen in an antedated Anglo-Irish mansion, comments that ' "The Fall of the House" has been a dramatic subject from the Greek Theatre onwards; in miniature it is the fall of dynasties, of nations. It is a tragic wheel that turns incessantly.'[4] For Bowen, the last inheritor of Bowen's Court, this wheel turned full circle when she sold the house to its destroyer. *Bowen's Court* the book thus stands as a funerary monument to Bowen's Court the house, razed to the ground in 1960. In 1964, when the second edition was published, Bowen included a new preface explaining her decision to preserve descriptions in the present tense, as if the building were still standing. Its fate, however, seems to be foretold in the wreckage that surrounds it. The barracks at nearby Fermoy, evacuated by the British after the Treaty of 1921 and burned down during the subsequent Civil War, spread 'acres of ruin' to 'frighten the eye.' Most of the local populace has vanished, yet it is not just lack of people that makes the countryside seem empty, but 'an inherent emptiness of its own' (*BC* 3, 11, 5, 78).

In a literal sense, then, *Bowen's Court* is a book about nothing. And Bowen likens the Big Houses themselves, imposed upon the island by her English forebears, to Flaubert's ideal book about nothing, which 'sustains itself on itself by the inner force of its style.' 'The creation of a new society requires not only force but taste,' Bowen argues, and the Anglo-Irish therefore needed an '*idea* of living' in order to complete their conquest (*BC* 21, 87). This is the historical process described by Yeats in 'Meditations in Time of Civil War' (1923):

> Some violent bitter man, some powerful man
> Called architect and artist in, that they,
> Bitter and violent men, might rear in stone
> The sweetness that all longed for night and day,
> The gentleness none there had ever known . . .

Reared in stone, the Big Houses embodied the 'European idea' of civilisation, the sweetness and gentleness of classical form and flowering lawns masking the violence that brought them into being. Each of these 'house-islands,' with its intense, centripetal life, placed a 'frame' around the lives of its inhabitants, providing an aesthetic in default of rootedness. Within these frames, the Anglo-Irish lived like only children, isolated from the native population by religion, nationality, and social class – 'singular, independent and secretive.'

As 'the family story-teller,' Bowen examines how her family's ups and downs reflected the vicissitudes of the ascendancy. Yet the Bowens themselves remained unconscious of their role as both the 'products' and the 'agents' of this larger history. For this reason, Bowen explains, 'I can only suggest a compulsion they did not know of by a series of breaks, contrasts and juxtapositions – in short, by interleaving the family story with passages from the history of Ireland' (*BC* 20, 69, 452). She admits that she is not a historian, and her sketches of Irish history, although considerately brisk, can still be tedious. Yet the breaks and interpolations of Bowen's narrative convey the force with which major events of Irish history – the Ulster Plantation, the Act of Union, the Great Famine – impinged upon the Bowens' lives, without their knowing it. Ensconced in their proud mansion, the Bowens took little interest in the plight of the supplanted peasantry or in the insurrections that shook the countryside from time to time. Agrarian rebellion scarcely touched the house. Even during the Troubles of 1921, when three of the neighbouring Big Houses were burnt down in a single night, Bowen's Court was spared. In 1798, 'the tip, and the very poor shoddy tip' of the United Irishmens' uprising reached Bowen's Court, when local rebels attacked the house, but were driven off by its forewarned inhabitants. The next morning, 'charnel fruit' was found in the branches of the pear-tree: the dead body of one of the insurgents who had climbed the tree to fire at the house. At a house-party in Bowen's Court in 1935, Bowen shushed a conversation about this incident in order to protect the feelings of her serving maid, who had an ancestor suspected of involvement in the raid 137 years ago.[5] The Irish have long memories: as we have seen, Bowen wished the Irish would remember less, the British more.

Isolation is the keynote of the family history, an isolation more profound than that of other Anglo-Irish landlords, for the Bowens were not important gentry and took no part in the wheeler-dealing that produced the Act of Union. Nor did they show any passion for the nationalist cause. They minded their own business, throwing parties, marrying their cousins, and trying to live up to their expensive house. Their story – with its births, deaths, marriages, estrangements, gains, and losses – resembles that of many landowning families. But the Bowens were remarkable for their litigiousness. A recurrent and disastrous lawsuit, combined with the occasional black sheep who squandered funds on 'horses, drink, and women,' all helped to 'kill the house' – a crime that Yeats condemns in *Purgatory* as 'a capital offence.'[6] One of Bowen's ancestors gambled away the side of a mountain. From time to time the family coffers were replenished by an advantageous marriage, only to be emptied by a further renewal of the lawsuit. The legal documents arising from these cases, along with 'hearsay and some certain retrieved facts,' provide the resources for Bowen's reconstruction of the past (*BC* 452). Out of the turgid legal prose 'successive lives show their tips, their little conscious formations of will and thought' – tips that Bowen re-embodies into vivid patriarchs and matriarchs.

Bowen's antecedents were neither English nor Irish, but Welsh. The name was originally 'ap Owen,' 'ap' meaning 'son of,' but this Welsh chrysalis was shed by Henry Bowen in the sixteenth century (*BC* 35). Two generations later Henry Bowen's grandson and namesake travelled to Ireland as lieutenant-colonel in Cromwell's army. Legend has it that Colonel Bowen, as an atheist and a Celt to boot, infuriated Cromwell, who strangled one of his treasured pair of hawks. But Cromwell must have thought better of it, because he later offered Bowen all the lands that the remaining hawk could fly over. The hawk flew south, and it was in the isolated lands around Farahy that the Bowen dynasty established its estate. The fact that a hawk flies up straight and hangs, until it plunges on its prey, did nothing to dislodge the legend. A hawk remained the family crest.

Colonel Bowen's son John Bowen married the daughter of a rich Cromwellian called Nicholls, the owner of Kilbolane Castle, some twenty-six miles from Farahy. When Nicholls died, it was whispered that a large fortune was buried in his castle, and the Bowens filed a lawsuit against the Nicholls family with the aim of recovering the treasure. No one ever knew how much the hoard was worth, but the longer it remained missing 'the greater its visionary proportions grew,' and the Kilbolane treasure became a hereditary obsession with the Bowens, their real resources squandered in pursuit of these imaginary riches. Bowen comments, 'Bowens have always been prone to avoid or baulk at facts only to torment themselves with fantasies . . .' (*BC* 100).

The Henry Bowen of the next generation, whom Bowen calls Henry II, introduced some money into the family, much impoverished by legal expenses, by marrying a rich heiress, Jane Cole, in 1716. Her surname was permanently absorbed into the family tree: hence Bowen's name was Elizabeth Dorothea Cole Bowen. Unfortunately Jane's son, Henry III, resurrected the ill-fated lawsuit, incurring vast debts. But Bowen forgives him this folly because it was Henry III, known in the family as 'Henry the Builder,' who erected Bowen's Court in 1775. This date, carved in the foundation stone, marked the height of the 'great century' of the Anglo-Irish, the age of Grattan, Burke, and Swift. It was also the year that the American Revolution began, inspiring another Anglo-Irish Protestant, Wolfe Tone, to lead the republican insurrection that ended with his suicide in 1798. Henry III, like all the Bowens, paid little attention to these earth-shaking events. He was busy trying to beget a child for every window of Bowen's Court, and succeeded in fathering fourteen, in addition to seven who did not survive. He left his offspring debts amounting to £40,000.

The term 'Big House' suggests a certain irony towards the pretensions of the Anglo-Irish: bigness is not the same as greatness, nor can square footage be equated with cultural capital. 'One may call a man "big," ' Bowen comments, 'because he seems to think the hell of himself.' Even in terms of size, many Irish houses were 'not big at all' by English standards. Yet Bowen insists that there was 'a true bigness, a kind of impersonality' in the conception of these mansions:

> After an era of greed, roughness and panic, after an era of camping in charred and desolate ruins (as my Cromwellian ancestors did certainly) these new settlers who had been imposed on Ireland began to wish to add something to life . . . They began to feel, and exert, the European idea – to seek what was humanistic, classic and disciplined.

'It is something to subscribe to an idea,' Bowen adds, 'even if one cannot live up to it.'[7]

The remainder of *Bowen's Court* traces the failure of the Anglo-Irish to live up to this idea, a failure prefigured in the absence of the north-east corner of the house, which was left unbuilt for lack of funds. This 'missing corner' lends itself to metaphorical interpretation: the Anglo-Irish could be said to represent a missing corner in the British empire, amputated both from England and from Ireland. Bowen's Court was meant to be a square, but in its unfinished state it evokes the famous gnomon – an oblong with a missing corner – mentioned in the first paragraph of Joyce's *Dubliners*:

> Every night I gazed up at the window I said softly to myself the word *paralysis*. It had always sounded strangely in my ears, like the word *gnomon* in the Euclid and the word *simony* in the Catechism. But now it sounded to me like the name of some maleficent and sinful being. It filled me with fear, and yet I longed to be nearer to it and to look upon its deadly work.[8]

Whatever Joyce's intentions, these three terms, gnomon (the missing corner, with its implication of unfinished business), simony (the traffic in sacred things), and most of all paralysis, with its double sense of immobility and dissolution, seem to encapsulate the fate of Anglo-Ireland, its irresistible 'descendancy.'

Julian Moynahan has remarked that 'the Irish Big House is about as convincing a symbol of community as the House of Usher.'[9] And the fissures in the Big House began to show long before the ostentatious imposition was destroyed. The Act of Union of 1800 meant that Ireland, ruled across the seas by Westminster, was obliged to yield much of its wealth in taxation to the English state, in return for the protection of a small minority. It was at this juncture that the Anglo-Irish, long established in their ill-gotten acres, came to be resented as an alien garrison. Their society broke up: although it persevered 'in detail – comings-and-goings, entertainments, marriages,' the 'main healthy abstract' of the eighteenth century was gone (*BC* 260, 258–9). Like Swift's airborne island, the world of Anglo-Ireland was now suspended in the void. '*Farouches*, haughty, quite ignorant of the outside world,' and handicapped by their 'divorce from the countryside,' the Big House people 'edged back upon a tract of clouds and of obsessions.'[10]

At least they kept their obsessions to themselves. Bowen argues that the isolation of the Anglo-Irish landlords prevented them from taking up the English habit of moralising at the poor. 'The Irish and the English squire are very differently placed,' Bowen explains:

> the first is imposed and the second indigenous. The English squire considers God gave him a function, the Irish considers himself his own end, put where he is by some sport of the Divine will – in fact, an aristocrat. The English squire can, or could until quite lately, combine with the parson in dragooning the lower classes into healthy activities; exceedingly conscientious, he feels he is where he is to teach the poor what is what . . . The Irish landowner, partly from laziness but also from an indifferent delicacy, does not interfere in the lives of the people round . . . The greater part of them being Catholics, and he in most cases being a Protestant, they are kept from him by the barrier of a different faith . . . he pursues, inside his demesne and mansion, his centripetal and rather cut-off life . . . There exists between classes, at least in the country in Ireland, a good-mannered, fairly cynical tolerance, largely founded on classes letting each other alone.
>
> (*BC* 125–6)

Whereas the English landowner was indigenous, the Anglo-Irish was imposed, gratuitous, installed by a divine caprice rather than a rational or moral masterplan, and hence a true aristocrat, cut loose from any purpose or responsibility. Abstracted from the world of fact, he tormented himself with fantasy. The philosophy of Berkeley (1685–1753), the Anglo-Irish Bishop of Cloyne, which questions the existence of a material world independent of our sense-impressions, seems to reflect the political predicament of the ascendancy: divorced from the daily life of Ireland, sequestered in a time-warp, and consequently doubting the reality of the surrounding world.

The Act of Union deepened the isolation of the Anglo-Irish, cutting them off decisively from their empirical surroundings, and thus intensifying their propensity to fantasy. In the Bowens' case, fantasy took the form of reviving the Kilbolane lawsuit in the 1840s, with the usual disastrous consequences. But the legal fiasco was immediately overshadowed by the Great Famine. At this crisis in history, Bowen argues that her family found an opportunity to prove themselves 'slightly better' than others of their class (*BC* 278). They were not absentees: in the year known as Black '47, when many landlords fled the country, Bowen's great-grandmother Eliza Wade Bowen opened a soup-kitchen, feeding beggars through a trap in the cellar-door. When the soup was used up she was forced to lock the trap, while the bolted door heaved with the pressure of the starving multitudes. The soup was a nice gesture, but useless. The avenue to Bowen's Court was strewn with corpses of those too weak to reach the kitchen, and the mass grave at Farahy was stuffed chock-full. Many of the dead were strangers to the small community, but even those whose names were known vanished without record: there was no time for funerals, no money for tombstones. Nonetheless, folk-memory of Eliza's charity may have saved Bowen's Court from arson later during the Troubles. Of England's apathy to the Famine, Bowen writes caustically that it was hard for England 'to see the native Irish as anything but aliens, and as worse, sub-human – potato-eaters, worshippers of the Pope's toe. The squalor in which the Irish lived was taken to be endemic in their mentality: it would have seemed fantastic to reform their conditions' (*BC* 263).

Elizabeth's grandfather Robert, the last of the 'high-voltage' Bowens, was at school in Cheltenham during the Famine (*BC* 291). Since the English blamed the Anglo-Irish for the Famine (whereas the Anglo-Irish blamed the English), Robert as an Anglo-Irish landlord must have been taunted at school for the suffering that he was not allowed to see. To this experience Bowen attributes his 'dislike of the "morbid," so mastering as to become morbid in itself.' A hard man and a hard rider, exemplifying Brendan Behan's famous definition of the Anglo-Irishman as a Protestant on a horse, Robert was also a great planner. After taking his degree at Trinity College, he made many improvements to Bowen's Court, including the installation of watercloset (bathrooms were added only in 1949, financed by the popular success of *The Heat of the Day*). When Robert married he filled the house with children – who crowded into the world, 'congested and isolated' – and with furniture, whose bulk and weight devoured light and air. Bowen comments:

> Though Robert liked the solidity of the Bowen's Court structure, its unemotional plainness was not grateful to him. I think he disliked light (he had much of that out of doors), despised space (as a form of vacuity) and had a half-savage feeling, apart from fashion, for the protuberant, the glossy and the ornate. The object of furniture was, in his eye, to betray expensiveness, to denote extreme solidity and to fill up rooms.
>
> (*BC* 315, 324, 320)

Elizabeth Bowen later cleared out much of this furniture from Bowen's Court, but it returns to clutter her fictional interiors.

Henry Bowen, father of the novelist, was the first of Robert's thirteen children, only nine of whom survived. Father and son were drastically opposed, the elder being rigid and despotic, the younger civil, intellectual, and vague. Their animosity intensified when Henry contracted smallpox on a European tour. Robert fled the house with the remaining children in a panic of self-preservation, while his wife, who remained to nurse her son, saved him and died of the disease herself. Henceforth Henry reacted against his father's 'success regime' in every particular. When he decided to become a barrister, refusing to devote his life exclusively to Bowen's Court, Robert exploded. He could not disinherit Henry, because the estate was entailed on the eldest son, but he tried to punish the young man by damaging the property, cutting down timber and selling off parts of the demesne. The 'headlong decline' of Bowen's Court was implicit in his will:

> in the dark in which he now increasingly dwelled he planned the destruction of his life's work. To-day, his fine iron field-gates rusting off their hinges, his metalled avenues grass-grown, his roofless farm-buildings, his 'machines,' that used to fill the yard with their humming, now with belts snapped, teeth rusting into the ground, make me feel a pang – on Robert's behalf. I think of the Giotto figure of *Anger*, the figure tearing, clawing its own breast.
>
> (*BC* 365, 376)

After Robert's death, Henry married Florence Colley, whose family had been in Ireland since Queen Elizabeth's reign and shared the Bowens' 'landowning Protestant outlook.' At the time of the marriage, the Colleys' estate at Castle Carbery, County Kildare, had lain in ruins for many years, and the family lived at Mount Temple, Clontarf, in a Victorian house overlooking Dublin Bay. Handsome and dreamy, Florence loved to read and think, but her 'evident pleasure in the pretty and gay' protected her from being taken as an 'intellectual,' in an era when the stereotype of the blue-stocking prevailed (*SW* 9). One of the most vivid moments of Bowen's chronicle is her account of the arrival of the newly-weds at Bowen's Court. The tenants surged round the couple, unhooked the horses, and drew the bridal carriage up the avenue themselves.

> Florence, her eyes swimming, unable to speak, was seen in the flashes of lantern-light – she wore a long dark-red caped cloak, which has never been forgotten. They praised her beauty and wished her happiness. Ireland is a great place to die or be married in.
>
> (*BC* 393)

Elizabeth Bowen enters this story in 1899, nine years after her parents' marriage. Had she been born the boy her family had expected, she would have been named Robert to preserve the alternation between Roberts and Henrys that went back to the beginning of the dynasty. The obsessive recurrence of the name Robert in Bowen's fiction, along with Roderick, Rodney, and Ronald, suggests a lifelong preoccupation with the man she might have been. But Elizabeth's birth was celebrated in Bowen's Court with great rejoicing: jigs were danced on the kitchen table, and no one, from the moment that the sex of the baby was announced, ever reproached Elizabeth for being a girl. The Bowens were 'not bound by the Salic law,' and her father had gained a high opinion of women from the heroic example of his mother (*BC* 405, 404).

But Bowen presents herself as a minor figure in this chronicle: she frames her individual life within her family's, much as she frames her family's within the history of the Anglo-Irish. The true hero of *Bowen's Court* is the house itself – although perhaps it is the villain too. The most important rule that Bowen made – and broke – in writing *Bowen's Court* was not to leave the house 'for more than a page or so.' The house dominates the book as it dominated its inhabitants and its demesne, stamping 'its character on all ways of living.' Henry the Builder may have made the house, but the house, 'with a rather alarming sureness,' made 'all the succeeding Bowens.' Bowen tells us little of her childhood, for instance, except when it impinges on the house. Her father's career obliged the family to spend winters in Dublin, thus deserting Bowen's Court and condemning its furniture to 'exile.' As a result of these absences, 'for the first time since Henry III had moved his family in, a break came in the house's continuous human life . . . it is to these first phases of emptiness that I trace the start of the house's strong *own* life' (*BC* 449, 32, 403).

There is something sinister about this 'strong *own* life,' as if the house had grown more animate than its proprietors, reducing them to ghostly revenants. Despite her admiration for the Big Houses, Bowen recognises that they drained their owners' resources:

> many of these genial builders died badly in debt and left their families saddled with mansions that they could ill afford. Then, decline set in almost at once. A more modest plan of living would have made, in the end, for very much more peace: big houses that had begun in glory were soon only maintained by struggle and sacrifice.
>
> (*MT* 27)

The Big House vampirised its owners; at the same time, it nourished the vampires of Irish fiction. The lonely mansions of Sheridan Le Fanu and Bram Stoker are set in countries as far-flung as Transylvania, and belong to an international Gothic tradition, but the Undead bear a strong resemblance to the Anglo-Irish: coffined in their Big Houses, feeding off their tenant farmers, and sentenced by the Act of Union to living death.[11] How the Big House bled the local peasantry is not a question Bowen raises: the plight of the labourers always lay beyond the Bowens' field of vision, beyond the landscape imprinted with their eye-beams. And if the Big House made the Bowens blind, there is a strong suggestion that it also made them mad, by encouraging their tendency to fantasy. Yet Bowen transforms this hereditary curse into a gift, enlisting fantasy to reconstruct in words the great stone edifice of Bowen's Court. It was this edifice, she argues, that saved the Bowens from the worst excesses of their will to power.

> One may say that while property lasted the dangerous power-idea stayed, like a sword in its scabbard, fairly safely at rest. At least, property gave my people and people like them the means to exercise power in a direct, concrete and therefore limited way. I have shown how their natures shifted direction – or the nature of the *débordement* that occurred – when property could no longer be guaranteed. Without putting up any plea for property – unnecessary, for it is unlikely to be abolished – I submit that the power-loving temperament is more dangerous when it either prefers or is forced to operate in what is materially a void. We have everything to dread from the dispossessed.
>
> (*BC* 455)

As political theory Bowen's argument scarcely holds water; but it conveys an imaginative truth that re-emerges throughout her fiction. The house incarcerates, controls, and even sucks the lifeblood of its inmates, yet also gives them boundaries, shape, and substance. 'Nothing can happen nowhere' – and nor can nobody.

While the Bowens created their own centre of gravity in Bowen's Court, they never overcame their dislocation from the countryside they dominated, and the term 'dislocation' recurs like a chronic symptom throughout Bowen's work. It was dislocation, she contends, that drove the Anglo-Irish landlords from the real world into fantasy. Her analysis of their mentality offers some insight into the sources of her own imagination. For the dislocation endemic to her people's plight, with its compensatory dreams of integration, is the theme and motor of her fiction. It is a tale she tells time and again, particularly in her wartime stories, in which the fact of upheaval engenders fantasies of perfect worlds. Among the finest of these stories is 'Mysterious Kôr,' in which the heroine conjures up Rider Haggard's city of Kôr out of the moon-drenched ruins of London. In 'The Happy Autumn Fields,' also written during this period, the narcoleptic heroine, dislocated in the war-torn present and dozing in her bombed-out house, takes refuge in a dream-world conjured up out of an Anglo-Irish family photograph. It was Bowen's own sense of dislocation, endemic to the Anglo-Irish condition, but intensified by her experience of war, that prompted her to resurrect her family history. In her Preface to the second edition of 1964, she recalls that the composition of *Bowen's Court* began in the early summer of 1939 and was completed in 1942, in 'the savage and austere light of a burning world.' At this time the past mattered more than ever: 'it acquired meaning; it lost false mystery . . . details leaped out with significance' (*BC* 454).

While Bowen felt she must record the past in order to preserve it from destruction, she also sensed creative possibilities in the upheaval. In her extraordinary Postscript to the American edition of *The Demon Lover* (1945), Bowen suggests that the dislocation caused by war awakened the collective imagination, transforming the civilian population into visionaries. She describes the cumulative effect of her own stories as 'a rising tide of hallucination':

> The hallucinations are an unconscious, instinctive, saving resort on the part of the characters: life, mechanized by the controls of wartime, and emotionally torn and impoverished by changes, had to complete itself in *some* way. It is a fact that in Britain, and especially in London, in wartime many people had strange deep intense dreams.
>
> (*MT* 96)

Characters require frames; but it is when these frames collapse, and walls come down, that dreams are born. The ruins of the Blitz, like the ruins of the Big House, open up a missing corner in reality, which can be completed only in a vision or a work of art.

Two decades before the Blitz, Bowen's Court survived the fires of the Troubles, but Bowen's fear that the house would be destroyed inspired the creation of the *The Last September*. This was the work of art that rose out of the imaginary ruins of the house, ruins more real to Bowen than any of the wreckage she actually experienced. Her second novel and her funniest – despite its melancholy theme – *The Last September* was of all her books, she once confessed, 'nearest my heart' (*MT* 122). Published in 1929, the year before her father's death, the novel may have been a way of coming to terms with her imminent inheritance of Bowen's Court. Set in a Big House called Danielstown in County Cork, the home of Sir Richard and Lady Naylor, the novel's romantic plot unfolds against the backdrop of the Troubles of 1920. As the Naylors and their visitors drink tea, play tennis, pick raspberries, go dancing, and get engaged, Black and Tans roar through the countryside in armoured cars, and Irish rebels lurk in ruined buildings, ambushing unwary passers-by.

The Big House novel has a long tradition in Irish literature, reaching back to the eighteenth century, and encompassing such masterworks as Maria Edgeworth's *Castle Rackrent* (1800) and the Gothic writings of Le Fanu and Maturin. But Bowen's immediate predecessor was Edith Somerville, particularly her novel *The Big House of Inver*, which was published in 1925 under the pseudonym Somerville and Ross ('Martin Ross' was the *nom de plume* of Violet Martin, Somerville's cousin, who had died ten years before). Illegitimate Shibby Pindy, also known as Isabella Prendeville – whose garbled name bespeaks her confused parentage – struggles to restore the Big House of Inver to its former glory by marrying her legitimate but good-for-nothing brother to an heiress. Instead the handsome Kit gets his low-life mistress pregnant, only to abandon her to madness and death. Having lost his chance to marry the heiress, he sells the House of Inver to her wealthy fiancé. But the house burns down before the purchaser can take possession, which was the fate of many such Big Houses in the early 1920s. In this case, however, the fire has been accidentally ignited by old man Prendeville, rather than by rebel arsonists. This careless act completes the self-destruction of the dynasty: 'five generations of mainly half-bred and wholly profligate Prendevilles rioted out their short lives in the Big House, living with country women, fighting and drinking, gambling.'[12]

In imputing the fall of the house to the corruption of its owners, Somerville seems to take a harsher view of the ascendancy than Bowen, who endows the Naylors with a keen sense of propriety. Neither debauched nor profligate, the Naylors are anachronisms, destroyed by the grandiose ambitions embodied in their house, rather than by any personal defects of character. In contrast to the traditional Big House novel, which tends to blame decline on the moral dissolution of the landowners, Bowen recognises that the world of the ascendancy was doomed to self-destruction, regardless of its owners' vices – the forces of disintegration were historical, not personal. In *The*

Last September, the Big House people do their best to ignore these historical forces, but Bowen shows how their affected nonchalance is riven by conflicting loyalties. Although the Naylors fear attack by raiders, they also deplore the British Army, with its menacing patrols, its murderous reprisals. Sir Richard fulminates against the Army for 'poking old women out of their beds' to search for guns; an encounter with a British tank rouses him to comic indignation:

> 'I was held up yesterday for I wouldn't like to say how long, driving over to Ballyhinch, by a thing like a coffee-pot backing in and out of a gate, with a little brute of a fellow bobbing in and out at me from under a lid at the top. I kept my temper, but I couldn't help telling him *I* didn't know what the country was coming to – and just when we'd got the horses accustomed to motors. "You'll do no good," I told him, "in this unfortunate country by running about in a thing like a coffee-pot."'

Such outrages intensify Sir Richard's suspicion that 'there's a great deal of socialism now in the British Army' (*LS* 25–6).

But the Naylors' pleasures also depend upon the Army, for the young soldiers provide tennis players and dancing partners for their parties, gallantly offering themselves up as flirtation-fodder. In this imperilled enclave, the sudden influx of dancing soldiers causes great excitement, as it does in Austen's *Pride and Prejudice.* Indeed Lady Naylor expresses the opinion that if the soldiers 'danced more and interfered less, I dare say there would be less trouble in the country' (*LS* 164). The trouble in the country is the other plot, most of which transpires behind the scenes, while the love plot dominates the stage. Yet both are stories of paralysis: Lois Farquar, the central character, fails to fall in love with any of the men available, just as the Naylors fail to take sides in the struggle that decides their fate. Both plots conclude in *disengagement,* romantic in the one case, political in the other.

Lois remembers that she once 'cried for a whole afternoon before the War because she was not someone in a historical novel' (*LS* 75). But that is precisely what she is: *The Last September* is the only novel that Bowen deliberately sets back in a former time. The second paragraph begins: 'In those days, girls wore crisp white skirts and transparent blouses clotted with white flowers; ribbons, threaded through with a view to appearance, appeared over their shoulders' (*LS* 7). It is telling that Lois's costume is introduced before its wearer, for Lois herself feels trapped in this appearance, trussed up to embody 'youth' and 'freshness,' yet afraid to contemplate a life outside such roles. 'So Lois stood at the top of the steps looking cool and fresh; she knew how fresh she must look, like other young girls, and clasping her elbows tightly behind her back, tried hard to conceal her embarrassment.' In this sentence the word 'must' introduces a suspicion of coercion: embarrassed and self-conscious, Lois is contemplating how she looks to others, but also how she is compelled to look; 'like other young girls,' she *must* look fresh in order to disguise the staleness of a dying order.[13] In homage to *The Last September,* J. G. Farrell's novel *Troubles* (1970), set in the same political context as Bowen's novel, opens with the echo: 'In those days . . .'[14] But the oddity of Bowen's usage of the phrase is that the action of *The Last September,* which is set in 1920, takes place only nine years before its date of publication. In that short interim the Naylors' world has disappeared: 'Lois's ribbons, already, were part of history,' Bowen later commented. The months from 6 December 1922 to 22 March 1923 saw 192 Big Houses destroyed by fire in the south of Ireland. Although Bowen's Court was not destroyed, Bowen watched it burning 'so often in my mind's eye . . . that the terrible last event in *The Last September* is more real than anything I have lived through' (*MT* 124, 126). The novel, which begins with Danielstown opening its door to visitors, ends with the house in flames, opening its door 'hospitably upon a furnace' (*LS* 206).

Sean O'Faolain has described the atmosphere of Danielstown as 'marmoreal,' but more precisely it is clenched to breaking-point.[15] The Naylors have not turned to stone, but they are stuck in a historic impasse: the novel abounds with images of nets and traps. Caught between warring factions, the Naylors cannot take sides with the British Army, imported to 'protect' them from their friends and neighbours, any more than they can champion the rebels. While entertaining British soldiers at their parties, they conceal their suspicion that rebel guns have been buried in remote parts of the estate, and their certain knowledge that a fugitive with a price on his head is hiding out at his family's nearby farm. In a letter to her friend the novelist William Plomer, Bowen explained that *The Last September* describes the 'equivocal position' of a Big House family. 'Interest and tradition should make them support the British,' but 'affection ties them to the now resistant people of their surrounding community.'[16] The novel exposes this equivocal position in a series of epiphanies. One occurs when Sir Richard, informed by a triumphant British soldier that the rebel Peter Connor has been arrested, winces, 'His mother is dying.' The soldier, Gerald Lesworth, is horrified in turn. 'His duty, so bright and abstract, had come suddenly under the shadowy claw of the personal' (*LS* 91–2). Behind the scenes, the rebels are also torn between their cause and their traditional consideration for their neighbours. When Laurence, Sir Richard's nephew, is attacked by rebels who strip him of his shoes and wristwatch, the wristwatch is returned to his uncle three days later, still ticking and in perfect order. ' "Which just shows," said Sir Richard, holding the watch to his ear with satisfaction' (*LS* 189). Thomas Henn recalls a similar experience during this period of history, when rebels who had raided weapons from his family's Big House came back with a package of cartridges, then unobtainable, so that young Tom might enjoy a bit of shooting during the school holidays.[17]

There are so many layers to this conflict that Catholics find themselves as compromised as Protestants. Mrs Fogarty, a middle-class Catholic and an ardent Unionist, whose drawing-room is thronged with photographs of British soldiers (the 'dear boys' barracked at Clonmore, many of whom perished in the Great War), swears that she will never put away her Union Jack cushions. Never – 'not if They came at night and stood in her room with pistols.' Her Protestant visitors reflect that 'this was all the more noble in Mrs Fogarty in that she was a Catholic, with relations whose politics were not above reproach at all' (*LS* 71–2). This comic vignette shows that there are no clear frontiers in this scramble, no foolproof way of telling Them from Us. The British soldiers also feel confused and sullied. Daventry, who suffered shell-shock during the Great War, fears that he will lose his mind in Ireland:

> He had received special orders to ransack the beds, and to search with particular strictness the houses where men were absent and women wept loudest and prayed. Nearly all beds had contained very old women or women with very new babies, but the N.C.O., who was used to the work, insisted that they must go through with it. Daventry still felt sickish, still stifled with thick air and womanhood, dazed from the din. Daventry had been shell-shocked, he was now beginning to hate Ireland, lyrically, explicitly; down to the very feel of the air and smell of the water. If it were not for dancing a good deal, whisky, bridge, ragging about in the huts, whisky again, he did not know what would become of him, he would go over the edge, quite mad, he supposed.
>
> (*LS* 144–5)

Bowen had witnessed the effects of shell-shock at first hand by working in a veterans' hospital in 1918, which she later described as her first year of 'looking life in the eye.' In an unpublished radio play called *A Year I Remember*, she looks back on her experience as 'a pink, rattled, inexpert VAD,' working in a special hospital 'for men wounded where I had not foreseen – in the mind.'

Shell-shock cases. Eighty or so of them, up and about all day. Scotsmen, Welshmen, Devon men, Midlanders, North Country men, Cockney Jews – each with some inner queerness a little heightened. Nobody quite mad – nobody, as one came to see, quite curable. A gimcrack house in the country, overlooking a river – that was the place.

Patients slept in huts, under our windows. At nights, the silence used to be broken by the chattering and chattering of a sleeper. Or a sudden loud cry.[18]

In her portrayal of the haunted Daventry, Bowen shows how the trauma of the trenches erupted in the barbarism of the Black and Tans, ex-soldiers hastily recruited to the RIC in 1921. Half mad with shell-shock, these broken men in their bi-coloured makeshift uniforms proceeded to re-inflict their nightmares on the Irish populace. At one point Sir Richard dreams that he has joined the Black and Tans, which suggests that he is implicated in their violence, but also that he finds these battle-crazed recruits more nightmarish than rebel arsonists (*LS* 107).

The British soldier Gerald Lesworth is naïve enough to think that the good guys can be firmly distinguished from the bad guys. If war were openly declared, he blusters, 'we could clean these beggars out in a week' (*LS* 38). Such bravado is one way of resisting ambiguity; smugness is another, as exemplified in Betty Vermont, the silliest of the British officers' wives. Betty 'was not disappointed in Ireland . . . She had never before been to so many large houses with so small a sense of her smallness. Of course, they were all very shabby and not artistic at all' (*LS* 36). She longs to give Danielstown a lick of paint. 'We came to take care of all of you – and, of course, we are ever so glad to be able to do it,' she gushes. 'I do think you're so sporting the way you just stay where you are and keep going on. Who would ever have thought the Irish would turn out so disloyal – I mean, of course, the lower classes!' she adds hastily, remembering that the Naylors regard themselves as Irish (*LS* 46–7).

Betty Vermont epitomises everything that the ascendancy despises in the English middle-class. Lady Naylor complains that the English have no relations and no roots: 'for no reason at all they will pack up everything and move across six counties' (*LS* 58). They visit in the morning – an unconscionable breach – and when they come they talk about their insides. Estranged from both the English and the Irish, the Naylors' political predicament is represented by the ante-room at Danielstown, whose occupants can be ambushed from four directions, their conversations overheard throughout the house. With its multiple exits and entrances, this ante-room also resembles the stage set for a farce, enabling Bowen to expose the farcical element of war, the incendiary element of romance. In this besieged domestic space, lovers become guerrillas, their rumours and intrigues mirroring the furtive logistics of insurgency. And it is love, as well as war, that threatens to destroy the Naylors' way of life: Lois's engagement to Gerald Lesworth risks miscegenation with the English middle-class, and the unthinkable prospect of in-laws in Surrey. Faced with such threats, the Naylors cling to traditions long defunct, their formidable will focused on not noticing the ferment in the countryside. ' "Will there ever be anything we can all do except not notice?" ' one visitor exclaims (*LS* 82). Elsewhere Bowen writes that by 1920 the ascendancy was 'a ghost only' – and the Naylors' life, although they do not know it, is an afterlife (*BC* 430). At one point Lois glances at her fingernails, 'the only part of one's person . . . of which it was possible to be conscious socially,' and marvels at the 'yards and yards of inexhaustible nail coming out of one' (*LS* 10). The persistence of the Anglo-Irish compares to the posthumous elongation of these nails.

In this posthumous world, the dead seem more substantial than the living. Here as in Bowen's Court, the dead count double: for what they were and for what they are. The family portraits that loom over the cavernous dining-room 'cancelled time, negatived personality and made of the lower cheerfulness, dining and talking, the faintest exterior friction.' Under the gaze of these lofty ancestors, the six people seated at the table seem 'unconvincingly painted, startled, transitory,' ephemeral as the six peas floating in the soup that Laurence gobbles up with six accurate spoonfuls (*LS* 24). The shabbiness of Danielstown also implies the obsolescence of this way of life. Nothing ever gets repaired. When the company are playing tennis, a net designed to prevent the balls escaping from the court into the shrubbery is 'full of rents' that these stray missiles find 'unerringly.' Needless to say, the defences of the Big House are comparably frayed. But the same net has malfunctioned for so long that many of the balls recovered date back to before the Great War. Lost balls come to signify lost gumption: a ball missing since 1906 reminds a guest of his failure to emigrate to Canada. The ball-hunt inspires Laurence to improvise on the resurgence of lost objects:

'Imagine, sir, a small resurrection day, an intimate thing-y one, when the woods should give up their tennis balls and the bundles of hay their needles: the beaches all their engagement rings and the rivers their cigarette cases and some watches. The sea's too general, an affair of furniture and large boilers, it could wait with the graves for the big day . . .'.

(LS 41–2)

This passage pokes fun at the procedures of the narrative itself, for Bowen – with her meticulous inventories of household objects – performs an 'intimate thing-y' resurrection in her prose.

It is not just tennis balls that bounce back from the past. Fearing ambush by guerrillas from without, the characters are ambushed from within by the incursions of their undead forbears. The house is 'pre-inhabited,' not only by the ancestors whose portraits loom over the dinner-table, but more assertively by Lois's mother Laura, Sir Richard's sister, who died young 'without giving anyone notice of her intention.'[19] Laura has left her signature, quite literally, on both the house and the demesne. Laurence finds her name scratched on the windowpane, leaving prints on the scene that he surveys – like the eye-prints left by Bowen's ancestors in Bowen's Court (*LS* 160). Lois, snooping round the house like Catherine Morland in *Northanger Abbey*, stumbles on her mother's trunks mouldering in storage, inscribed with the monogram LN (*LS* 132). Scrawled like graffiti on the field of vision, Laura is too ubiquitous to be a ghost: she occupies the house so palpably that the living suffer from her presence, rather than her absence. Laurence finds her closeness in his room oppressive, her misspent life having 'clotted up the air.' Lois's father, on the other hand, is so insignificant that Bowen never bothers to explain his absence. 'The rudest man in Ulster he was, with a disagreeably fresh complexion and an eye like a horse' – this is the most we ever hear of him (*LS* 107). It is typical of Bowen's fiction that fathers recede into the background, whereas mothers seize the limelight: Sir Richard is overshadowed by his imperious wife, just as Lois's absent father is eclipsed by her dead mother. Yet dead or alive, the characters occupy the same dimension, as if they had been dreamed into existence by the house.

In her preface to *The Last September*, Bowen speaks of 'the difficulty of assembling a novel's cast – bringing the various characters to the same spot':

> generally, in the novel the characters are maintained in the same orbit by some situation which sets a trap for them – some magnetic interest, devilment, quest or passion. My solution was a more childish one . . . in *The Last September*, as in *The Hotel*, I have used the device of having my men and women actually under the same roof . . .

(MT 123)

Danielstown therefore functions as the 'magnet' that draws the cast of characters together (*LS* 67). The subtitles of the sections formally announce comings and goings, like a butler: 'The Arrival of Mr and Mrs Montmorency,' 'The Visit of Miss Norton,' and 'The Departure of Gerald.' The last of these is butlerishly euphemistic, for Gerald's departure is a mortal one. But the subtitle subordinates his death to its impact on the house, which is not just the backdrop of the novel but its central consciousness. It is notable that all the characters, with the exception of the lord and lady and their overbearing ancestors, visit rather than reside in Danielstown, whose 'strong *own* life' goes on without them. The younger generation, Lois and her cousin Laurence, are the niece and nephew – not the children – of Sir Richard and Lady Naylor, respectively. This indirect line of descent hints, if hints were needed, that the Anglo-Irish have no future, no posterity.

The novel begins with the arrival of Hugo and Francie Montmorency, or more precisely with the sound of their motor in the countryside:

> About six o'clock the sound of a motor, collected out of the wide country and narrowed under the trees of the avenue, brought the household out in excitement on to the steps. Up among the beeches, a thin iron gate twanged; the car slid out from a net of shadow, down the slope to the house. Behind the flashing windscreen Mr and Mrs Montmorency produced – arms waving and a wild escape to the wind of her mauve motor-veil – an agitation of greeting. They were long-promised visitors. They exclaimed, Sir Richard and Lady Naylor exclaimed and signalled: no one spoke yet. It was a moment of happiness, of perfection.

What is striking about this prose, as Sean O'Faolain has observed, is its diminishment of human agency.[20] It is not the Montmorencys, nor even their car, but the sound of its motor that heralds their arrival, a sound 'collected' and 'narrowed' by invisible forces. Later on we realise that this sound, at a distance, could have been mistaken for the roar of armoured vehicles. Deprived by the syntax of volition, the 'household' is 'brought out' by this sound, summoned forth like a hypnotic subject. The passive verbs have the effect of emphasising the subordination of the individual to fate, while the metonymies (the sound of the motor, the twang of the thin iron gate) shift onto objects the power of determination normally reserved for subjects. We are told that this is a moment of happiness, but for whom? The second paragraph assigns the happiness to Lois, but in the first it floats free of any human consciousness. The emphasis upon the moment intimates its brevity: forces are gathering within this landscape to erase such moments, just as the syntax conspires to erase the human will.

Lois Farquar is an early example of Bowen's awkward, often lethal innocents whose need for love wreaks havoc in the drawing-room. In this novel, the terrorism of innocence mirrors the innocence of terrorism – for the rebels are Lois's childhood playmates, victims turned victimisers. Where Lois differs from Bowen's lovelorn adolescents, such as Portia in *The Death of the Heart,* is that she suffers from the inability to be infatuated. 'She really prays for somebody to be fatal; she eyes doors. And you are all disappointments,' says Marda Norton, whose ill-fated visit occupies the middle section of the novel (*LS* 82). Lois first sets out to fall in love with Hugo Montmorency, the idea of an 'older man' appealing to her taste for melodrama. In the prehistory of the novel, Hugo was the lover of her mother Laura, but failed to marry her, which is one of many undone deeds that trail behind him. In the figure of Hugo, Bowen portrays the ascendancy reduced to Beckettian futility. Heir to a Big House which he sold to 'travel light,' and married to the sickly Francie, ten years his senior, Hugo wallows in his disappointments: the woman he never married, the move to Canada he never risked, the bungalow he never bought, the furniture that will never be unstored.[21] His life with Francie has degenerated into a cycle of visits, with Hugo building castles in the air only for the gloomy satisfaction of demolishing them. Lois remembers him most vividly from childhood as fast asleep, a 'kindly monolith' (*LS* 27).

Hugo uses his wife's ill-health as an excuse for his paralysis, and Francie cannot fend off his solicitude. 'How she had tried, but had not been able, to keep him – first from marrying her, then from giving up Canada, leaving his friends when she had to go to the south of France, or from brushing her hair in the evenings' (*LS* 18). Francie, 'wonderfully unselfish,' has given herself up to Hugo's care to justify his purposeless existence, a shady deal described in the therapeutic jargon of today as 'co-dependency' (*LS* 122). Lady Naylor is convinced that Hugo will beat Francie to the grave: 'he will die first, he has just that way of avoiding things. Look how he didn't marry Laura . . .' (*LS* 115). Hugo Montmorency is by no means an appetising figure – 'his negativeness was startling' (*LS* 80). But Bowen understands the magnetism of depression, the sex-appeal of its volcanic inhibitions: 'anger did illuminate him becomingly: brighter and harder, for the first time he could be conceived as lovable' (*LS* 122). With his raging self-pity, Hugo is a forerunner of Markie Linkwater in *To the North,* the most sadistic of Bowen's smouldering depressives.

Rebuffed by Hugo, Lois tries to fall in love with Gerald Lesworth, who is at least convincingly in love with her. His name (as Heather Bryant Jordan has observed) is 'worthless' back to front.[22] Handsome, well-meaning, brainwashed, and obtuse, Gerald takes the English view that 'Irish fighting is not cricket' (*LS* 185). His affections for 'mother, country, dog, school, a friend or two, now – crowningly – Lois,' are 'rare and square – four-square – occurring like houses in a landscape, unrelated and positive' (*LS* 41, 40). Gerald has no missing corner. Lacking nothing, he stifles the imagination: 'He is so terribly *there,*' Lois complains (*LS* 52, 69). He personifies the kind of talk he likes, 'square and facty, compact with assumptions' (*LS* 84). Laurence teases jingo out of him like yards of fingernail. 'Well, the situation's rotten. But right *is* right,' Gerald declares. 'Why?' Laurence snaps back.

> 'Well . . . from the point of view of civilization. Also, you see, they don't fight clean.'
>
> 'Oh, there's no public school spirit in Ireland. But do tell me – what do you mean by the point of view of civilization?'
>
> 'Oh – ours.'
>
> Laurence smiled his appreciation: the conviction, stated without arrogance, had a ring of integrity. Gerald, embarrassed by this benevolence, had recourse again to the back of his head, so gratifyingly polished. 'If you come to think,' he explained, 'I mean, looking back on history – not that I'm intellectual – we *do* seem the only people.'
>
> 'Difficulty being to make them see it'.
>
> (*LS* 92–3)

For Lois, Gerald is always out of focus: 'concrete' and 'shadowless,' he lacks the chiaroscuro that could bring him into view (*LS* 13). Nonetheless she is disappointed by her inability to burn for him. Reared like Emma Bovary on romantic novels ('those biological books,' as Lady Naylor calls them), Lois is perplexed to find herself immune to kisses, at least to those 'administered' by Gerald (*LS* 167, 152). 'But surely love wouldn't get so much talked about if there were not something in it?' she wonders. 'I mean even soap, you know, however much they advertise . . .' (*LS* 97). Later on, however, Gerald's kisses take deferred effect, bringing Lois a vision of 'a quiet beyond experience, as though for many nights he had been sleeping beside her' (*LS* 89). For a brief interlude Lois, motherless daughter of a dying house, mistakes this 'back-to-the-wombishness' for love.[23] She agrees to marry Gerald.

As soon as Lady Naylor learns of the engagement, she brings it to a brutal halt. In one of the funniest scenes in the novel, she engineers an interview with Gerald to force him into retreat. They meet in Mrs Fogarty's drawing-room, surrounded by her photographs of British soldiers, so that the tête-à-tête is witnessed by the 'candid eyes of dead young men' – a ghostly regiment that Gerald is soon to join. Lady Naylor is scandalised that Gerald comes from Surrey (Surrey!), and that his family may be in *trade*, although she would 'never say a thing like that without foundation.' Besides, if they were in trade, 'there would be money; money on English people shows so much and he quite evidently hasn't any. No,' she concludes, the Lesworths must be 'just villa-ry' (*LS* 58). To Gerald she smiles:

> 'We must seem ridiculous to you, over here, the way we are all related.'
> 'Topping, I think,' said Gerald.
> 'Oh, I don't know! Now you people seem to have no relations at all; that must feel so independent.'
> 'I have dozens.'
> 'Indeed? All in Surrey?'
> 'Scattered about.'
> 'That sounds to *me*, of course,' remarked Lady Naylor, pulling her gloves off brightly, 'exceeding restless. But you all *came* from Surrey, didn't you?'
> 'More or less,' said Gerald, who was not sure.
>
> (*LS* 178)

When Gerald protests that he loves Lois, Lady Naylor retorts, harshly but accurately, that Lois does not love him, even though 'she would have loved to love him' (*LS* 52). Besides, he has no money. But Gerald's unaffected love for Lois lends him humanity, and bruised by Lady Naylor's cruelty, he transcends his former role as cardboard henchman of the British Empire. The price of gaining flesh and blood, however, is mortality: a few days later, Gerald is shot dead by a rebel bullet. 'Heroic,' says Lady Naylor briskly. 'Although . . . he could not help it . . .' (*LS* 205). As for Lois, she is bundled off to art school. 'There's a future for girls nowadays outside marriage,' Lady Naylor declares. 'Careers – how *I* should have loved one' (*LS* 174). There is little reason to believe that Lois will flourish as an artist; whether she will turn to writing, like her author, Bowen does not divulge. At this point it seems unlikely, for Lois complains that writing is too self-revealing: 'Even things like – like elephants get so personal,' she stammers (*LS* 98). Yet whatever path she chooses, it is clear that Lois has a future, whereas Gerald has only a grave, the house – a pyre.

There is an old joke that in Anglo-Ireland the time is always mid-afternoon after a heavy Sunday meal. Torpor is certainly the feeling that predominates in Danielstown. Laurence feels 'all gassy inside from yawning,' and yearns for 'some crude intrusion of the actual' (*LS* 44). But the house immures itself against reality: the massed trees at the boundary of the demesne are 'spread like a rug to dull some keenness, break some contact between self and senses perilous to the routine of living' (*LS* 67). In this muffled world, peopled by sleep-walkers, Marda Norton introduces human agency. 'She's very positive,' Laurence remarks (*LS* 80). Marda's visit to Danielstown takes place in the middle section of the narrative, where her charm electrifies the deadened household – it is not for nothing that her name is an anagram of 'drama.' One guest after another falls in love with her. Lois, who has so much trouble loving Gerald, falls for Marda with the greatest ease. Even Laurence, briefly distracted from his narcissism, gives Marda a book. But Hugo smoulders for her so volcanically that Lady Naylor is obliged to send her packing.

Marda is too open to experience to last long in this anaesthetised environment – it spits her out. This is a world where objects masquerade as people. In Hugo and Francie's bedroom, 'two arm-chairs faced round intently into the empty grate'; and when Hugo sits down on a chair outside, 'creaks ran through the wicker, discussing him' (*LS* 12, 29). While objects menace or oppress the other characters, they make no impact on Marda's vitality. For Lois, 'the simplest objects' are 'tinged with consequence,' but Marda simply does not notice them, and treats them with a nonchalance her host finds agonising (*LS* 162). Sir Richard spends most of her visit bemoaning the suitcase that she lost on the way; at the end of her foreshortened stay, she forgets the book that Laurence gave her. On a previous visit she lost an engagement ring, and has discarded fiancés with blithe abandon. The Naylors think her engagements fantastic, for 'they have all come to nothing' (*LS* 85).

Marda's body is strangely prone to penetration; she has what she wryly terms 'a high standard' of bleeding (*LS* 127). Lady Naylor has never forgiven her for bleeding extravagantly at a children's party. True to form, Marda manages to burn herself by drinking coffee as soon as she arrives at Danielstown. Her opportunity to bleed occurs when she insists on exploring an abandoned mill, with the infatuated Lois at her side, while Hugo lurks resentfully outside. Entering the ruin they disturb a sleeping rebel, who points a pistol at them. For a comic instant, the young women are distracted by its puniness: 'it was short-looking, scarcely more than a button' (*LS* 124). The rebel slinks upstairs, muttering that they should stay inside their house while they still have it. But his pistol goes off accidentally, and the bullet grazes Marda's hand. 'I seem to have lost some pieces of skin,' she observes – a loss that she accepts with much the same aplomb as the losses of her suitcase and her suitors (*LS* 126). When she emerges from the mill, her injured hand pressed against her mouth, the sulking Hugo, 'in an incredible half-glimpse,' thinks he sees 'blood round the lips' (*LS* 126). This image is obviously sexual, but Julian Moynahan suggests that it could also be vampiric, associating the ascendancy with the Undead. In any case, both women undergo a kind of defloration in the mill: Marda's body is literally penetrated by the Troubles, and Lois's innocence is shattered by her glimpse of Hugo's erotic obsession with her friend. It is this realisation, as William Heath has pointed out, that initiates Lois into 'the conspiracy of adulthood and adultery.'[24] She stammers, 'I've had a . . . a revelation' (*LS* 128).

Marda's thin skin is the only membrane in the household to be pierced by politics. The other characters shield themselves against all shocks. When the company is sitting outside in the evening, the ladies swathe themselves in shawls, as if 'a touch of dew on the bare skin would be fatal.' Lady Naylor warns Lois, sitting cushionless on the front step, that 'at this time of night stone will strike up through anything,' causing rheumatism in later life. 'It will be my rheumatism,' Lois retorts. Meanwhile the massed trees pillow and blanket the demesne, 'muffling the senses' – as if the Anglo-Irish had resolved to sleep through the nightmare of history (*LS* 29, 106). Lois protests: 'How is it that in this country that ought to be full of such violent realness, there seems nothing for me but clothes and what people say? I might as well be in some kind of cocoon' (*LS* 49).

The narrative also cocoons itself, in the sense that most events occur offstage, as in Greek tragedy. We hear, rather than see, the gunshot that wounds Marda, because Bowen removes us from the scene of action, placing us with surly Hugo on the outside of the ruined mill. Similarly, Laurence's capture by rebels is reported after the event, the danger past. Those actions that take place before our eyes tend to be aborted: questions unasked, gramophones silenced, kisses unadministered, engagements broken, and conversations 'torn off rough at [the] edge' (*LS* 93). Even inaction is inhibited: 'There was to be no opportunity for what he must not say to be rather painfully not said' (*LS* 138). On the rare occasions when actions are carried out, they detach themselves from their performers and hover in the past-clogged atmosphere. Gerald's kisses, lost on Lois, float suspended in the living-room or 'asterisk' the evening sky (*LS* 158). 'Queer,' Lois muses, how men throw off action without a quiver at severance from the self that goes into it. They remain complete, the action hangs in the air of the place, above the grass or furniture, crystallizing in memory; eternal, massive and edged to the touch of thought as, to the bodily touch, a grand piano. (*LS* 91)

But Lois's cocoon is soon to be in flames.

In *The Last September*, as in *Bowen's Court*, the house is the hero of the tragedy. In the end it is the house that suffers for its founders' greed. But just as Gerald cannot be murdered until he has been brought to life, so the house cannot be executed until it has acquired consciousness. Constantly described as staring, the house seems to gain face as the inmates lose it. Lois prefers the back of Gerald's head to his full frontal, and wonders why men are so rarely photographed in profile ('Do they have to look frank?' (*LS* 107, 101)). Hugo's failures are also described in terms of facelessness: 'the perspectives of his regret opened fanwise, profound avenues each white at the end with a faceless statue' (*LS* 105). While the characters are threatened with loss of face, in every sense, the facial features of the house grow more defined: out of its 'window sockets,' 'a square black eye of the house – three – four – looked down . . . through the branches . . .' (*LS* 124; 86–7). In *Bowen's Court*, Bowen insists that character is shaped by architecture; but in *The Last September*, architecture takes the place of character, usurping personality from the protagonists – Danielstown acquires face and consciousness while human faces turn into blank walls. The use of the term 'sockets' to describe the doors and windows of the house implies that its face has already turned into a skull.

The last paragraph of the novel turns back to the first, but replays it in reverse as if a film had been rewound. Once again, the roar of a motor rips across the silent landscape, but this time the noise that heralded the Montmorencys' arrival decrescendos as it carries off the arsonists.

> At Danielstown, half-way up the avenue under the beeches, the thin iron gate twanged (missed its latch, remained swinging aghast) as the last unlit car slid out with the executioners bland from accomplished duty. The sound of the last car widened, gave itself to the open and empty country and was demolished. Then the first wave of a silence that was to be ultimate flowed back, confident, to the steps. Above the steps, the door stood open hospitably upon a furnace.
>
> (*LS* 206)

Here the sound of the last car widens, whereas the sound of the Montmorencys' car had narrowed, until it is demolished in the landscape. A 'wave of silence' takes the place of the waving arms of the Montmorencys' arrival, and flows over the steps on which the household had awaited its long-promised visitors. But the arsonists seem as robotic as the household seemed at the beginning, when it was summoned forth hypnotically onto the threshold. Even the final atrocity occurs with a minimum of volition, the perpetrators, 'bland with accomplished duty,' swept by their cars into the silence. The use of passive verbs conveys the sense that both the burners and the burned are subject to the nameless, faceless force of history. Everything in Bowen's prose conspires to efface the human subject. Action is imputed only to unliving things: the gate that twangs, the car that slides, the door that welcomes its destroyers, and the silence that flows over the stairs. This syntax mocks the notion that human beings can command their destiny.

Bowen also hints that the writer is controlled by unknown forces. Her Preface to *The Last September*, published in 1952, argues that the novelist cannot foresee the outcome of the work. 'To write is to be captured,' Bowen declares. 'The writer, like a swimmer caught in an undertow, is borne in an unexpected direction.' Thus it was the novel, not the novelist, that chose September as its month (*MT* 125, 123). Fall is the season for the fall of houses, but also for the fall of words into their places on the page, a fall that eludes the writer's mastery. All these falls, in Bowen's view, depend on forces that dwarf the will of individuals: the writer is as 'captured' as the victim and the executioner, caught in the undertow of unknown agencies. 'Caught' – the title of Henry Green's wartime novel of 1942 – epitomises the predicament of Bowen's characters, entrammeled in the nets of history, their vision of the world tattooed by prints of previous lives. The novels discussed in the next chapter, *The Hotel* and *Friends and Relations*, examine what it means to be caught in the impasse of desire.

Notes

1. Joyce, *Ulysses* (1922; Harmondsworth: Penguin, 1986), ch. 14, p. 323, lines 398–400.
2. James, *The Spoils of Poynton and Other Stories* (Garden City, New York: Nelson Doubleday, 1971), ch. 21, p. 157.
3. In both Maria Edgeworth's *Castle Rackrent* (1800) and Sheridan Le Fanu's *Uncle Silas* (1864), there is a play on the double meaning of execution: Sir Condy Rackrent, after suffering the execution of his

property, plays dead in order to witness his own funeral; Uncle Silas tells Maud Ruthyn that an execution is about to take place in his house, when it is she that he intends to execute.

4. T. R. Henn, 'The Big House' (1967), in *Last Essays: Mainly on Anglo-Irish Literature*, p. 207.
5. *BC* 20, 69, 452, 218; Glendinning, *Elizabeth Bowen*, p. 8.
6. *Purgatory* (1939), in *The Collected Plays of W. B. Yeats* (London: Macmillan, 1952), p. 683.
7. Bowen, 'The Big House' (1940), *MT* 26–7.
8. *BC* 31; Joyce, 'The Sisters,' in *Dubliners* (1914; New York: Viking, 1969), p. 9.
9. Moynahan, 'Elizabeth Bowen: Anglo-Irish Postmortem,' p. 84.
10. *MT* 27; *BC* 258.
11. In her Preface to Sheridan Le Fanu's *Uncle Silas*, Bowen described the novel as 'an Irish story transposed to an English setting. The hermetic solitude and the autocracy of the great country house, the demonic power of the family myth, fatalism, feudalism and the "ascendancy" outlook are accepted facts of life for the race of hybrids from which Le Fanu sprang' (*MT* 101).
12. E. Œ. Somerville and Martin Ross, *The Big House of Inver* (1925; reprinted London: Quartet, 1978), p. 135.
13. I am grateful to Sarah Mesle for pointing out the ambiguity of 'must' in an essay on *The Last September* written for my class on Irish Modernism, Northwestern University, 2002.
14. J. G. Farrell, *Troubles* (1970; Harmondsworth: Penguin, 1975), p. 7.
15. O'Faolain, *The Vanishing Hero*, p. 178.
16. Quoted in Jordan, *How Will the Heart Endure*, p. 51.
17. Mark Bence-Jones, *Twilight of the Ascendancy*, p. 190.
18. Bowen, 'A Year I Remember – 1918,' broadcast on 10 March 1949, HRHRC.
19. *WL* 48; *LS* 19.
20. O'Faolain, *The Vanishing Hero*, pp. 173–4.
21. In *The Heat of the Day*, Colonel Pole advises Stella that her son should get rid of his Big House and 'travel light' (*HD* 82).
22. Jordan, *How Will the Heart Endure*, p. 49.
23. This was Bowen's term for her yearning to return to Hythe, her childhood home, in a letter to Charles Ritchie, cited in Glendinning, *Elizabeth Bowen*, p. 222.
24. William Heath, *Elizabeth Bowen: An Introduction to Her Novels*, p. 40.

3

Impasse: The Hotel, Friends and Relations, *and 'The Shadowy Third'*

The Last September was the only novel Bowen set in Ireland until *A World of Love* in 1955, although there are significant excursions to Anglo-Irish houses in *The House in Paris* and *The Heat of the Day*. Otherwise her early novels turn away from Ireland: the first, *The Hotel*, exports an English cast of characters to Italy; the third, *Friends and Relations*, takes place exclusively in England. In both novels, Ireland – which Lois Farquar imagines as a fragment broken off the coast of England and cast adrift in the Atlantic Ocean – recedes from view (*LS* 34). Bowen's decision to locate her first full-length novel on the continent, and most of her subsequent novels in England, indicates that she intended to establish her credentials as a European novelist, asserting her affinity to Forster, Flaubert, Proust, and James, rather than to Edgeworth, Le Fanu, or Somerville and Ross.

The Hotel in the Riviera seems a world away from the Big Houses of County Cork, but similar dilemmas re-emerge. Sydney Warren, the heroine of *The Hotel*, is an updated, spiky version of beribboned Lois Farquar. Both are adolescents on the verge of womanhood; while Lois is an orphan, Sydney has no father, nor is a mother ever mentioned. The first (and last) of Bowen's heroines to entertain professional ambitions, Sydney hopes to become a doctor, and to this purpose has completed an exhausting gauntlet of exams. Now she has been sent away on holiday, with a hypochondriac cousin as a chaperone, for fear that the idleness expected of young ladies will drive her to a nervous breakdown. Both Sydney and Lois have reached a turning-point, not only in their personal development but in the history of their sex. In *The Last September* Lady Naylor pontificates,

'There's a future for girls nowadays outside marriage' (*LS* 174). But what does the future hold? Must the thrill of romance be sacrificed for the chill of a 'career'? And how can the novel, which traditionally ends in death or marriage, accommodate itself to women's new and unpredictable trajectories? Henry James foresaw that the novel would be re-shaped fundamentally by 'the revolution taking place in the position and outlook of women.'[1] But just as Bowen's adolescents are stuck between generations, unwilling to imitate their mothers but unable to imagine other destinies, so *The Hotel* climaxes in an impasse, both literal and metaphorical. At this point the only way forward for either the novel or the heroine is to jettison traditional romantic endings. An obstruction brings a car drive to a standstill; Sydney withdraws from her short-lived engagement with a parson; and connections established in the novel unravel stitch by stitch until the characters are strangers once again. This deconstructive logic compares to the chess game in Beckett's *Murphy*, which the madman Mr Endon plays with the maniacal intention of manoeuvring his pieces back to their original positions on the board.

Each of Bowen's early novels confronts the impasse of romance and devises an ingenious strategem for getting round it. In *The Last September*, as in *The Hotel*, the marriage plot evaporates, leaving the heroine facing an uncertain future, her innocence distressingly intact. Even in *Friends and Relations*, where the heroine gets married at the outset, romantic aspirations end in impasse. Not until *To the North* are lovers allowed to consummate their passion, with disastrous consequences – 'a splinter of ice in the heart is bombed out rather than thawed out' (*N* 47). But the ice never breaks in Bowen's first two novels: Sydney and Lois suffer from the inability to fall in love, and have read too many novels not to be perturbed that they are missing something. Yet neither finds young men particularly 'inspiring,' and both are drawn to older women of the world: Sydney is obsessed with Mrs Kerr, a languorous enchantress at the Hotel, much as Lois is obsessed with Marda. At one point Lois finds herself wishing Gerald was a woman, exasperated by his saying her hair is 'lovely' when she wants to know if there are twigs in it (*LS* 97, 172). Yet in spite of innuendoes of lesbian desire, outing the heroine is not the point, for Bowen is more concerned with number than with gender. Sydney longs to share a universe of two with Mrs Kerr, but the arrival of a third person, in the form of Mrs Kerr's son Ronald, shatters the dyad, and Sydney has to go out hunting for a fourth to avenge herself against the second for favouring the third. On one level these supernumerary presences pose an impediment to love, but on a deeper level they generate its energy, as love ricochets between the four points of the quadrangle. If any of these corners drops away, love short-circuits. This is what happens at the end of *The Hotel*, when Sydney breaks off her engagement, and all the planets in this brief erotic constellation drift apart.

Normally romance involves the quest for an *object* of desire, but Bowen's first two novels lack a *subject* of desire – neither Sydney Warren nor Lois Farquar can work herself up into the passion traditionally required of a heroine. If these novels confirm Yeats's view that 'the desire that can be satisfied is not a great desire,' this is because Bowen questions the very possibility of a desiring subject.[2] Sydney, who suffers from a 'strange anaesthesia,' could be seen as a living embodiment of impasse, blocked from without and from within. Described by her tennis-partner as 'subject to a deplorable kind of paralysis,' this ailment extends to her emotional relationships: in her romantic life as in her tennis, 'love' means no points scored (*H* 143, 12). In Bowen's third novel, *Friends and Relations*, love bumps up against a different kind of impasse: there are two married couples in the book, but the wife of one pair is entangled with the husband of the other. In addition to these double couples, two free-floating women, a lesbian and a retired adulteress, stretch the four-cornered love affair into a hexagon. These shadowy presences inhibit the fulfilment of desire but also enable it to circulate, fanning its flames while hindering its satisfaction.

Freud's theory of the role of the third person in the dirty joke sheds some light on Bowen's triadic structures of desire. In *Jokes and their Relation to the Unconscious*, Freud argues that the dirty joke originates in the desire to seduce a woman. If the woman yields, seduction obviates the need for speech; but if she resists, the act of sexual aggression is redirected into the linguistic detour of a joke. With characteristic chauvinism, Freud takes it for granted that the woman, left to her own devices, inevitably falls for the seducer. Her flimsy resistance must therefore be reinforced by 'another man,' for it is this 'third person' who prevents the sex act, forcing the seducer to resort to jokes instead of deeds. The presence of a third party precludes seduction (for the first person cannot assault the second under the observation of an onlooker), yet ensures the perpetuation of sexual excitement through its transformation into verbal play. Hence the third person acts as both an obstacle and an incentive to desire. By deflecting sexual violence into language, he inaugurates the chain of substitutions whereby everyone who hears the joke is induced to pass it on. Thus savage lust is converted into social intercourse.

But notice that Freud conceives of joking as a male preserve: the third person is always assumed to be 'another man.' By dislodging the woman from her place, the third person becomes the 'ally' of the joke, whereas she is reduced to being its butt. He is to be tickled, she debased. Adding social to sexual chauvinism, Freud argues that woman's role becomes redundant as the joke moves up the social ladder. Among the 'lower orders,' the presence of the woman encourages obscenity; but in the higher levels of society, her presence brings the joking to an end, for men of rank 'save up' their smut for times when they can be 'alone together.' Thus the original impulse to seduce the woman is transformed into the desire to amuse another man with words. Heterosexual aggression gives way to homosocial bonding, in which men get together to tell dirty jokes at the expense of the absent woman.[3]

This structure reappears in Bowen's works, but she often turns the Freudian triangle upside-down, making an absent man into the bridge between two female characters.[4] Her late novel *A World of Love* presents two women, Antonia and Lilia, locked together in a tug-of-war over the ghost of their dead lover. A similar dynamic may be found in *The Hotel*, in which two minor characters, 'the Honourable Mrs Pinkerton and her sister-in-law the Honourable Miss Pinkerton,' have been thrown together by the death of 'the Honourable Edward Pinkerton' ('Poor Edward,' as he is always called, not because he died too young but because he did so little). His widow and his sister are 'more closely allied to one another in the memory of Edward than they had either of them been to Edward himself' (*H* 19, 24). In other words, the female Pinkertons are joined together by an absent male; this is a reversal of Freud's dirty joke, in which two men are joined together by an absent female. While Bowen avoids Freud's gender stereotypes, she shares his intuition that a third person is required to create a circuit of desire. Operating as both an obstruction and a conduit between lovers, this shadowy third holds couples together precisely by disrupting their duality, diverting two-way love into a three-way relay system.

In an intriguing passage from *The Heat of the Day*, quoted in chapter 1, Bowen insists that the heterosexual couple is always haunted by a mysterious third presence. 'No, there is no such thing as being alone together,' she writes:

Daylight moves round the walls; night rings the changes of its intensity; everything is on its way to somewhere else – there is the presence of movement, that third presence, however still, however unheeding in their trance two may try to stay. Unceasingly something is at its work.

This enigmatic third has a hybrid literary ancestry and manifests itself in different ways in Bowen's works. Derived in part from Gothic fiction, it bears some resemblance to 'the third person' in Henry James's story of that name, in which the ghost of a hanged smuggler comes between two staid old ladies.[5] In Bowen's work, the third presence serves to draw attention to the writer's interference in the story, as in the above quotation from *The Heat of the Day*, where the voice-over intrudes into the narrative to comment on the intrusion of the shadowy third. In Bowen's story 'The Secession,' discussed below, the third presence is associated with the writer's power to murder her creations. In *Friends and Relations*, on the other hand, the third presence is subjected to hectic permutation, dividing into fourths, fifths, and sixths.

Freud's model of the dirty joke mirrors the Oedipal triangle, in which the primal dyad of mother and child is disrupted by the third term of the father. But Bowen often adds a fourth term to this triangle, and sometimes adds a further fifth or sixth. Although the holders of these places are constantly reshuffled, the fourth position tends to be associated with a captivating mother-figure. To the traditional trio of lover, rival, and beloved, Bowen adds a witch – Mrs Kerr in *The Hotel*, Elfrida in *Friends and Relations*, Madame Fisher in *The House in Paris* – who lures the heroine away from the erotic triangle into a four-sided configuration of desire. This fourth woman plays a role similar to that which Freud attributes to Frau K in his case-history of Dora. Throughout this case Freud insists that Dora is in love with her father or her father-substitute Herr K, but afterwards he realises her greatest passion was reserved for Frau K, her father's mistress: 'her homosexual (gynaecophilic) love for Frau K was the strongest unconscious current in her mental life.'[6] Frau K therefore represents the missing corner of the quadrangle that Freud has mistaken for a triangle; she stands for a supplementary desire that cannot be dragooned into the Oedipal paradigm. In Bowen's fiction, the fourth woman represents both supplement and lack: she is lacking in the sense that she withdraws from the erotic field of action, and by so doing inaugurates the chain of substitutions that ensures the circulation of desire; but she is also supplementary in that she adds an extra shadow to the love affair. In the following pages we shall see how the shadowy presence, the mysterious intruder at the heart of love, provides the impasse that impassions Bowen's lovers.

In the Preface to *The Last September*, Bowen describes both the Big House and the Hotel as 'childish' stratagems for trapping characters under one roof. But the Hotel represents a very different kind of trap from Danielstown, a family home whose visitors are magnetised by blood-ties or long-standing friendship. In hotels it is strangers, not friends and relations, who 'jiggle apart and together.' Tourists become strangers even to themselves, leaving their identities at home in pursuit of an 'innocent holiday taste for incognito.' Only in the Hotel could Milton shed his dog-collar, or Sydney agree to be a parson's wife. In this transient assemblage, gossip and surveillance, rather than kinship or affection, hold the characters in volatile synthesis. The 'hundred windows of the Hotel' exercise a constant vigilance. The Hotel is overlooked in turn: 'Eyes from the villas could have peered down into the vacant eyes of newly awakened sleepers.' Like Jeremy Bentham's panopticon – his blueprint for a prison in which every cell would be exposed to the surveillance of an unseen watchman – the Hotel enforces conformity through paranoia.[7]

Yet the novel opens by flinging the characters apart, rather than by drawing them together. Miss Pym, having quarrelled with her companion Miss Fitzgerald, rushes down the stairs to find the lounge vacated: 'There was not a soul down there; not a movement among the shadows . . . Not a shadow crossed . . . Not a sound came . . . Miss Fitzgerald was not there.' With this litany of 'nots,' the narrative begins by voiding the mise-en-scène of characters. A moment later Mrs Kerr arrives, calling out for Sydney, as if to summon her out the 'limbo to which forgetfulness had consigned her . . .' Miss Pym retorts: ' "Miss Warren isn't here" ' (*H* 5–6). Underneath this farce of missed encounters lurks a sense of the fragility of presence, the imminence of loss. More of an end than a beginning, these opening paragraphs foreshadow the diaspora with which the book concludes, scattering its characters across the seas.

It is striking that the novel should begin with women looking for women, not for men. In *The Hotel*, love between women dominates the action, while heterosexual attachments fizzle out on contact with reality. The story opens with the rift between two middle-aged spinsters, Miss Fitzgerald and Miss Pym, and ends with their reconciliation. This means that all the intrigues between men and women take place within the fracture opened up between these female friends. At the conclusion, Bowen evades what Forster, in *Aspects of the Novel,* calls the 'idiotic use of marriage as a finale,' and places a reunion between women at the terminus traditionally accorded to the wedding ceremony.[8] Patricia Juliana Smith has pointed out that Bowen goes to inordinate lengths to prevent her characters from getting married, often by killing off the would-be grooms: Gerald Lesworth in *The Last September* is shot dead by a rebel bullet; Max Ebhart in *The House in Paris* stabs himself to death; Robert Kelway in *The Heat of the Day* jumps or falls off Stella's roof.[9] In *The Hotel,* the slaughter of the suitors is accomplished without violence, but the eligible men back off with their tails between their legs, leaving operatic passion to the women.

Geometrically speaking, an erotic triangle develops, which then expands into a quadrangle but suddenly contracts into a gnomon after the excision of the fourth imagined corner. First Sydney falls in love with Mrs Kerr, who indulges her young admirer as far as lethargy allows. Mrs Kerr 'has no interests,' a gossip grumbles. 'She hasn't a large correspondence, she does nothing at all for herself' (*H* 51). But Sydney, prey to paralysis herself, is fascinated by her idol's immobility. The 'violent friendship' between Sydney and this femme fatale is disrupted when Mrs Kerr's long-neglected son Ronald arrives at the Hotel, to be showered with overdue maternal adoration (*H* 53). Now it is Sydney's turn to feel neglected. The flirt Veronica Lawrence thinks Sydney a 'queer girl . . . to sit brooding cheerlessly on a parapet because a middle-aged woman hadn't asked her to go for a drive' (*H* 33). 'I would far rather she lost her head about a man,' another busybody comments (*H* 53). But Sydney chafes at the idea that women must always be angling for husbands. Why should she and Mrs Kerr, she wonders, be 'supposed to assume . . . that that man down in the garden could be more to either of us than the other'? (*H* 60). Even the married women in the Hotel agree that 'the best kind of man is no companion.' 'Still, he is someone *there*' is the best that anyone can say in favour of a husband (*H* 54). But thereness can also be a nuisance in a man: in *The Last September,* Gerald Lesworth is 'so *there*' that he imprisons Lois's imagination and spoils any possibility of romance.

Sidelined in Mrs Kerr's affections, Sydney accepts a proposal of marriage from James Milton, a middle-aged vicar as virginal as she. Now the triangle turns into a rectangle. The fourth corner drops away at the climax of the novel, when the company assembles for a valedictory car drive in the mountains. Their descent is brought to an abrupt stop by 'a long wagon of timber jammed crossways, shouting men, backing, terrified horses.' In this traffic jam, modernity is blocked by tradition: the motorcar, emblem of the new, bumps up against the 'dead wood' of the past, and no future can go forward until the resistance has been cleared. The cruelty inflicted on the horses harks back to the terrible nightmare in Dostoevsky's *Crime and Punishment* where Raskolnikov dreams about the savage beating of a helpless carthorse.[10] Bowen's horses are also kicked and thrashed until they bleed, but the witnesses' reactions differ tellingly. Milton gets furious, while Sydney keeps her cool, a cool that verges on necrosis. Before this impasse the heroine, unable to contemplate the future, has been yearning for the car to plunge over the precipice: ' "If it could be the next corner," she thought, "we should go over clean – there is that clear drop. Let it be the next corner . . ." ' Instead of falling, however, the car gets stuck, and this sudden arrest jerks Sydney out of her somnambulism. Life pierces through her carapace of anaesthesia – 'life as keen as death to bite upon the consciousness, pressed inexorably upon her, held to her throat like a knife' (*H* 159–60). Impeded from without, she realises that she has also been impeded from within – 'dammed up' – her progress thwarted by outmoded narratives (*H* 13). In a flash it dawns on her that marriage to Milton is impossible. ' "I suppose it was the shock of being alive – oh, how can I explain to you?" ' she cries. ' "I had no idea we were as real as this." ' Up to now the lovers have been shadow-dancing like illusions dreamed up in the mind of the Hotel. ' "I think we have been asleep here," ' Sydney muses; 'you know in a dream how quickly and lightly shapes move, they have no weight, nothing offers them any resistance. They are governed by some funny law of convenience that seems to us perfectly rational, they clash together without any noise and come apart without injury' (*H* 162).

On one level, the impasse in the mountain symbolises sexual inhibition: faced with the prospect of carnal passion, where bodies clash with sound and injury, Sydney retreats into paralysis. In this sense she resembles Eveline in Joyce's *Dubliners*, the book that he regarded as his vivisection of the Irish malady: paralysis.[11] Eveline, a Dublin shop girl, is invited to embark on a new life in Argentina with a plausible bounder, but she fails to board the ship at the last minute, arrested by an inhibition that she cannot explain. While the way forward for Eveline is probably seduction and abandonment, the way back is a lifetime of what-ifs. Sydney's paralysis, on the other hand, aligns her with the Anglo-Irish sleepwalkers of Bowen's fiction, by evoking the spellbound state of the ascendancy. Yet Sydney is not

Irish but English (although her name associates her with Australia, as if to exculpate her from both islands). Bowen's decision to create an English heroine, distanced from the Irish stalemate, implies that Sydney is fixated on a personal, rather than political, catastrophe. Her symptoms – insentience, de-realisation, suicidal fantasies – suggest that she has undergone a psychic trauma. Her favourite accessory – a flame-red scarf, bound around her forehead like a bandage or streaming from her neck like blood – signals a wounding more mysterious than defloration, a 'queer appetite for pain' that puzzles her self-appointed mentors. For Milton, 'the colours of her scarf burnt' (*H* 139, 152).

Despite the risks of psychobiographical analysis, it is hard to resist the suspicion that Sydney's 'strange anaesthesia' reflects Bowen's state of shock after her mother's death: 'the sense of disfigurement, mortification, disgrace' that goes with 'total bereavement.'[12] Motherless, at least for the duration of the narrative, Sydney finds a mother-substitute in Mrs Kerr, who is described as 'vague': a word that Bowen often uses to describe her own faraway mother.[13] There is something ghostly about Mrs Kerr's vagueness (has she grown vague in the survivor's memory?), just as there is something moribund about her indolence that testifies to her affinity to the dead mother. But instead of dying, Mrs Kerr rejects Sydney in favour of her son. At this crisis Sydney fails to follow the trajectory mapped out by Freud, whereby the daughter abandons the mother for the father and graduates from homosexual to heterosexual desire. If one accepts Freud's recipe for maturation, Sydney's impasse could be interpreted as arrested sexual development, resulting in fixation on the mother. But there is no evidence that Bowen thinks the sexes predestined to desire one another. Sydney, watching newly-weds solicitously watching one another eat, finds it 'odder that ever . . . that men and women should be expected to pair off for life' (*H* 18). In fact Sydney never relinquishes the dead mother; her breakthrough in the mountains testifies to her acceptance of bereavement, for she casts away all substitutes for the lost object.

Impasse is not restricted to Sydney's personal psychology, but extends into the detail of the narrative, where actions are repeatedly arrested or aborted: cars stop dead, brakes jam fast, lifts break down. The intermittency of life at the Hotel makes Milton wonder if he will ever see Sydney as a whole, rather than a 'succession of moments' (*H* 148). These constant interruptions resemble the torn-off conversations, unadministered embraces, and Prufrockian volte-faces of *The Last September.* They also invite comparison to 'Circe,' the dream

chapter of *Ulysses*, which Joyce associated with the locomotive apparatus of human body. 'Locomotor ataxy.' 'O, my dictionary,' chirp the
prostitutes in Circe's brothel.[14] The dictionary explains that locomotor ataxia is a neurological affliction marked by spasms, cramps,
tremors, seizures, lapses, and paralyses. Needless to say, there is no
place in Bowen's realism for the rambunctious hallucinations of the
'Circe' episode. But life in *The Hotel* is also shaken by ataxic, epileptic
rhythms. To Milton the social intercourse of the resort resembles 'the
maze of a gnat's dance, an aimless passionate jiggle apart and
together.' Jiggling, jerking, seizing up, the characters are constantly
short-circuiting, their locomotion suddenly arrested and their consciousness suspended, emptied out. After her contretemps with Miss
Pym, Miss Fitzgerald is 'frightened by an interior quietness and by the
thought that she had for once in her life stopped thinking and might
never begin again.' Here Miss Fitzgerald's mind is clearly out of
order, on the blink; later Sydney is associated with the broken
elevator: 'distracted, mechanical, and at a standstill.' One lady confesses she is often surprised when the telephone rings to discover that
she still exists. It is as if she must be plugged in or dialled up for her
machinery to function (*H* 108, 5, 121, 53).

If Sydney is a broken elevator, stuck between the heights of
romance and the depths of sexuality, she also projects her own
paralysis onto the world. In her imagination, she transfixes the
inhabitants of the hotel with the petrifying gaze of a Medusa. At
one point she pictures the Hotel as a dolls' house, flung open like a
tomb on Judgement Day to expose its occupants in rigor mortis:

> 'I have often thought it would be interesting if the front of any house, but
> of an hotel especially, could be swung open on a hinge like the front of a
> doll's house. Imagine the hundreds of rooms with their walls lit up and
> the real-looking staircase and all the people surprised doing appropriate
> things in appropriate attitudes as though they had been put there to
> represent something and had never moved in their lives.'

Is this a dolls' house or a catacomb? In this rhetorical set-piece, stiff as
the vision it describes, Sydney peoples the Hotel with motionless
corpses, bound to 'the compulsion of their furniture.' Perhaps it was
the churches already existing, she suggests, with their pews and
pulpits waiting to be filled, that turned Milton into a parson.
' "I'm afraid I don't agree with you at all," ' Milton retorts, with
impressive finality. If Milton is disconcerted by Sydney's flight of
fancy, it is because she has flung open the 'warren' of her psyche,

revealing the impasse of her inner world, tenanted by lifeless car-
icatures of the family: 'the father-doll propped against the library
book-shelves' (*H* 68–9). Melanie Klein has argued that the ego
'introjects' the objects of its outer world into the inner world of
fantasy, alternately attacking and propitiating these 'internal objects.'[15] From a Kleinian perspective, Sydney's dolls could be interpreted as her internal objects punitively turned to stone. But the
dolls' house also mirrors the procedures of the narrative itself, for it is
Bowen who swings open the façade of the Hotel, inviting us to pry
into its chambers; and it is Bowen who rigidifies her characters,
transforming them into 'still lives', to borrow Bennett and Royle's
term for Bowen's art of petrifaction.[16]

It is possible that Bowen was drawn to painting in her early youth
because of the petrifaction it inflicts on life; later she described her
writing as a form of word-painting.[17] Using words to paint pictures is
one way of arresting their linear momentum, creating asylums of
stasis in the narrative. It is notable that *The Hotel* is punctuated by
tableaux, in which the scene of action is suddenly immobilised into a
picture. Milton, searching unsuccessfully for Ronald, imagines his
frustration captured in a composition called 'Temptation to Murder'
(*H* 109). Ronald, meanwhile, is frequently compared to statues and
paintings: a 'Donatello,' a 'Laocoön' imprisoned in his mother's
tentacles, and the 'young Sebastian of painters . . . strung to a tree'
(*H* 141, 164, 130). Such images operate like freeze-frames in a film,
jamming the progress of the narrative. Another means of stilling life
is the demotic artform of the snapshot, mentioned once or twice in
the Hotel, which petrifies its victims at their most banal – much as
Sydney petrifies the family in her vision of the dolls' house. And it is
petrifaction that Sydney desires above all: her attraction to Mrs Kerr
indicates a preference, not for women over men, but for stasis over
locomotion. In the Hotel, men 'jiggle apart and together,' whereas
Mrs Kerr remains stock-still. This inertia appeals to Sydney's death-
drive, her suicidal urge to shortcut all the hairpin turnings in the
mountain road and to dive headlong into the abyss.

Much has been written about similarities between *The Hotel* and E. M.
Forster's *A Room with a View*, the bulk of it to Bowen's disadvantage.
Even Bowen's most influential advocate, Hermione Lee, accuses her
of imitation in this debut performance. The accusation is not entirely
unjust: echoes of Forster do reverberate, but these are orchestrated
with a symphony of other echoes, ranging from Jane Austen (*Emma*)

to Virginia Woolf (*The Voyage Out*), Thomas Mann (*The Magic Mountain*), and Henry James (*Daisy Miller*), to name only a few. Moreover Bowen does not merely parrot her precursors, but argues with them. Her treatment of *A Room with a View* (which Forster wryly dubbed his 'nicest' novel) alternates between homage and satire.[18] The resemblances are striking: both Forster and Bowen gather English tourists under one Italian roof, partly to poke fun at foibles like 'the traditional British struggle with macaroni' (*H* 21). But Forster also introduces locals in order to contrast Italian passion to English prudery, thus reinforcing, rather than dislodging, national stereotypes. Bowen shows a different – although perhaps a more pernicious – xenophobia in keeping her Italians largely out of sight. They hover round the margins of the novel like the rebels in *The Last September*, unseen and inscrutable.

A Room with a View begins in Florence, where the English tourists find themselves surrounded by the glories of the Renaissance. Bowen's Hotel, by contrast, stands beside the empty sea, where a gaudy graveyard is the only vestige of Italian genius. In Forster's novel, Lucy Honeychurch complains that she is missing Italy; in Bowen's, Italy is missing altogether, for it is difficult to tell where the unnamed Hotel is situated.[19] Bowen's novel begins *in medias res*, as if the reader were already well-acquainted with the place and clientele. Modes of address, by shifting unexpectedly from formal to familiar (Miss Fitzgerald is suddenly plain Emily), confuse rather than identify the characters. We find ourselves in much the same position as James Milton, the latest arrival, who blunders into a bathroom commandeered by Mrs and Miss Pinkerton, and splashes blithely in the bathtub singing hymns – a lapse for which these Honourable ladies never forgive him.

Bowen's heroine also resembles Forster's: both Sydney Warren and Lucy Honeychurch are middle-class, over-protected ingénues desperate for greater independence. It is easy to imagine Sydney crying out in unison with Lucy: 'Nothing ever happens to me.'[20] Both are sleeping princesses unconscious of their own desires. William Heath has pointed out that crucial scenes in both novels involve 'a discovery of sexual passion during a pastoral excursion.'[21] Yet how different these discoveries and passions are. Bowen fulsomely acknowledged her indebtedness to Forster, declaring, 'I can think . . . of no English novelist who has influenced me more.'[22] But *The Hotel* challenges many assumptions embedded in *A Room with a View*. For instance, Bowen reverses Forster's gender-stereotypes: it is Sydney, with her 'hard-sounding' androgynous name, who becomes the mouthpiece for the coruscating honesty that Forster assigns to George Emerson, the impetuous young man whose kiss awakens Lucy's sexuality (*H* 174). And it is Sydney, emblazoned in red scarves (like the proverbial red rag to a bull), who scorches Milton's emotional virginity. Bowen also slips in a barb against male novelists. When Sydney's future is discussed, she stands between her mentors 'as inanimate and objective as a young girl in a story told by a man, incapable of a thought or a feeling that was not attributed to her, with no personality of her own outside their three projections upon her . . .' (*H* 158).

Kisses also reveal differences between Bowen and Forster. Outdoor kisses always run the risk of being overseen: George and Lucy's kiss is interrupted by Lucy's chaperone, Miss Bartlett, who reports it to the novelist Miss Lavish, who appropriates it for her latest romance. Despite this farcical chain-reaction, the kiss still works its magic, if only by deferred effect, for it releases Lucy from her Victorian hang-ups, awakening her nascent sexuality. But Bowen allots the first kiss not to the heroine but to Veronica, the coquette who flirts half-heartedly with Victor Ammering, a shiftless young veteran of World War I. During a picnic that owes as much to Austen's *Emma* as to Forster, Victor and Veronica break away, interrupting Mr Lee-Mittison (who takes the part of Austen's motor-mouth Miss Bates) as he embarks on one of his interminable anecdotes. The lovers gambol down the hill to indulge in 'a delectable water-battle,' their antics 'watched with covert but passionate interest' by those above. When the lovers kiss, each voyeur reacts according to type. To Sydney, disconnected and benumbed, the scene looks like a 'perfect piece of cinema-acting, emotion represented without emotion.' Other picnickers pretend not to have noticed: they seem 'to be stupefied by something and to be at the same time scrutinizing one another and avoiding each other's scrutiny.' Some blush, some fidget. Milton's cheeks burn – he has never seen a man and woman kiss before and is 'battering in a kind of despair against the glass wall that divided him from experience' (*H* 41–2). The younger people assume that the older people must be shocked, and move instinctively away; the older people, on the contrary, are mortified by their desertion. Loyal Mrs Lee-Mittison is too upset about her husband's interrupted anecdote even to notice the kiss that lures his audience away.

What separates the kiss in *A Room with a View* (1908) from the kiss in *The Hotel* (1928) is World War I. After this cataclysm kisses, however idyllically located, can never be the same. George's all-conquering love has given way to Sydney's anaesthesia, her sense of being merely a spectator at the movie of her life. Her numbness represents a kind of shell-shock – 'the shock of being alive' – the shock of the survivor who cannot quite believe she is still breathing. Coming of age in the aftermath of war, she is embarking on adulthood in a shattered world, where people cling to wreckage of the past in order to avoid the question of the future. Ronald Kerr, a convinced feminist, cannot understand why women, freed from the necessity of marriage, persist in grovelling for husbands. ' "There is nothing now to prevent women being different," said Ronald despondently, "and yet they seem to go on being just the same. What is the good of a new world if nobody can be got to come and live in it?" ' (*H* 94, 111).

As for Victor Ammering, the only reason he gets kissed at all is that there is a shortage of young men at the Hotel. Thousands of potential kissers, flirts, and cads lie buried underneath the local cemetery's garish masonry. A victor in name alone, Ammering has survived the bloodbath only to be relegated to the masses of the unemployed. '*Can't* young Ammering get a job?' Colonel Duperrier demands. 'No, he can't,' Joan Lawrence, Veronica's sister, replies defensively, and adds, 'It worries him awfully. The War's come very hard indeed on our generation. I don't think people understand a bit.' 'Perhaps they don't,' says Colonel Duperrier, who had also fought. Joan then cries, 'What's the good of being ambitious? There may be another war' (*H* 47–8). Indeed there was another war – unless it was the same war temporarily suspended, as Joan's forebodings suggest. This dialogue implies that the whole of Europe is arrested in an impasse, not just the young men stuck without a job or the young women stuck without a husband. Meanwhile Sydney thinks Victor 'a dreary young man,' and Veronica, although temporarily engaged to him, agrees. Veronica sounds more like Molly Bloom than Lucy Honeychurch when she complains, 'Everybody's the same and I must have somebody.' ('As well him as another' is Molly's verdict on Leopold Bloom.)[23] Sydney is disgusted by this attitude: 'Women, she thought, are all tentacles: this last remark suggested a wide but horribly purposeful groping about' (*H* 99). In any case, Veronica's father intends to whisk her away from the Hotel, making sure that her engagement, like Sydney's, comes to nothing.

Sydney's first love scene, like Veronica's kiss, takes place outside the circumference of the Hotel, set on a plateau with no prospect.[24] The match is even less auspicious than the setting, Sydney and Milton having little in common but a penchant for self-punishment. Sydney thinks Milton 'feels spikes everywhere and rushes to impale himself'; while Milton thinks Sydney has a 'queer appetite for pain' (*H* 59, 139). Nonetheless Milton plucks up the courage to ask Sydney for a walk, but to his fury she invites the child Cordelia Barry to tag along.[25] Milton gets rid of Cordelia long enough to blurt out a proposal, which is instantly rejected, although Sydney later has a change of heart and accepts him on the rebound from Mrs Kerr. Milton proposes in the same way that he sweats; he can't help but 'express himself,' as Sydney puts it. She, by contrast, must endure 'the burning discomfort of those who cannot perspire'; she is 'dammed up' whereas he is torturously 'fluent' (*H* 34). Mortified by the rejection, Milton slinks away.

After this comically ill-staged proposal, Sydney and Cordelia pay a visit to the local cemetery (reversing the sequence of Lawrence's *Women in Love,* in which the tortured Gerald makes love to Gudrun after trampling through muddy graves). The girls survey the monuments to fallen soldiers: 'the rank and file of small crosses staggered arms-wide in the arraignment of sunshine.' With its ribbons, marbles, flowers, and porcelains, the cemetery bears a curious resemblance to a 'salon' – a macabre counterpart of the Hotel. The analogy is disconcertingly precise. Like the occupants of the hotel, the dead are strangers forced into a transient community. Transient, because the dead are also guests, not permanent residents; neither the grave nor the hotel provides a final resting place, except for the wealthiest of skeletons. 'Did you know . . . that it costs a great deal of money to be buried permanently?' Cordelia asks. In Cordelia's turns of phrase, the living change places with the dead: Italian graves look 'lived in,' whereas people in hotels are 'hardly *alive*' (*H* 86, 88, 81). Her second observation corresponds to Sydney's vision of the hotel as a dolls' house, its inmates frozen to their furniture, 'as if they had never moved in their lives.' In comparison to these stiff figures, supposedly alive, the portable corpses in their fly-by-night accommodation seem positively sprightly.

Ronald Kerr (according to his mother) cannot believe 'in any satisfactory *modus vivendi* between two people that's based on an attraction' (*H* 135). *The Hotel* corroborates his pessimism. With the exception of Miss Pym and Miss Fitzgerald, no sexual relation, whether gay or straight, comes to fruition in this narrative; all reach impasse. No barriers are really broken down. The novel ends as it begins, with evacuation and dispersal, as the guests depart in dribs and drabs, while the reader is left in the position of the hangers-on, wondering what happened to the story. Rather than endorsing Forster's motto, 'only connect,' this narrative suggests the alternative proposed by Gertrude Stein: 'only, only excreate, only excreate a no since.'[26] And far from aping Forster's (Lawrencian) celebration of the liberating power of libido, Bowen confirms Lacan's verdict that 'there is no sexual relation.'[27]

There is, however, sexual geometry. Bowen is no matchmaker; nor does she write about what people do in bed; but she is fascinated by the 'abstract pattern' of desire, by triangles and quadrangles and gnomons. In *The Hotel* the erotic quadrangle explodes, flinging its four corners to the winds, as Sydney, Milton, Mrs Kerr, and Ronald go their separate ways. As we shall see, *Friends and Relations* also sets up a four-sided structure, in which the symmetry between the couples is endangered by intruders from without, as well as by recombination from within. Yet to understand the workings of the foursome in *Friends and Relations*, it is important to explore the threesomes in Bowen's short stories of this period. To this purpose the next part of this chapter traces the emergence of the shadowy third.

'The Shadowy Third,' first published in 1923, is the story of a serial killer. Yet Martin, the protagonist, is an unlikely Bluebeard.

> He was a pale little man, with big teeth and prominent eyes; sitting opposite to him in a bus one would have found it incredible that there could be a woman to love him. As a matter of fact there were two, one dead, not counting a mother whose inarticulate devotion he resented, and a pale sister, also dead.

> (*CS* 75)

The very blankness of this pale commuter is his murder weapon: the women who have loved him – one pale, one dumb, two dead – seem to have been blanked out of existence, nullified. In fact it is difficult to tell the living from the dead in Bowen's awkwardly contracted sentences: one wife, never named, is dead, another, named Pussy, still alive; there is also a pale sister, who is dead, and a silent mother, who is scarcely living. But we soon learn that the dead wife is by no means dead enough – she makes her disappearance felt in furnishings long since removed. Absent curtains flutter in the windows, an absent *portière* blocks the hall, and an absent clock, with an infuriating tick, torments Martin with its silence.

As they passed through the archway into the hall he put out his hand to sweep something aside; then smiled shamefacedly. It was funny how he always expected that *portière. She* had declared that a draught came through from the kitchen, and insisted on putting it up. *She* had filled the house with draperies, and Pussy had taken them down . . . Funny how he could never accustom himself to the changes; the house as it *had* been was always in his mind, more present than the house as it *was.* He could never get used to the silence half-way up the stairs, where the grandfather clock used to be.

In this passage, as in Daphne du Maurier's *Rebecca,* the dead wife asserts herself in furniture, but in Bowen it is not the things themselves, but the chasms that they leave behind, that haunt the living tenants of the house. Poor Pussy's efforts to redecorate are hopeless: they vandalise the old rather than create anew, leaving gashes and silences where furniture had been. In the garden, too, her flowerbed looks 'scratched-up and disordered', a wounding rather than a fecundation of the earth (*CS* 78, 75).

If the dead masquerade as living, the living also masquerade as dead, assuming both the stillness and the restlessness commonly attributed to ghosts. Although Bowen's characters are frequently arrested in an impasse – transfixed, struck dumb, and 'at a standstill' – they also tend to be frenetically in motion.[28] Pussy's restlessness, her habit of pacing round the house, alarms her husband, who attributes her agitation euphemistically to her 'state of health.' He means, of course, that she is pregnant, but this state of health is presented in the story as a state of death, of purgatorial noctambulation. Later we learn that her predecessor, too, was always in 'an aimless bustle,' rummaging through drawers in the upper reaches of the house, until her child came, unnamed and presumably still-born, after which 'she did nothing, nothing at all . . .' There is a strong suspicion that Pussy is also destined to give birth to death – she already engenders 'morbid' thoughts. At the end of the story she foresees her own nemesis. ' "I think," ' she stammers, ' "that not to want a person must be a sort, a sort of murder. I think a person who was done out of their life like that would be brought back by the injustice much more than anybody who was shot or stabbed." ' Unwanted in life, Martin's murdered wife is wanted painfully in death, in the sense that she is lacking, missing, gaping. One might say she is the gap that gapes - like the hidden skull in Holbein's painting *The Ambassadors,* which gapes at its unseeing spectator. Even when she was alive, her husband's emotional anaemia had sentenced her to ghostly vigilance:

'All the time he had felt Her watching his face; always on the verge of saying something . . .' (*CS* 77, 81, 82).

Yet Bowen does not let us get away with dismissing Martin as a fiend. She forces us to feel his inability to feel, the torment of knowing he is missing something, which makes his vampirism almost poignant. As Hermione Lee has pointed out, Bowen has the rare ability 'to persuade the reader of what it feels like to be a damned soul.'[29] Prey to 'the inconvenient cruelty of passion,' Martin cannot choose to be enchanted by Pussy's horticultural incompetence or infuriated by his dead wife's squint (*FR* 119). Nor can he control the paling of his own desire, destined to reduce Pussy, like her nameless predecessor, to a watchful shadow. 'Just the littlest differences in you would make me eat my heart out,' Pussy cries. 'I should never be able to ask you for things. I should just look and look at you, trying to speak, and then you would grow to hate me.' At this juncture the reader realises that Pussy – like the last duchess of this 'coldly distempered' house – is doomed to dissolve into the furniture (*CS* 82, 75).

'The Shadowy Third' is an immature work, but it nonetheless taps into the 'addictions' underlying Bowen's fiction. The most conspicuous of these addictions is to killers of the heart – bloodless Martin anticipates the ruddier monsters of her later novels: the callous Eddie of *The Death of the Heart* (1938), or the satanic Markie of *To the North* (1932). Pussy and Martin are prototypes of 'the kid and the cad,' whose destructive passion drives the plots of later works.[30] Both kids and cads, however, are subordinated to a third presence, which in this story takes the form of a nameless ghost, familiar and alien at once. *Unheimlich*, this intruder violates the couple's privacy, but also intimidates them into closing ranks, uniting them through paranoia. Their intimacy therefore depends upon the 'extimacy' of the vengeful other. This structure reduces persons to the status of algebraic variables, as in Freud's anatomy of dirty jokes: Pussy, now cast in the position of the second, is doomed to be demoted to an absent third.

'The Secession' (1926) is another early story in which the second person turns into a missing third. Miss Selby has invited Mr Carr to join her at a *pensione* in Rome, expecting him to renew his proposal of marriage. In the meantime she has befriended Miss Phelps, a beautiful American girl who comes 'quickly and frothily to the boil, like milk' (*CS* 161). Humphrey Carr arrives, but instead of trying to re-enchant him, Miss Selby perversely plays the go-between, using every opportunity to lure her would-be lover and her friend into betraying her by falling for each other. When her manipulation takes effect,

Miss Selby 'secedes,' vanishing unaccountably from the hotel. The guilty couple, searching her vacated room for clues, find her diary lying open at the final entry. Here Miss Selby, having recorded word-for-word her final conversation with Miss Phelps, contemplates the ease with which she could have thrown the young girl out of the window. Horrified, Miss Phelps takes flight, and the love affair, so craftily premeditated, comes to nothing.

In this story, the absent third or 'missing woman' sets the lovers up but prevents them from acting on their passion; her shadow both facilitates and thwarts their love.[31] It is intriguing that the third person assumes the position of the writer in this story: Miss Selby (like Jane Austen's Emma) wants to be the author rather than the heroine of the romance, but after bringing her protagonists together she drafts an alternative conclusion in her journal, in which the leading lady is killed off. In effect this death sentence rebounds upon its writer, for it is Miss Selby rather than her creatures who vacates the scene, as if the diarist had been obliterated by her diary. 'The Secession' provides a prototype for Bowen's later works, in which the third presence tends to mirror the liminal position of the writer in the text – both outside and inside, absent and present, dead and vindictively alive. Bowen's thirds perform the role that Derrida attributes to the 'hymen,' an antithetical word meaning 'marriage' that also designates the 'maidenhead'; that is, the anatomical impediment to marriage.[32] In Bowen the third presence, like the hymen, both fosters and hinders marriage, bringing lovers together while also driving them apart. In *Friends and Relations*, however, marriage is endangered not only by the rogue third presence, but by half a dozen spectres of adultery. The result is an impasse in which no love affair gets off the ground, and the star-crossed lovers end up tamed into friends and relations.

In an interview with Jocelyn Brooke in 1950, Bowen described *Friends and Relations* as the 'book of mine which most nearly wrote itself.'

> Oh, but in some ways that novel was more exterior to me than any other I've ever written before or since, and that did make for a sort of psychological ease. On the whole I looked on the story rather than felt it. But then again one can't have it both ways. Frankly, I've got less feeling for "Friends and relations" than I have for any other of my books. I quite enjoy [the] book when I re-read it and in a way I could be impressed by it. In so far as I have any abstract conception of what a novel should be "Friends and relations" seems to conform to that. Perhaps it reminds me slightly of the Edwardian new novels I used to read when I was a child.[33]

Bowen's comments help to explain why *Friends and Relations* is the weakest of her novels, exhibiting good structure without compelling feeling. This structure resembles that of James's *The Golden Bowl*, which also deals with two overlapping couples hovering on the verge of incest and adultery. But the lifelessness of *Friends and Relations* suggests that James's fiction posed an impasse to Bowen, which she had to tackle in order to move forward as a writer.[34] Awkwardly schematic, *Friends and Relations* is nonetheless instructive to the critic because it provides the clearest blueprint of the multifaceted dynamics of desire.

The novel opens with a wedding, ominously marred by rain, in which Laurel Studdart marries Edward Tilney. The groom bears a striking disresemblance to the famous Tilney of *Northanger Abbey* who demystifies Gothic conventions for the naïve heroine's edification. Bowen's Tilney, by contrast, is a hysteric who embodies his creator's taste for melodrama, cramped by her commitment to the comedy of manners.

Among the wedding guests is Laurel's sister Janet, the stillest of Bowen's arrested characters: 'a positive no-presence'; 'almost utterly silent'; 'dead, but not disembodied'; 'oblivious sentinel of oblivion'; possessing the 'power of being nowhere.'[35] Since Janet is secretly in love with Edward, her stillness suggests that the impasse of this romance has condemned her to a form of living death. Some weeks after Laurel's wedding Janet marries Rodney Meggatt, heir to his uncle's large estate at Batts Abbey (like many of Bowen's protagonists, Rodney seems to have mislaid his parents). This uncle, absurdly named Considine, and even more absurdly represented as a former big-game hunter, was once in love with Edward Tilney's mother, Elfrida. Their scandalous affair, although long since extinguished, overshadows the marriages of their descendants. To avoid their elders' catastrophe, both the younger couples have foresworn the 'inconvenient cruelty of passion' for the sake of a 'miniature happiness.' ' "Life after all," ' thinks Edward, 'hearing tea approach, the gay dance of china on the silver tray, "is an affair of charm, not an affair of passion" ' (*FR* 119, 104, 99).

In the second part of the novel, ten years have passed and each couple seems to have produced the other's children. The Tilneys' sturdy youngsters resemble Rodney, whereas the Meggatts' hysterical daughter Hermione – 'a preposterous child for Janet' – takes after the troubled Edward (*FR* 56). These changelings deepen our suspicion that their parents could have been or should be recombined. A crisis erupts when Janet, against Edward's wishes, invites Elfrida to rejoin her former lover Considine at Batts Abbey. When Edward finds out about this invitation, he storms into his elders' bittersweet reunion, bent on rescuing his children, also visitors at Batts, from the corrupting influence of the ex-lovers. To his astonishment – and ours – he finds himself overwhelmed instead by his long-suppressed love for Janet. At this point, 'the present relaxed its grip on the house,' and Edward and Janet are compelled to re-enact the dead-end passion of their forebears. Their love, never consummated, is renounced in a few weeks, after which the 'dear conventions' close over the wound (*FR* 71, 145).

The present also relaxes its grip over the reader, compelling a reversion to the past – for the clues to 'this large non-occurrence' lurk in the recesses of the novel's overture (*FR* 131). Reading backwards we discover – or rediscover – that Theodora Thirdman, a juvenile guest at Laurel's wedding, has already intuited the plot. 'Theodora, intently listening, inferred that Janet loved Edward, that his mother preferred Janet; that for Janet this was a day of chagrin, possibly of despair.' Because this insight is attributed to the boorish Theodora, whose 'personality was still too much for her, like a punt-pole,' the reader is inclined to overlook the premonition (*FR* 13). On a second reading, however, other omens re-emerge: we are told that Edward 'was determined that his wedding, like the execution of Julien Sorel, should go off simply'; and a few pages later we find the newly-weds separated by a 'chasm' in single beds compared to 'tombs' (*FR* 9, 21). All this sounds distinctly inauspicious, but the narrative is so elusive that such portents can easily be missed. Nonetheless, when the crisis finally happens, it is presented as a kind of déjà vu: Janet and Edward have always already been in love, if only they (or we) had spotted its pre-indications. In Bowen's fiction, love always predates its realisation, catching up with lovers when they least expect it. Oddly, Theodora alone, 'intently listening,' is granted the power to detect its symptoms. The other characters either read too quickly (like Elfrida, 'a rapid and superficial reader') or too slowly (like Janet, who 'read, at all times, with an annoying slowness') to penetrate each other's secrets, or their own (*FR* 17, 93).

In spite of these clues, the climax flops. This 'belated flowering' of passion leaves us embarrassed rather than convinced (*FR* 120). Inert and undeveloped, Edward and Janet cannot carry off the repetition of their elders' downfall, and their elders also seem too nonchalant for tragedy. Yet it is worth noting that the blossoming of love is immediately blasted by the shadowy third. In Bowen's fiction, a coupling need only be mooted in order for a tripling to occur. Janet, rushing to London under the hypnotic compulsion of her love for Edward, feels she is fragmenting into a third person:

> These weeks, a grotesque, not quite impossible figure, had come to interpose between herself and Laurel. A woman, an unborn shameful sister, travestying their two natures, enemy to them both . . . Never overt, less than a sinner, worlds apart from Elfrida, she was the prey of all speculation, the unpitiable quarry of talk . . . this horrible illusory figure had materialised on the upward train journey.

> (*FR* 122–3)

Clearly Janet is projecting on to the third sister her guilt for her betrayal of the second.

Yet notice that as soon as this third presence makes itself felt, the fourth presence of Elfrida is invoked, if only by negation – 'worlds apart from Elfrida.' Elfrida's position in the novel corresponds to that which Freud assigns to Frau K, the fourth term that subverts his triangular model of desire. Only in a later footnote does Freud acknowledge Frau K as the strongest love of Dora's life, stronger than any of the girl's triangular attachments. He traces this lesbian desire back to infantile attachment to the mother, which he else-where likens to the Minoan-Mycenean civilisation buried underneath the patriarchal culture of Greece.[36] Like Frau K, Elfrida figures as a kind of footnote in the younger generation's love affairs, in that she marks a debt to something lost, archaic, matriarchal.

It is Elfrida's visit to Batts that brings Janet and Edward together, but she also functions as an impasse to their love. She resembles other older women in Bowen's fiction, such as Madame Fisher in *The House in Paris*, who at once awaken and repress the sexuality of younger characters. Bowen associates Elfrida with Dickens's Miss Havisham, that great manipulator of the younger generation, through mischie-vous allusions to stale or ruined cake: 'the half-ruined cake went golden; the faces flame-coloured – Lady Elfrida's was for a moment ravaged . . .'[37] Unlike Miss Havisham, however, Elfrida was not jilted; it was she who jilted Edward's father, but when she found herself alone with Considine at last, both lovers suddenly experienced a 'stupefying cessation of love, positive as the passion itself' (*FR* 82). The failure of their passion corroborates Bowen's dictum that 'there is no such thing as being alone together.' The couple, released from the interference of a shadowy third, or a shadowy fourth, cannot sustain what Bowen calls its 'trance.'

Elfrida's great passion may have foundered, but her conception of love as 'a very high kind of ruling disorder' still looms over the younger generation like an unpaid debt, reproaching them for their erotic poverty. In fact Elfrida comes to represent what everybody thinks they do not have. Laurel cries:

> this idea of Elfrida, what she had, what she was, has been fearful; it's ruined us all. We've been certain of missing something, we've all watched the others. Like that game, a ring going round and round on a circle of string under everyone's hands – you never know where it is, who may have it.

(FR 104, 129)

Elfrida stands for something missing, for a sense of lack that circulates among the parties to this merry-go-round. It is this missing something (Laurel's simile suggests) that strings the characters together, creating geometries of love – like the purloined letter, in Poe's much-psychoanalysed short story, which orbits round the cast of characters, conscripting everyone into the circulation of desire.[38]

Theodora Thirdman unwittingly joins forces with Elfrida in sabotaging heterosexual couples. It is Theodora as a child who intuits, or perhaps invents, the passion between Janet and Edward; and it is Theodora as an adult who stage-manages the belated flowering of their romance. But her machinations are more roundabout than cunning: first she descends on Batts during the elderly lovers' reunion with the aim of declaring her love for Janet. Miffed by Janet's heavy-lidded impassivity, Theodora vents her frustration in a letter to Laurel which inadvertently reveals Elfrida's presence at Batts Abbey. It is this letter that infuriates Edward into his confrontation with Janet, which concludes with the traumatic admission of their love. The name 'Thirdman' smacks of sexual ambiguity (neither man nor woman but 'third man'), as does Janet's characterisation of Theodora as the 'odd man out.' Through 'one or two vital interpolations,' Theodora engineers a plot out of ingredients remarkable for their inertia. Without her intervention, combined with 'the Elfrida business,' there would be little to galvanise these torpid thirtysomethings into passion (*FR* 94, 119, 138).

It is significant that Theodora's interference tends to be associated with communication at a distance, particularly with the letter and the telephone. As a child her favourite pastime is impersonating adults on the telephone:

> The telephone became at once her distraction and torture. She would not go out with her parents, but solitary in the flat remained for hours with the directory . . . Then, having bolted the door, she rang up several prominent people and, skilfully passing secretary or butler, maintained with each a conversation of some seconds, under the pseudonym of Lady Hunter Jervois. She had a pleasant, mature voice: an asset. Passionately passing along the wire she became for those moments the very nerve of some unseen house.
>
> (*FR* 28)

The French word *parasitaire*, denoting the corrosive work of parasites but also interference on the telephone-line, encapsulates the role of Theodora – the sponger, 'bounder,' stalker who devours her protectors, and prevents them, through telephonic or epistolary terrorism, from insulating either the home or the self against the other.[39] Since her role is to disrupt relations between couples, she holds the place that Freud assigns to the castrating father, the shadowy third who shatters the primal dyad of mother and child. But the Thirdman in this novel really represents a fourth man – a shadowy fourth who interferes with triangular relationships, and reveals another configuration of desire older than the threesomes of the Oedipus complex.

Older, but also newer. The shadowy fourth harks back to the archaic mother, like the Furies of Aeschylus's *Oresteia*. But there is something startlingly modern about Bowen's Fury, particularly in her penchant for the telephone – Theodora combines primeval vengeance with cutting-edge communicational technology. Remember that a guest in *The Hotel* admits to being surprised when the telephone rings to discover she is still alive, as if her personal identity depended on a 'call.' In *Friends and Relations*, however, the call foreshadows death rather than affirming life, for any mention of the telephone elicits intimations of mortality. At the climax of the novel Laurel, lunching in a restaurant, is interrupted by a call from Janet: 'The messenger, like death, approached. A call to the telephone?' Laurel instantly vanishes, leaving her companions gazing at her 'empty place with the chair awry, the poor sweet-pea lying across her plate,' suggestive of a floral tribute on a grave. We next see Laurel 'shut in with her sister's voice in the strait little telephone box like a coffin upright.' Meanwhile Janet wonders why she has interrupted her own tryst with Edward merely to traumatise her sister with a telephone call. 'Why speak *now*, at all, to Laurel?' Janet asks herself. 'From now he and she would not feel alone any more' (*FR* 117–18). In effect,

Janet answers her own question: lovers in Bowen can never be alone together. Love involves at least three persons – and a telephone.

In his famous Baltimore address of 1966, Lacan asks his audience to consider the genesis of two. 'The *two*,' he argues, ' is here to grant existence to the first *one*: put *two* in the place of *one* and consequently in the place of *two* you see *three* appear.' At the risk of over-simplification, I would venture this translation: by establishing one, you thereby establish that-which-is-not-one, an unaccountable remainder. Lacan continues: 'When you try to read the theories of mathematicians regarding numbers you find the formula "*n* plus 1" ($n + 1$) as the basis of all the theories. It is this question of the "one more" that is the key to the genesis of numbers . . .' As we have seen, the 'one more,' or one too many, also provides a key to the 'arithmomania' of love in Bowen's works. While Lacan boasts that he has taught his students how to count to five, Bowen's early novels teach us how to count at least to six, by alerting us to the one more that fractures any structure of containment.[40] At once a barrier and an incitement to desire, this one-too-many leads to impasse, for it means that the couple can never be alone together; but it also conduces to mobility, for it ensures that love is constantly in transport rather than at rest. It is transport that becomes the major theme of Bowen's next two novels, *To the North* and *The House in Paris*.

Notes

1. Henry James, *Literary Criticism: Essays on Literature, American Writers, English Writers*, ed. Leon Edel and Mark Wilson (New York: Library of America, 1984), p. 109.
2. W. B. Yeats, *Mythologies* (1959; London: Macmillan, 1989), p. 337.
3. Freud, *Jokes and their Relation to the Unconscious* (1905), SE, vol. 7, pp. 97–102.
4. Much has been written, from René Girard to Eve Kosofsky Sedgwick, about erotic triangles in Western literature, demonstrating that the bond between male rivals is often more intense than the bond that draws them both to the desired woman. See René Girard, *Deceit, Desire and the Novel: Self and Other in Literary Structure* and Eve Kosofsky Sedgwick, *Between Men: English Literature and Male Homosocial Desire*. These matters are discussed at further length in Chapter 4.
5. Henry James, 'The Third Person' (1900), in *The Complete Tales of Henry James*, ed. Leon Edel, vol. 11 (London: Rupert Hart-Davis, 1964), pp. 133–69.
6. Freud, *Fragment of an Analysis of a Case of Hysteria* (1905), SE, vol. 7, p. 120n.

7. *H* 108, 34, 9, 22. See Jeremy Bentham, 'Panopticon Papers,' in *A Bentham Reader*, ed. Mary Peter Mack (New York: Pegasus, 1969), pp. 194–208.

8. E. M. Forster, *Aspects of the Novel* (1927; Harmondsworth: Penguin, 1970), p. 45.

9. Patricia Juliana Smith, *Lesbian Panic*, pp. 78–9.

10. Fyodor Dostoevsky, *Crime and Punishment* (1866), trans. Richard Pevear and Larissa Volokhonsky (London: Vintage, 1993), pt I, ch. 5, pp. 54–9.

11. Joyce wrote to Constantine P. Curran in 1904: 'I am calling the series Dubliners to betray the soul of that hemiplegia or paralysis which many consider a city', *Letters of James Joyce*, vol. 1, ed. Stuart Gilbert (1957; New York: Viking Press, 1966), p. 55.

12. *H* 143; *MT* 289.

13. *H* 20, 113; *SW* 8.

14. Joyce, *Ulysses* (1922; Harmondsworth: Penguin, 1986), Ch. 15, p. 425, lines 2,592–4.

15. See Melanie Klein, 'A Contribution to the Psychogenesis of Manic-Depressive States' (1935), in *Love, Guilt and Reparation and Other Works 1921–1945*, pp. 262–89; and 'Notes on Some Schizoid Mechanisms' (1946) in *Envy and Gratitude and Other Works 1946–1963*, pp. 1–24.

16. 'Still Lives' is the subtitle of Andrew Bennett and Nicholas Royle, *Elizabeth Bowen and the Dissolution of the Novel.*

17. Bowen, 'Autobiographical Note' (1947), HRHRC.

18. E. M. Forster, 'A View Without a Room' (1958), reprinted in Forster, *A Room with a View*, ed. Oliver Stallybrass (1908; Harmondsworth: Penguin, 1978), p. 231.

19. In the longer of two versions of her 'Autobiographical Note' (1947), HRHRC, Bowen recalls her travels in Italy between art school and marriage, and remarks that 'A winter at Bordighera inspired, subsequently, my first novel, *The Hotel.*'

20. E. M. Forster, *A Room with a View*, p. 61.

21. Heath, *Elizabeth Bowen*, p. 23.

22. Elizabeth Bowen, 'A Passage to E. M. Forster,' p. 12.

23. *H* 198, 99; Joyce, *Ulysses*, ch. 18, pp. 643–4, lines 1,604–5.

24. Petra-Utta Rau makes this point in *Moving Dangerously: Desire and Narrative Structure in the Fiction of Elizabeth Bowen, Rosamond Lehmann and Sylvia Townsend Warner*, pp. 113–14.

25. *H* 59. As the unwanted third, it is appropriate that Cordelia bears the name of the third daughter dispossessed by Lear; at the same time her surname evokes 'the Barrie play,' *Peter Pan*, which to Sidney reeks of 'middle-aged whimsicality' (*H* 68).

26. Forster, epigraph to *Howards End* (1910); Gertrude Stein, 'Food,' *Tender Buttons* (1914), in *Selected Writings of Gertrude Stein*, ed. Carl Van Vechten (New York: Vintage, 1972), p. 496.

27. Jacques Lacan, 'God and the Jouissance of ~~The~~ Woman,' in Juliet Mitchell and Jacqueline Rose (eds), *Feminine Sexuality: Jacques Lacan and the École Freudienne* (London: Macmillan, 1982), p. 143.
28. The term 'at a standstill' is used at least three times in *Friends and Relations* (*FR* 7, 9, 27, and others). See also *MT* 286, where Bowen agrees with a reviewer that her characters are 'almost perpetually in transit.'
29. Hermione Lee, *Elizabeth Bowen: An Estimation*, p. 69. This phrase is altered in the revised edition of this book, *Elizabeth Bowen*, p. 69.
30. Quoted in Patricia Craig, *Elizabeth Bowen*, p. 59.
31. In her Preface to the collection in which 'The Secession' first appeared, *Ann Lee's* (1926), Bowen wrote: 'The fate of the missing woman in "The Secession" is not hinted at . . .' (*A* 94).
32. See Jacques Derrida, 'The First Session,' in *Acts of Literature*, pp. 161–9, where he describes the hymen as 'an operation that *both* sows confusion *between* opposites *and* stands *between* the opposites "at once" '; it is associated with both 'virginity' and 'consummation.'
33. Elizabeth Bowen and Jocelyn Brooke, broadcast on 3 October 1950, HRHRC.
34. Asked in an interview of 1959 for her opinion of Henry James, Bowen admitted to her difficulties with his later work: 'I admire him in the dramatic way. I can't read the more complicated [books]. I haven't ever read *The Ivory Tower*, he's quite beyond me there, I really belong to *Portrait of a Lady*. I wouldn't care to read him while I was writing a novel because I think his type of style is extremely infectious' (Broadcast interview with Elizabeth Bowen by John Bowen, William Craig, W. N. Ewer, 11 September 1959, HRHRC). In the light of these comments it is possible (although improbable) that Bowen never tackled *The Golden Bowl*, but the novel centred on two couples has many precedents in English literature, including *Middlemarch* and *Women in Love*.
35. *FR* 33, 41, 128, 58, 57, 10.
36. Freud, *Fragment of an Analysis of a Case of Hysteria* (1905), SE, vol. 7, p. 120n.; 'Female Sexuality' (1931), SE, vol. 21, p. 226.
37. *FR* 14. Later on, in Bowen's most gnarled syntax, we are told that Elfrida 'disturbed the stale enclosed afternoon that like a cake under glass night after night had covered without renewing' (*FR* 86).
38. See John P. Muller and William J. Richardson (eds), *The Purloined Poe: Lacan, Derrida, and Psychoanalytic Reading*.
39. The French term for interference on the telephone line is *un effet parasitaire*; the term 'parasitics' is also used in English in electronics.
40. The term 'arithmomania,' meaning obsessive counting, is used by Freud in 'Obsessions and Phobias: Their Psychical Mechanism and their Aetiology' (1895), SE, vol. 3, pp. 77–8; Jacques Lacan, 'Of Structure as an Inmixing of an Otherness Prerequisite to Any Subject Whatever,' pp. 190–1.

4

Transport: To the North *and* The House in Paris

If paralysis is the keynote of Bowen's early novels, locomotion is the dominant motif of *To the North.* The novel opens and closes with excursions, the first in a train, the last in a car, and the characters are 'driven' in every sense. Psychologically, they are driven by desire, or more precisely by the death-drive disguised as romantic love; physically, they are driven by every mode of transportation available in 1928 – by trains, buses, taxis, private cars, and even aeroplanes, which had only recently begun to operate commercially.[1] Finally, they are driven by the plot which, streamlined and remorseless as a non-stop flight, expedites them to catastrophe. Even the author, driven by the fatal momentum of the narrative, felt unable to rescue the heroine from downfall. 'Poor Emmeline!' Bowen later commented. 'It was inevitable.'[2]

In *The House in Paris,* the characters are also 'perpetually in transit.' In her 'Notes on Writing a Novel,' Bowen confesses to having imparted to her characters 'an enthusiastic naivety with regard to transport which in my own case has not dimmed. Zestfully they take ship or board planes: few of them are even blasé about railways. Motor-cars magnetize them particularly' (*MT* 286). *The House in Paris* begins in a taxi and ends in a railway station, with a dizzy to-and-fro of ferry journeys in between. But it is time-travel that distinguishes *The House in Paris* from Bowen's previous novels: the middle section, called 'The Past,' plunges back into the prehistory of the present crisis. *To the North,* as its title implies, moves relentlessly in one direction, teleological in the extreme, whereas the movement of *The House in Paris* is centripetal, circling back to the enigmas of the past.

Taken together these two novels bring out every nuance of the term 'transport.' The *Oxford English Dictionary* lists four definitions for the noun and three definitions for the verb 'transport,' as well as many further shades of meaning. Derived from the Latin *trans* (across) and *portare* (to carry), to transport is to carry across: this is the same meaning as the Greek word 'metaphor,' which is still used in its literal sense on Greek removal vans. Puttenham's *English Poesie* defines 'transport' as a synonym for metaphor:

> To call the top of a tree, or of a hill, the crowne of a tree or of a hill . . . because such a term is not applied naturally to a tree, or to a hill, but is transported from a mans head to a hill or tree, therefore it is called by metaphore, or the figure of transport.

To transport is also to transfer property; to remove oneself to another place of abode (to emigrate); or more often to be forcibly deported as a criminal. One may be 'transported' from this world into the next. Finally to transport is 'to carry away with the strength of some emotion; to cause to be beside oneself, to put into an ecstasy, to enrapture' (*OED*).

Transported by their passions, Bowen's lovers are also uprooted from their safe abodes, condemned to wander like unquiet ghosts through the labyrinths of modern transportation. Edward and Janet's realisation in *Friends and Relations* that 'their love was homeless' applies to most of Bowen's peripatetic lovers (*FR* 145). But her creatures also suffer 'transport' in another sense: the transference of human properties to inanimate prostheses, especially to machines that carry bodies and voices across distances, such as the motor car, the telephone, and the telegraph. These transferences between human beings and machines often take a playful form: in *The Hotel*, the elevator is described as 'sick,' whereas Sydney is described as 'mechanical'; in *Eva Trout* a transistor radio is jealous of a tape-recorder; in *The Little Girls*, the 'telephone, after its brief good time, had to go back on to the shelf' (*LG* 150).[3] But such 'transports' also have an ominous dimension, overturning the supremacy of mind to matter. In *To the North* and *The House in Paris*, the characters find themselves enmeshed in the vast relay systems of modern travel and communication – 'hooped round with roads and netted with railways' (*FR* 136). The transport of messages via post, telephone, and tele-graph, combined with the transport of persons via motorways, ship-ping routes, and flight paths, has the effect of alienating speech and motion from the human will. Extending into every area of private life, these networks override the boundaries that separate one person from another, creating mysterious and uncontrollable relations of dependency. 'Even what I think isn't my own!' Lois Farquar cries (*LS* 191).

One symptom of this interconnectedness is the jitters: Bowen's characters are 'wired' in every sense, as if their nerve-ends, fused to the surrounding networks, are crepitating with the dips and surges of an unknown current. Another symptom is collective guilt, for the erosion of personal autonomy means that everyone is implicated in the act of betrayal that propels the narrative. Indeed, betrayal and adultery are melodramatic side-effects of the promiscuity endemic to these networks, in which 'relations stop nowhere,' in Henry James's words.[4] Wired to a world of others, Bowen's characters inevitably get their wires crossed, and find themselves transported into alien selves. Sexual betrayal is the visible tip of this insidious violation of boundaries.

In *The House in Paris*, this violation is re-enacted at the level of diction. In particular, the terms 'violet' and 'poison' cut across the boundaries between characters, resurfacing throughout the text like tics or chronic symptoms. In the case of violets, their reiterations resemble those of the enigmatic 'rosebud' of Orson Welles' movie *Citizen Kane*, except that the repeating violet is not presented as a symbol with a hidden meaning, whose decipherment could cure or free the characters, but rather as a link in an inescapable chain. Criss-crossing plot and subplots, indifferent to temporal or psychological consistency, violets intertwine the characters into a complicity beyond their knowledge or control. This is the strangest 'transport' of all: the displacement of intersubjective guilt – the guilt attached to intersubjectivity per se – on to the compulsive repetition of the signifier.

What all Bowen's forms of transport have in common is that they sabotage 'free will,' a concept dismissed by the heroine of *To the North* as 'a mistake' (*N* 54). Despite the constant movement of the characters, they rarely act off their own bat; another force controls their restless choreography. Both *To the North* and *The House in Paris* show how 'transport,' in all the senses of the word, deprives the characters of agency, reducing them to puppets of their own technology. As Walter Benjamin has written: 'all technology is, at certain stages, evidence of a collective dream.'[5]

The most striking difference between *To the North* and Bowen's earlier novels is that Emmeline Summers surrenders to the 'transport' of passion, whereas her predecessors, Lois, Sydney, even Janet, remain paralysed in the impasse of innocence. In one of her most quoted axioms, Bowen proclaimed: 'No, it is not only our fate but our business to lose innocence, and once we have lost that it is futile to attempt to picnic in Eden' (*MT* 50). Despite this dictate, Emmeline is the first of Bowen's heroines to venture out of Eden, tempted by the satanic Markie, whose serpentine features are somewhat overstated: he has 'the impassive bright quick-lidded eyes of an agreeable reptile' (*N* 7). Eden, on the other hand, is the loving home that Emmeline shares with her widowed sister-in-law, Cecilia Summers. Like Mrs and Miss Pinkerton in *The Hotel,* or Antonia and Lilia in *A World of Love,* Emmeline and Cecilia are bound together by a dead man, Henry Summers, brother to Emmeline and briefly husband to Cecilia before he died unheroically of pneumonia, shortly after World War I. 'How lively a bond was their loss?' wonders Lady Waters, the Summers' meddlesome relation; the novel leaves her question hauntingly unanswered (*N* 13). After Henry's death Emmeline and Cecilia moved 'to the North,' specifically to St John's Wood, where they set up house together in Oudenarde Road. Judging by Bowen's meticulous directions, and by the anagrammatic similarity between the names, the likely prototype for Oudenarde Road is Boundary Road, NW8.

Most of the characters in *To the North* are parentless, and there is something Edenic about their orphanage, in that they seem absolute beginners, thrust without precedents into the world. Emmeline and Henry lost both parents at an early age, while Cecilia's mother, her only living parent, has abandoned her daughter to join a second husband in America. Lady Waters, indirectly related to the Summers girls, has imposed her 'fine, massive figure' *in loco parentis* (*N* 15). Driving round in a Daimler 'massive as a conservatory awheel,' she bulldozes into other people's lives, 'quick to detect situations that did not exist,' and gloriously blind to those that do (*N* 152, 12). She collects no-hopers, and pries into their secrets, dolloping misguidance on their troubled souls. Having attended lectures on Adler, and absorbed a little half-baked Freud, Lady Waters clamps her captives down with psychoanalytic clichés. When a young visitor who wants to take an airplane says she 'dreams of flying,' Lady Waters drops the heavy hint: 'That may have nothing to do with flying' (*N* 154). Neither Lady Waters nor Cecilia notices that Emmeline is heading for a crash. Cecilia's 'incuriosity was immense,' whereas Lady Waters's curiosity is purely theoretical. 'One may do so much,' she gloats, 'with a little judgement, by bringing theory to bear on life' (*N* 50, 171).

Inevitably Markie betrays Emmeline for a good-time girl called Daisy – 'he liked women lowish' (*N* 179). But Cecilia also betrays Emmeline, forsaking their 'quiet marriage,' based on 'unspoken good faith,' to secure a husband she does not even love (*N* 148). Conventionality, combined with restlessness, compels her to cast away the 'one dear exception' to her loveless life (*N* 9). 'Poor Cecilia's horrid, isn't she,' Bowen wrote to her friend Alfred Coppard in 1932. 'But I have quite a feeling for her.'[6] Cecilia's worldliness contrasts sharply with Emmeline's 'air-mindedness' (*N* 144). When Cecilia half-heartedly agrees to marry Julian Tower, her lukewarm suitor, she chooses Edgar Linton, whereas Emmeline is fatally enthralled to Heathcliff. But Cecilia's experience has taught her to accept half-measures; Emmeline's innocence, by contrast, makes her ruthless in exacting 'a heroic happiness' (*DH* 106). 'One can't live on the top of the Alps,' Markie protests (*N* 183).

After Cecilia's engagement, the Summers' day is over, and Emmeline loses her last refuge from the North. Once the most enterprising of Bowen's heroines, having co-founded a successful travel agency, Emmeline forfeits everything but her obsession. Ravaged by Markie's 'curves of caprice,' she allows her business to disintegrate, while her home, abandoned by Cecilia, falls apart at the same time (*N* 145). In a passage reminiscent of the ending of *The Last September*, Emmeline contemplates the fall of her house:

> Timber by timber, Oudenarde Road fell to bits, as small houses are broken up daily to widen the roar of London. [Emmeline] saw the door open on emptiness: blanched walls as though after a fire. Houses shared with women are built on sand. She thought, 'My home, my home'.
>
> (*N* 207–8)

At the end of the novel Emmeline, driving north towards Baldock (an ominous destination), kills herself and Markie in a car crash, leaving Julian and Cecilia in St John's Wood, waiting. 'I agree: it was tough on Markie, having to come in on that death,' Bowen commented to Coppard, showing a surprising sympathy for the man that Lady Waters calls a 'basilisk' (*N* 44).[7]

Bowen claimed that the idea of the novel came to her when she was driving out of London with her husband, and spotted a road sign saying 'TO THE NORTH' outlined against the sky.[8] Such signs, still

common in the South of England, amuse visitors from larger countries, where 'the North' would be far too vast for signposting. Only in
a 'small island,' as Ford Madox Ford described it, could such directions be intelligible.[9] But Bowen contrasts the smallness of the island
to the immensity of northernness, which is not a mappable locale but
an eschatological condition. It is the polar hinterland of passion,
where fire meets ice, and Eros reveals itself as Thanatos, the death-
drive. While Emmeline and Markie, like Frankenstein and his monster, pursue each other northwards through the frozen wastes and
icebergs of the heart, southern England perseveres in its 'daily island
life,' and insulates itself as far as possible against the cold.[10] The novel
pits its Gothic melodrama of destructive passion against a comedy of
manners; in generic terms, Emily Bronte collides with Oscar Wilde.
The Wildean interludes take place in London and at Farraways, a
country house belonging to the queenly Lady Waters (reminiscent of
Wilde's Lady Bracknell) and Sir Robert, her intimidated husband.
Lady Waters prides herself on being a 'born islander.' She disapproves of travel, regarding Cecilia's wanderlust as 'neurosis.' 'All ages
are restless,' she pronounces, but '*this* age . . . is decentralised. From
week to week, there is no knowing where anyone is. Myself, I move
very little . . .' When the prospect of a Channel tunnel comes up in
conversation, Lady Waters protests, 'God must have meant us to be an
island.'

Emmeline, by contrast, is 'claustrophobic.'[11] Her business as a
travel agent enables her to focus her imagination on escapes from
Britain. The first of Bowen's heroines to embark on a career, she has
been shrewd enough to join an industry that burgeoned during the
interwar years. Travel had become much cheaper: the refinement of
mass-production had brought down the real cost of cars, enabling
young women like Emmeline to purchase – and to crash – their own.
During World War I many soldiers had learned to drive and some to
fly, and in the 1920s they began to realise the market value of these
skills. In consequence the expansion of commercial airlines created
an opportunity for travel agents. While the railways had traditionally
issued their own tickets at the station, the new airlines, obliged to
invest in airports inconveniently located out of town, lacked the
capital to set up retail outlets. Hence they relied on travel agencies
to sell their tickets. It was also during the interwar years that the
annual holiday became established as a right for most working people
in Britain, producing a boom in the tourist trade. As tension in
Europe increased, tourism was encouraged as a means of preserving

international peace, young tourists, in particular, being urged abroad as moral ambassadors for Britain.

Emmeline has established a special niche in this growing market. When it is suggested at a party that her travel agency is 'like Cook's,' she answers quite accurately 'No' (*N* 23). Thomas Cook hired his first train in 1841, but he began as a 'tour operator' rather than a travel agent, entering retail at the turn of the century mainly to enhance his tour business. Retail travel agencies emerged in force only after World War I, when the increase of air traffic required the establishment of local retail outlets. The difference between such agencies and Cook's, which was still essentially a tour operator, was that the travel agent acted on behalf of a principal, that is, the original provider of tourist services, such as a hotel company, an airline, a tour operator, or a shipping company. Travel agents sold the principal's services and were rewarded by a commission on each sale, but undertook no liability for the original provider.[12] Emmeline and Peter, her business partner, make a selling point of this impunity. Flaunting the ridiculous slogan 'Move dangerously' ('But do your railway companies like that?' Julian wonders), they challenge their clientele to brave the unknown. 'Life, even travel, is losing its element of uncertainty,' Emmeline explains; 'we try to supply that. We give clients their data; they have to use their own wits. "Of course" – we always say to them – "you may not enjoy yourselves."' But the business partners also pride themselves on the 'personal care' they lavish on their customers (*N* 23–4). 'Arriving at one's destination one found a postcard, stamped with the office slogan, wishing one every pleasure.' One tourist, who was sent to Silesia, having mixed it up with Sicily, returned after a dreadful fortnight to wreck the office, but ended up entreating Emmeline not to cry. '"There, there," he said, "a girl like you's not fit for this sort of life"' (*N* 92). In point of fact Emmeline was not crying, but had merely blinked myopically behind her spectacles. The agents' solicitude, however, earns them large commissions.

Large enough to hire a secretary, aptly named Miss Tripp, who provides a comic counterpoint to Emmeline's operatic passion. Recently graduated from Oxford and hopelessly inefficient, Tripp (as she prefers to call herself) develops an alarming crush on Emmeline, who is too short-sighted to detect its symptoms. But one day, when Emmeline is trying to dictate a letter, Tripp lets rip: 'all this time in Miss Tripp the juices of an unduly prolonged adolescence had violently been fermenting: now with a pop they shot out the cork from the bottle.' Tripp protests that she is 'human' and accuses Emmeline of wanting an 'automaton' ('we couldn't afford one,' Emmeline is tempted to reply). To Emmeline, 'it was as though the very furniture had complained' (*N* 120–4). She gives the lovelorn Tripp a holiday and employs the inexorable Miss Armitage instead. As befits its title, *To the North* is a novel of polar contrasts: Miss Tripp and Miss Armitage are as opposite as south and north, summer and winter, fire and ice. If Tripp parodies grand passion, Miss Armitage parodies the grim fatality that overshadows Bowen's world. 'Efficient as Nemesis and as unrelenting,' Miss Armitage's zeal produces extra drudgery, and the partners groan under the oppression of the mounting paperwork (*N* 174). Her ruthless competence terrifies the customers away.

Emmeline's myopia makes a comic contrast to the long-sighted vistas of her enterprise. Imagining herself a rocket scientist, rather than a lowly travel agent, she shoots her clients into unknown continents – 'such an exalting idea of speed possessed [her]' (*N* 135). If her faculties stray, however, her body remains stationed in the office in Woburn Place (*N* 125). Apart from a memorable flight with Markie to Paris, and a disastrous dirty weekend in a country cottage near Devizes, her travelling is largely done for her by her clients. Similarly, her partner Peter 'can't move.' Emmeline explains: 'He gets sea-sick and air-sick and quite often train-sick, and I haven't got time to go everywhere' (*N* 24). Both partners travel vicariously through their customers, who report back when they return, enabling future tourists to benefit from their experience.

Thus Emmeline moves by proxy while remaining at a standstill, static as the eye of a tornado. Bowen agreed with a commentator's observation that 'Bowen characters are almost perpetually in transit', yet they are strangely motionless at the same time (*MT* 286). In Bowen's world, as in Lewis Carroll's Wonderland, 'it takes all the running you can do to stay in the same place.'[13] Modern transportation, which features so prominently in *To the North*, enables Bowen's characters to be motionless in motion, relinquishing their will to the machines that drive them. In aeroplanes, for instance, passengers are squashed together, bound into their seats, and imprisoned for hours in an airborne tube. They travel like astronauts who, as Mary Ellmann has observed, bear more resemblance to pregnant women than to macho explorers of heroic times:

> Like a woman being carted to a delivery room, the astronaut must sit (or lie) still, and go where he is sent. Even the nerve, the genuine courage it takes simply not to run away, is much the same in both situations – to say nothing of the shared sense of having gone too far to be able to change one's mind.[14]

Bowen's characters have usually gone too far to change their minds; in fact they often seem devoid of minds to change. Even when Emmeline is driving her own car, she finds herself driven by an agency beyond control: the car's dizzy terror of its driver. 'She shot into gear, accelerated, and the small car went spinning, terrified, up the empty streets to St John's Wood' (*N* 50).

Most of the motion in *To the North* is circular; the final car drive is the only one-way journey. Although the characters may 'dream of flying,' in actuality they either shrink from travel or return as tourists to their starting-point. Cecilia frequently announces her imminent departure to America, yet never goes. Emmeline, on the other hand, finds herself whirled round in forms of transportation that usurp her will – her car, for instance, which spins her through the streets of London. Her penchant for 'spinning' – a recurrent term in *To the North* – connects her to Emma Bovary (whose name is daintified in Emmeline). In the famous scene in *Madame Bovary* when Emma waltzes with the Viscount at Vaubyessard, she turns 'like a disk on a pivot,' intoxicated by the spinning of the gorgeous ballroom. Emmeline enjoys a similar thrill when she and Markie are hurtling through Paris in a taxi, which 'steered between two lorries, bumped on an island and spun just clear of a bus. Emmeline laughed, seeing Paris spin round, and blinked at the crash of light' (*N* 149). This roller-coastering reminds Emmeline of Robert Browning's sexy poem 'The Last Ride Together.' But it also alludes to the famous cab journey in *Madame Bovary*, when Emma and her lover Léon insist on being driven around Rouen all day long, their driver wondering 'what furious locomotive urge prevented these people from ever coming to a stop.' A crucial difference, however, between *Madame Bovary* and *To the North* is that Flaubert's bodies have been superseded by Bowen's machines. Emma Bovary spins on her own two feet: those famous feet 'so swift when she had hastened to satisfy her desires . . . that would now walk no more' – as they are described on her deathbed in the ritual of extreme unction.[15] Even the cab in Flaubert's novel is pulled by living horses and navigated by a mind indignant at this aimless locomotion. Emmeline, by contrast, is spun around by motor vehicles whose drivers seem mechanised by their machines. In *To the North*, it is the taxi, not the taxi driver, which careers through Paris, just as Emmeline's car speeds off through London with a terror of its own.

The first journey of the novel is taken by Cecilia, who initially appears to be the heroine. Returning by train from Italy, Cecilia is dining in the restaurant-car when a stranger, beckoned by her half-involuntary glance, sits down to join her. They engage in awkward conversation, while the dark lakes of Switzerland whiz past, the train 'lashing about its passengers as though they were bound to a dragon's tail' (*N* 9). To Cecilia the landscape, with its torn mists and toppling rocks, looks like an afterworld, and the stranger seems a suitable companion in damnation: 'square and stocky, clean shaven, thickish about the neck and jaw, with a capable, slightly receding forehead, mobile, greedy, intelligent mouth and the impassive bright quick-lidded eyes of an agreeable reptile' (*N* 7). Yet Markie (the name inscribed on his cigarette case – he is '*that kind* of young man') has the brutish magnetism of a Rochester, stocky and moody as Charlotte Bronte's romantic hero (*N* 19). A barrister, Markie is reputed to be ' "rising" with the inevitability of a lighted balloon' (which implies that he is also bound to burst). When Cecilia reluctantly invites him to dinner with Emmeline in Oudenarde Road, Markie takes over the party with a 'rapid fire of talk' – 'incisive, spectacular, mordant.' Despite his brilliance, Cecilia's post-mortem is that 'it was one of those one-man evenings which, though successful, leave one rather depressed.' She confesses herself 'worn out listening to Markie; it's like watching something catch too many flies on its tongue' (*N* 48–9). When we are later told that his reflection in a kettle looks like the 'Frog Footman, shockingly globular,' it is all too clear that Markie is a frog that Emmeline disastrously misrecognises as a prince (*N* 106).

Markie's effect on Emmeline is shattering: 'a splinter of ice in the heart is bombed out rather than thawed out' (*N* 47). Yet her innocence is as dangerous as his depravity, their combination deadly: 'Innocence walks with violence,' Bowen states somewhat portentously (*N* 185). Throughout their love affair, Emmeline's myopia blinds her to the monster she has charmed. One morning Markie, looking like the picture of Dorian Gray, visits Emmeline after an all-night orgy, reeking with 'the whole fumy void of a night which, like hell, had no clocks, in which no remission was to be hoped of the hours.' Ashamed of his hideousness, he attacks her beauty, finding fault with her spectacles, which she submissively removes. With or without spectacles, however, Emmeline cannot see what Markie is: 'it was as though some ragged and bulky cloud interposed a moment between herself and her fixed idea of him' (*N* 102–4). Cecilia has no patience with Markie's 'Byron complex.' 'All this *âme damnée* is such a bore,' she exclaims (*N* 164). But Emmeline resembles Graham Greene's protagonists in that she must undergo the torments of the damned in order to become a moral being. Her demon lover is her passport to the northernmost extremities of pain.

Emmeline's loveliness makes Markie conscious of his own deformity, and he lashes out at her with all the fury of his injured narcissism. Yet he also blames her, with a barrister's facility for twisting facts, for his tantrums. Take the horrid quarrel that concludes the lovers' clandestine weekend in the country. Still hung-over from the night before, Markie sets out to spoil the idyll; he refuses to eat the treats that Emmeline has brought from Fortnum's and insists on dining in public at Devizes. Here the lovers are observed, and the scandal is reported back to Lady Waters. The next day Markie throws a wobbly when Cecilia, thrilled with the news of her engagement, telegraphs Emmeline to come home early. Markie refuses to budge: Cecilia's selfishness provokes his rivalry for Emmeline's attention, and he insists that they stay put. After a few hours of his furious sulking Emmeline can bear no more and gives in to his demand to stay. By now, however, he has changed his mind. Emmeline cries:

> 'Listen, I give in, I give up. Cecilia'll just have to bear it. I'll let things be spoiled between her and me. Could you think I wanted to miss our day? Our minutes are all so precious I never know what to do with them. All I ever wanted, all I ask now is to stay. Every time you and I part it tears me to bits. There is no one but you.'
>
> 'If we really must go into all this – my dear Emmeline, you put no one first but yourself. Your will, your conscience, your lunatic sensibility. No doubt you are right, but you can't have it both ways, you know.'
>
> 'I love you. I beg you to stay here with me tonight.'
>
> 'Love?' said Markie. 'Love with you's simply a theory. You care for nothing but being right. It's a pity you can't be natural.'
>
> 'Oh, Markie. Natural . . .'
>
> 'You think you've done something extraordinary.'
>
> 'It made you happy.'
>
> 'Oh yes.'
>
> 'Whatever I am, forgive me. I only ask you to stay.'
>
> 'Quite frankly, I don't care to stay in a cottage this size with a cold and hysterical woman.'
>
> 'I see,' said Emmeline, dropping her voice suddenly.
>
> (*N* 211–12)

This nasty dialogue proves Markie a master of projection. The insults he flings at Emmeline boomerang upon himself – it is he who is cold, wilful, egotistical, self-righteous, lunatic, yet also paradoxically conscience-stricken. Emmeline fears his conscience more than his carnality: 'Though she had never met Markie's conscience she had heard it sometimes, creeping about the house' (*N* 183).

Markie cultivates incompetence in order to enslave women to his needs – 'on the principle that it is a mistake to do anything anyone else can do for one' (*N* 203). Why drive if someone else will do it for you? Why create a home, if your sister is willing to provide one, with a whistling cook thrown into the bargain? Markie's flat, located on the top floor of his sister's house, is 'completely cut off' from the world below: one sibling 'might have lain gassed for days before the other became suspicious' (*N* 66). When Markie's meals are ready, the cook whistles through a pipe, and the food arrives on the dumb-waiter. In his emotional life, as in his living arrangements, other people scarcely exist for Markie, except as spittoons for his projections, unless they interfere with his debaucheries – for instance, when his sister Mrs Dolman (a dolorous name) complains about the racket, or the wretched cook goes off on holiday.

It is arguable that Markie, the Jacobean villain of the melodrama, is too bad to be true, whereas Emmeline, the novel's angel, is too good. William Heath has pointed out that 'angel is a title she is given with almost annoying frequency'; it is Markie's pet name for her, and when he betrays her she becomes an angel of death.[16] But Emmeline is blank rather than good. Often dressed in silver, she is associated with transparent or reflective surfaces: windows, mirrors, glaciers, silver, glass, and ice. On the night of their last ride together, she dazzles Markie like the northern star: 'Very tall, silver and shining, her hair tonight at its brightest, face at its most translucent . . .' 'Were she dead,' he thinks, 'she could not have come from farther away' (*N* 229). Virginia Woolf, in *A Room of One's Own*, argues that 'women have served all these centuries as looking-glasses possessing the magic and delicious power of reflecting the figure of man at twice its natural size.'[17] Unfortunately Emmeline's magic mirror has the opposite effect, for Markie sees himself outshone, diminished in her silvery surface. It is telling that he spoils compliments to Emmeline by adding that she is 'too shiny,' admonishing her to powder her nose (*N* 105). Her shine shows him up too clearly.

Markie is a 1930s version of the great rakes of the eighteenth-century epistolary novel, such as Valmont in Laclos's *Dangerous*

Liaisons, or Lovelace in Richardson's *Clarissa*. Each of these villains finds himself outdone by the woman he seduces, debased by his own compulsion to debase. Similarly, Markie feels 'guilty and nervous' after seducing Emmeline in Paris:

> he had been oppressed since last night by sensations of having been overshot, of having, in some final soaring flight of her exaltation, been outdistanced: as though a bird whose heart one moment one could feel beating has escaped between the hands. The passionless entirety of her surrender, the volition of her entire wish to be his had sent her a good way past him: involuntarily, the manner of her abandonment had avenged her innocence.
>
> (*N* 142)

It is a testimony to Bowen's psychological intelligence that Markie's cruelty stems from conscience, not from callousness. Tormented by guilt, he cannot rest, like a shark that suffocates if it stops moving – 'missing repose vaguely he made it impossible' (*N* 145). Markie also resembles Lovelace and Valmont in being an epistolary predator who uses letters to seduce the innocent. As his name suggests, Markie's secret weapon is his writing or his 'mark.' It is the 'bumptious letter' that he sends to Emmeline at Farraways, rather than his froggy presence, which bombs the ice out of her heart (*N* 46). Later he clinches the seduction by writing notes. In the aeroplane to Paris, where the engine-roar makes speech impossible, Markie resorts to a one-way epistolary correspondence:

> The manner of this correspondence began to appeal to him: deliberation unknown in speaking, boldness quite unrebuked by its own vibration and, free of that veil of uncertainty and oblivion that falls on the posted letter, the repercussions upon her of all he said. The indiscretions of letter-writing, the intimacies of speech were at once his.
>
> (*N* 137)

For Markie – who shrinks from direct contact, channelling his relationships with others through prostheses like the telephone, the whistle, the dumb-waiter – this correspondence is ideal, for it combines indirection with peremptoriness. '*You must know what I want*,' he scrawls, adding with legalistic foresight, '*We could not marry.*' Emmeline merely smiles – his writing compels her like the runes of fate. 'She was embarked, they were embarked together, no stop was possible' (*N* 137–8). Months later he reminds her of his let-out clause – '*We could not marry*' – to justify his faithlessness. 'You are like an insurance company,' Emmeline replies (*N* 184).

Once Emmeline succumbs to Markie's letters in the aeroplane, she is branded by his writing like a virgin page: 'His being was written all over her' (*N* 180). In this novel, to be written *to* is to be written *on*, but also to be written *into* a pre-existent script whose outcome is irreversible: 'no stop was possible.' Marked by Markie, Emmeline is robbed (or relieved) of innocence, but she is also robbed of self-determination and marked out for doom. References to writing multiply as the novel speeds to its catastrophe. 'Across the mind's surface – on which a world's apprehension, strain at home and in Europe, were gravely written – the sense of a spoilt summer, so much prettiness wasted, darkly spread like split ink' (*N* 177). This passage indicates that it is not just the lovers, but the whole of Europe which is 'riding for a fall' (*N* 184). Meanwhile Emmeline is so possessed by Markie, in all the senses of the word 'possessed,' that she scarcely inhabits her own body: she does not 'have' a headache, as those who occupy their bodies do; instead 'headache was written over her forehead' (*N* 195). After the lovers' disastrous outing to the country, 'one more violent and wordless hour disjointed from life was written over the week-end cottage' (N 208).

These insistent images of writing build up an impression of the modern world as a palimpsest of marks, a 'mesh' of traces (*N* 177). These images are reinforced by those of transport, another form of marking that inscribes the world with roads and railroads, shipping lines and air routes, telegraph cables and telephone wires. The transport of voices by telecommunication, the transport of bodies by land, sea, and air, implicates the characters in relay-networks extending far beyond their consciousness. These networks commandeer their users' will, reducing speakers to automata. Emmeline feels whirled by words much as she is whirled by cars, dizzied by 'spinning sentences, little cogs interlocked, each clicking each other round' (*N* 98). Cecilia, like the unnamed guest in *The Hotel*, fears that she does not exist unless she is connected to the telephone, when she can 'crystallise over the wire' (*N* 29). Her telephone bill grows enormous because she cannot wait to be rung up: she must be plugged in or dialled up lest she should vanish 'into abeyance' – a constant risk in Bowen's world. If Cecilia fuses with her telephone, Emmeline fuses with the 'shadowy nets' of transportation: the railways, airlines, and shipping routes whose schedules she knows by heart (*FR* 82, 99). As a party trick she turns into a talking timetable, telling the guests exactly where the Simplon-Orient is travelling at eight forty-eight pm (*N* 231).

While characters behave like transportation systems, those systems retaliate by taking on the attributes of human beings. The funniest example is the number 11 bus. When Julian's blushing, spotty niece Pauline, who 'chaperones herself the whole time,' asks if it is proper for a girl of her age to go riding around London in a bus, the housekeeper replies that it depends 'entirely upon the character of the bus':

> The no. 11 is an entirely moral bus. Springing from Shepherd's Bush, against which one has seldom heard anything, it enjoys some innocent bohemianism in Chelsea, picks up the shoppers at Peter Jones, swerves down the Pimlico Road – too busy to be lascivious – passes not too far from the royal stables, nods to Victoria Station, Westminster Abbey, the Houses of Parliament, whirrs reverently up Whitehall, and from its only brush with vice, in the Strand, plunges to Liverpool Street through the noble and serious architecture of the City.
>
> (*N* 40)

While buses become 'moral,' human beings become mechanical – spinning, twitching, shivering, and stalling, as if driven by remote control. No wonder Tripp suspects that she has been mistaken for an automaton; even her name associates her with machinery, specifically with a trip-switch, or an automatic power-cut. Similarly, Markie ticks off Emmeline for speaking of his girlfriend Daisy as a 'cheap gramophone' (206).

Technologies of transport seem to reach into the inner nervous system, connecting characters to unknown frequencies. Emmeline's mind 'hums' like a telephone receiver, while Markie provides her with a kind of dial tone, a white noise that drowns out her volition.[18] 'He had the effect of suspending her faculties not unpleasantly, like some very loud noise to which one becomes accustomed' (*N* 49). Similarly, Cecilia's nerves – 'a living tissue of shadows and little insistent sounds' – suggest that she is suffering from faulty wiring (*N* 132). Nervousness is not unique to her, but spreads through *To the North* like an infection – even Lady Waters's dog is 'nervy' (*N* 155). Entrammeled in clandestine networks, vibrating with energies beyond control, Bowen's characters are jittering wrecks whose only respite from nervousness is numbness. In this respect they resemble Simmel's conception of the metropolitan subject, dazed into apathy by constant bombardment of the nerves. Simmel argues that the nerves, when agitated to their strongest reactivity for too long a time, finally cease to react at all, producing what he calls the 'blasé' attitude – a kind of Bowenesque insentience.[19]

George Miller Beard, writing in 1881, attributes what he calls 'American nervousness' to five aspects of modern civilisation: 'steam power, the periodical press, the telegraph, the sciences, and the mental activity of women.'[20] At least three of these ingredients in updated form – combustion engines, the telephone, and female commercial enterprise – also feature memorably in *To the North*, inducing telltale side-effects of nervousness. Writing almost fifty years before Bowen, Beard anticipates the modern phobia that telecommunications, by speeding up the dissemination of information, overload circuits in individual nervous systems, transforming the human mind into a 'machinery of agitation' (*N* 98). Even the inventors of these new technologies perceived them as extensions of the nerves: Thomas Sömmerring, who presented the first electrolytic telegraph to the Munich Academy of Sciences in 1809, described it as 'a rough physical analog of a nerve centre'; Samuel Morse, who refined the telegraph, also called it a nerve system; while the *New York Times* hailed it as 'the international spinal connection.'[21] These metaphors also work the other way around, implying that the human nervous system is telegraphy incarnate.

In Bowen's fiction, nervousness reveals the interconnectedness of minds, enmeshed in transport networks that traverse the boundary between the human and the technological. Her characters, swinging between the jitters and the doldrums, present the symptoms Beard ascribed to 'neurasthenia', a term he coined in the 1860s to describe a new form of nervous fatigue, whose indications ranged from agitation to insentience. The key symptom was 'aboulia,' or diminution of the will. It is telling that the French psychologist Charcot associated this disorder with 'railway spine' and other hysterias arising from modern forms of transport. These mental illnesses had been the focus of medical and legal controversy since 1864, when British railway companies belatedly accepted legal liability for the health and safety of their passengers. It was widely recognised that railway accidents caused deeper and more lasting psychic injuries than preindustrial accidents, such as falling off a horse. John Eric Erichsen, in his 1866 study *On Railway and Other Injuries of the Nervous System*, commented that 'railway accidents have this peculiarity, that they come upon the sufferers instantaneously without warning, and that the utter helplessness of a human being in the midst of the great masses in motion renders these accidents peculiarly terrible.'[22] The 'aboulia,' or deterioration of the will, typical of Bowen's characters could be understood as a psychological effect of the industrialisation of transport, an expression of the utter helplessness of the human being in the midst of great masses in motion. Emmeline feels helpless even when driving her own car, her will subordinated to the agency of the machine. In the final car crash, she surrenders all volition to velocity – 'such an exalting idea of speed possessed [her].' Throughout the novel, her constant blinking intimates that she is on the blink, her will destroyed.

Sean O'Faolain has marvelled at the 'lengths to which Miss Bowen will go to deprive her characters of autonomy.' He attributes their passivity to the 'atmosphere of ancient fable' that pervades her novels, the sense of an overwhelming force of destiny.[23] Yet this passivity also reflects conditions peculiar to modernity, specifically the transport of the will into mechanical extensions, such as cars, taxis, aeroplanes, telegrams, telegraphs, radios, and gramophones – prostheses that reduce their users to bewildered residues. In Bowen's next novel, *The House in Paris*, the characters find themselves ensnared in networks that extend through time as well as space, transporting the scars of yesterday into tomorrow.

The House in Paris, like *To the North*, opens with a scene of transport, specifically a taxi ride through Paris. Henrietta Mountjoy, an eleven-year-old girl, is being driven in a 'skidding taxi' through the deep ravines of the Parisian streets, when dawn breaks and a gash of light assaults the darkness: 'In a sort of slow flash, Henrietta had her first open view of Paris – watery sky, wet light, light water, frigid, dark, inky buildings, spans of bridges, trees. This open light gash across Paris faded at each end' (*HP* 17, 21).

Why should Paris be perceived as gashed? Why should light be experienced as laceration? Is it the dawning sun, or Henrietta's act of seeing, that stabs the city with a blade of light? The image of the gash is associated, here and elsewhere in the novel, with the transport of the past into the present, the resurgence of obliterated histories. In this scene, the light gash, cutting through the 'fissures' of the streets, reopens the scars of history, reminding the child 'how much blood had been shed in Paris' (*HP* 22). To Henrietta, the passing vistas look identical to one another, like a movie stuck in endless replay: the past repeats itself ad infinitum. 'The same streets, with implacably shut shops and running into each other at odd angles, seemed to unreel past again and again. She thought she saw the same kiosks' (*HP* 17). At the end of the 'complex of deep streets, fissures in the crazy gloomy height,' lies the eponymous house in Paris, home of the Fishers, mother and daughter, and the matrix from which all the fissures in the novel radiate (*HP* 22).

But Henrietta's journey, like Cecilia's at the opening of *To the North*, is a decoy set up to mislead the reader. For Henrietta is not the heroine, nor is her destination Paris. Nor is the novel based on the familiar model of the journey, with a beginning, a middle, and an end, but rather on the model of the labyrinth. An anatomy of intersubjectivity, the novel traces the 'complex of deep streets,' the hidden networks that knit the characters into their quasi-tele-pathic intimacy. The striking image of a child thought-reading a missing letter from his missing mother epitomises the predicament of the protagonists. The house in Paris is the switchboard where their histories collide and interpenetrate.

On this fateful Thursday morning in November, two unrelated children accidentally converge upon the house, like letters in transit, in order to be forwarded to new addresses ('Thursday's child has far to go,' chants the old nursery rhyme). Henrietta has been sent to visit her grandmother in the South of France, but has paused in Paris to change trains. Her grandmother, Mrs Arbuthnot, has lined up a series of chaperones to accompany the motherless child, devising a 'dear little system of cherry-pink cockades' to be worn by Henrietta and her escorts for mutual identification (*HP* 43). Owing to a lengthy gap between trains, Naomi Fisher, long-suffering friend of the ma-nipulative Mrs Arbuthnot, agrees to meet Henrietta at the Gare du Nord and deposit her some hours later at the Gare de Lyon. In the interim Naomi takes the little girl home to the 'fatal house': a Gothic ménage dominated by her dying mother, Madame Fisher, the French widow of an English captain.

By chance, Henrietta's visit coincides with that of Leopold, a precocious ten-year-old who lives in Italy with his American adoptive parents, the Grant Moodys. The astonishing purpose of Leopold's trip to Paris is to meet his birth mother Karen Forrestier for the first time, under the auspices of Madame Fisher, her former landlady. To Leopold's dismay, a telegram arrives instead of Karen, announcing that she will not come. At this point a gash opens up within the narrative itself, and the past impales itself into the present in the form of a long flashback recounting the disastrous love affair that led to Leopold's conception and adoption. *The House in Paris* thus divides into three parts, of which the first and third take place in the present, while the second transports us back into the past. (Bowen described *The House in Paris* as the most 'shapely' of her novels, and re-deployed its temporal structure in her elegiac novel *The Little Girls*.)[24] After the flashback Madame Fisher beckons Leopold into her sickroom, where she divulges the secrets of his birth prudishly withheld from him by his adoptive parents. In the final episode, Karen's husband Ray Forrestier arrives at the Fishers' house, determined to restore Leopold to his blood mother. But the novel breaks off before this projected reunion has occurred, leaving the characters suspended on the verge of transport, whether to this world or to the next.

On one level, *The House in Paris* could be read as an allegory of socialisation. Both Henrietta and Leopold have lost their mothers, through death in the first case, abandonment in the second. Forsaken and farouche (to use a favourite Bowen gallicism), the children need to be reintegrated into bloodlines in order to repair the gashes in the web of genealogy. Like letters with illegible addresses, both children are returned to sender, posted back to their maternal origins: Henrietta rejoins her maternal grandmother, Leopold his natural mother. But this putative reintegration takes place only by inference after the narrative concludes. For the duration of the novel, while the children are suspended in the Fishers' 'waiting-room,' their origins, addresses, and identities are cast adrift (*HP* 100). Here they wait and wonder – 'Why am I? What made me be?' – in Leopold's unspoken words (*HP* 67). The boy's tormenting doubts dismantle Henrietta's certainties: 'Today was to do much to disintegrate Henrietta's character, which, built up by herself, for herself, out of admonitions and axioms (under the growing stress of: if I am Henrietta, then what is *Henrietta?*) was a mosaic of all possible kinds of prejudice.' Prim, matter-of-fact Henrietta has constructed her identity defensively, but her encounter with Leopold shatters this cocoon of prejudice, forcing her to recognise that there is more to being 'a someone' than 'disliking things' (*HP* 25–6).

Leopold, like Oedipus, knows nothing of his true heredity. 'Over understood' by his adoptive parents, who scrutinise his every bowel movement, he has been denied all knowledge of his birth, the Grant Moodys being determined at all cost 'to keep his childhood sunny and beautiful' (*HP* 34, 41). Leopold has to break 'the rule of "niceness,"' as his unknown mother did before him, in order to wake up from this dream-life (*HP* 108). If the novel has a moral, it is that niceness suffocates the spirit, whereas rejection and betrayal, whatever damage they inflict, also provide the 'opposition' necessary to distinguish self from other. Without the distance created by this opposition, there can be no transport and no love. By the standards of today's media, Karen would undoubtedly be deemed a 'dead-beat mom' – not only does she abandon her child but she stands him up, breaking her promise to be reunited with him. But Bowen precludes such banal judgements. For Leopold, his mother's defection proves that she is something other than the creature of his thought:

> Her will, her act, her thought spoke in the telegram. Her refusal became *her*, became her coming in suddenly, breaking down by this one act of being herself only, his imagination in which he had bound her up. So she lived outside himself; she was alive truly. She set up that opposition that is love.

(HP 193–4)

Henrietta, on the other hand, grows up 'to date her belief that nothing real ever happens from Leopold's mother's not coming this afternoon' (*HP* 191). The children's diverse responses show that any action, whether nice or cruel, brings forth incalculable consequences – 'those sad meaningless things that are called "effects."'[25]

The narrative itself eschews the logic of cause and effect, proceeding through cuts and interpolations rather than a chronological succession of events. These cuts tend to be triggered off by letters or telegrams, which disrupt the unities of time and place by introducing absent characters and offstage plots. The most important is Karen's telegram, which precipitates the transport to the 'The Past,' the central flashback of the novel. The children themselves arrive like letters, posted between their parents and parental surrogates. Although Miss Fisher dismisses her own suggestion that her house is 'a depôt for young people crossing Paris,' this is the service it performs in the novel, either facilitating transport or stalling it, with fatal consequences (*HP* 20). While it functions as a post office, relaying its visitors to and fro, it also threatens to become a mausoleum of dead letters.

Leopold is not a dead letter but a misdirected one, and it is by reading other people's letters that he discovers the role he plays in other people's plots. Specifically he raids Miss Fisher's handbag, 'with the immediate thought that inside there might be letters about him,' and finds three envelopes, already opened. (There is a possible allusion here to Wilde's *The Importance of Being Earnest*, in which a handbag holds the clue to the mystery of Worthing's origins.) The first envelope contains a 'copious letter' from Leopold's adoptive mother, Marian Grant Moody, exposing the well-meaning despotism of his upbringing. She entreats Miss Fisher to avoid unduly agitating Leopold, cursed as he is by his heredity: 'instability on the father's side, lack of control on the mother's.' She also instructs her to inspect his bowel movements, restrict him to the blandest fluids in the evening ('whatever he may say'), and encourage him to masticate. And she warns not once but twice that the child has received no 'direct sex-instruction' – 'though my husband is working towards this through botany and mythology' (*HP* 39–41).

Leopold finds the revelations in this letter shattering. For some time he remains 'quite blank,' then reaches for the second letter to assuage what Bowen calls the 'gash' inflicted by the first – an image that recalls the 'light gash' of the opening scene. 'The revulsion threatening him became so frightening that he quickly picked up Mrs Arbuthnot's letter and read it, as though to clap something on to the gash in his mind.' This letter addresses the spinsterly Miss Fisher as 'Kingfisher,' an epithet that seems absurd until we learn that Mrs Arbuthnot once spotted Naomi standing on a rock in a long blue coat, looking down intently as though she 'wanted to dive', but probably contemplating suicide. The point of this snide letter is to wheedle Miss Fisher into fetching Henrietta from the train station, and to post the child forward, through the chain of pink cockades, to her grandmother's villa in the South of France. 'This struck Leopold as a competent letter. He saw at once that Mrs Arbuthnot was wicked, and would succeed.' The third envelope, 'dead white' and addressed to Miss Fisher in Karen's handwriting, is empty. Leopold presses this envelope to his forehead, like a compress for the 'gash in his mind,' and attempts to thought-read the missing contents. At this point Henrietta interrupts him with the bizarre reprimand: 'you oughtn't to thought-read letters to someone else!'[26]

Shortly after this scene of illicit reading, Karen's telegram arrives, announcing that she will not come, and this is when the narrative skids backwards, like Henrietta's taxi, to the past. This narrative manoeuvre resembles the famous recognition scene in Homer's *Odyssey*, in which the hero, returning in disguise to Ithaca, is bathed by his old nurse Eurycleia who recognises his distinctive scar. At this point a scar or gash opens up within the narrative itself, and the poet, in one of his rare flashbacks, recounts the hunting accident in which Odysseus received his wound.[27] The three letters also hark back to the mythological theme of the three caskets famously analysed by Freud. In *The Merchant of Venice*, the most well-known version of the myth, Portia's suitors are obliged to guess which of three caskets, the gold, the silver, or the lead, contains her portrait. Bassanio wins Portia's hand by resisting gold and silver and opting for the third casket, made of 'meagre lead,' declaring that its 'paleness moves me more than eloquence.'[28] According to Freud, the third casket stands for death, and therefore corresponds to many other thirds throughout mythology, including the third daughter of King Lear, who responds with silence to her father's imperious demand for love, offering him 'nothing' when her sisters offer everything. 'In dreams dumbness is a common representation of death,' Freud claims. He also points out that Offenbach's opera *La Belle Hélène* assigns the third daughter to the place of silence: 'La troisième! ah, la troisième . . ./ La troisième ne dit rien.' In Freud's view, the three caskets stand for 'the three forms taken by the figure of the mother in the course of a man's life – the mother herself, the beloved one who is chosen after her pattern, and lastly the Mother Earth who receives him once more.'[29] Whatever the validity of Freud's analysis, it is intriguing that Leopold's third envelope should also be associated with the mother, and moreover that it should be empty, as if the corpse had been raided from its tomb – or womb. Like the third daughter, the third envelope says nothing: 'la troisième ne dit rien.' A casket within caskets, the 'dead white' envelope coffined in the handbag coffined in the house harbours an impenetrable core of silence.

The House in Paris itself is structured like an envelope, in that the first and third sections, both called 'The Present,' enclose the central section called 'The Past.' Like 'The Present,' 'The Past' begins with a scene of transport in which Karen Michaelis, travelling to Cork by ferry, watches the Irish countryside slip past, much as Henrietta watches Paris unreeling ten years later. Bowen borrowed her heroine's name from the Danish novelist Karen Michaelis, whose novel *The Dangerous Age* had caused a stir more than twenty years before the publication of *The House in Paris*.[30] Bowen reputedly disliked the heroine, but the novel and its sequel, *Elsie Lindtner*, were sufficiently forgotten by 1935 for the author's name to be recycled. Bowen's Karen Michaelis comes from an implacably nice English family, neither 'bigoted, snobbish, touchy, over-rich, over-devout, militant in feeling or given to blood sports,' for whom 'the Boer War, the War and other fatigues and disasters had been so many opportunities to behave well' (*HP* 70). Karen has agreed to marry Ray Forrestier, an equally nice young man, whose remote kinship to the Michaelises bestows 'that touch of inbreeding that makes a marriage so promising' (*HP* 71). The marriage has to be postponed, however, until Ray has sailed to the East and completed 'a mission so delicate that it must not appear to be a mission at all' (*HP* 69). In the meantime Karen is left waiting – the prevailing mode of being in this novel, not only for the characters but for the reader, who also waits amidst 'beforehand echoes' of a transport endlessly deferred (*HP* 65).

To escape the 'uninfectious' excitement aroused by her engagement, Karen travels to Ireland to take refuge with her most oblivious relative, Aunt Violet, and her husband Uncle Bill Bent (*HP* 69). The couple live in Rushbrook, a town full of Protestant gentry forced out of their Big Houses, either by arson or by poverty, and 'living down misfortunes they once had' (*HP* 75). Outside the bathroom door hang grisly photographs of the ruins of Montebello, Uncle Bill's Big House, which was burnt down during the Troubles. At first Karen relishes this afterworld, but its stillness is broken by a letter from Ray interrogating her commitment to their marriage, and later by Uncle Bill's revelation that Aunt Violet is dying of cancer. At this point the calm of Rushbrook becomes oppressive, and Karen, feeling the need 'to be with some gaunt, contemptuous person who twisted life his own way,' makes contact with her former landlady Madame Fisher (*HP* 79).

Karen's connection to the house in Paris dates back five years, when she was studying art and staying with the Fishers as a paying guest. At this time Madame Fisher ran an exclusive establishment for 'well-bred, well-fed, well-read English-speaking girls,' whose parents wanted their dependable daughters to enjoy 'freedom inside the bounds of propriety.' Like Madame Beck in Charlotte Bronte's *Villette*, Madame Fisher kept her young charges under discreet but ubiquitous surveillance: 'she asked no questions, but knew' (*HP* 102–3). As Flaubert says of the ideal author, Madame was 'everywhere felt but nowhere seen.'[31] Behind closed doors she used to entertain her intimate, Max Ebhart, a young Jewish man who fascinated Karen. 'Every movement he made, every word she heard him speak left its mark on her nerves.' This word 'mark,' which recurs at crucial moments of *The House in Paris*, much as the image of writing recurs in *To the North*, suggests that Karen has been marked by love and thereby marked out for catastrophe (*HP* 107). After her trip to Rushbrook Karen receives the news that Max has unaccountably proposed to Naomi Fisher, and that Madame Fisher opposes the match. Anxious, self-abasing, 'thin all over,' Naomi has little but a modest legacy to recommend her to a man of Max's ambitions (*HP* 25). But Max later denies that he is marrying for money, or even marrying the daughter to secure the mother. What he seeks in Naomi is the kind of stillness Karen sought in Rushbrook, the cessation of all transport: 'Naomi is like furniture or the dark,' he explains (*HP* 146, 155).

Eager that Karen should approve of her prospective husband, Naomi arranges to meet both of them at Twickenham, home of the dead aunt from whom she inherited her 'dot.' By bringing her lover and her friend together, Naomi engineers her own betrayal, much as Miss Selby does in 'The Secession,' for it is during this reunion that Max and Karen acknowledge their passion for each other. Nonetheless the reader suspects that it is Madame Fisher, everywhere felt but nowhere seen, who is pulling the strings behind the scenes. No declarations are made at Twickenham, but Max seizes a moment when Naomi's back is turned to press Karen's hand into the grass, which springs back blade by blade, leaving no 'mark' of the impulse which has flattened it – although the image of this obliterated mark returns to mark the text itself (*HP* 120). A desperate love affair ensues, involving so much transport back and forth across the Channel that there is little time for transport into ecstasy. The lovers meet only twice, and it is during a rainy night in a Hythe hotel room that Leopold is conceived; Karen later describes him as 'the mark our hands did not leave on the grass' (*HP* 155). When Karen returns home from her secret tryst, her alibi has already been discredited, yet the whole house seems to be colluding in her mother's 'deadly intention to not know' (*HP* 173). After a week of mutual evasion Karen forces her mother to acknowledge her love-affair. At this moment a telegram arrives from Naomi with the news that Max is dead.

Later Karen learns that Max returned to the house in Paris where he broke off his engagement to Naomi, only to discover her mother eavesdropping outside the door. This proof of her manipulation drove Max to despair. Realising that Madame Fisher had stage-managed his affair with Karen, he perceived that he could never free himself from her emasculating power. Madame Fisher resembles other shadowy thirds in Bowen's fiction, such as Elfrida in *Friends and Relations*, in that she functions as a pander ('fishmonger') to other people's love affairs but also as a deadly obstacle, destroying passion 'like acid on a plate' (*HP* 138). In one of the most melodramatic scenes in Bowen's novels, Max slashes his wrists over the Fishers' hearth and staggers out to die, leaving a trail of blood that disappears at the front door. The only 'mark' that remains of the affair is Leopold. Karen conceals the child's birth from everyone except her mother, who dies of the offence to niceness, and Naomi, who arranges Leopold's adoption.

Meanwhile Karen marries Ray Forrestier after all, his ardour having been intensified by her affair with Max. In this marriage, Max plays the role of 'hymen' – the copula that binds and separates – for Bowen's couples are always 'pinned together' by an interfering third. But Ray insists that Leopold should be sitting in the 'third chair left pushed in at a table set for a couple' (*HP* 219). Without the child, the third presence cannot be kept in place, but penetrates the deepest recesses of the couple's intimacy: 'we are never alone.' If Leopold were here, Ray pleads, 'he'd be simply a child, either in or out of the room. While he is a dread of yours, he is everywhere' (*HP* 217). This predicament resembles Graham Greene's *The End of the Affair*, in which the husband feels oppressed by the ubiquity, rather than the loss, of his dead wife: 'Because she's always away, she's never away. You see, she's never anywhere else. She's not having lunch with anybody, she's not at a cinema with you. There's nowhere for her to be but at home.'[32] Similarly, Leopold's absence means that he is all too present. Yet if Ray yearns for Leopold, it is principally as a conduit to Max: in this triangle, Ray is drawn to Karen and her missing son as a means of transport to her missing lover.

The final section of the novel cuts back to the moment when Leopold receives his mother's devastating telegram. Standing by the mantelpiece where his father bled to death, Leopold succumbs to a haemorrhage of tears – not only his own tears but 'all the tears that had ever been denied . . . arrears of tears starting up at one moment's unobscured view of grief' (*HP* 196). After this outburst Madame Fisher summons the child to her sickroom to tell him the secret of his birth. Every truth that she divulges drains her ravaged body of its life, and by the time she finishes her face is nothing but 'a flaccid mask.' Yet her words, like 'cold slow drops,' shower over Leopold, helping him to 'grow like a young tree' and 'crack the tomb' in which he is immured (*HP* 207, 203). Through a moral reversal typical of Bowen's fiction, the Gothic ogress turns out to be the child's liberator: only Madame Fisher has sufficient contempt for niceness to give Leopold the knowledge that he hungers for. 'How right of Mrs Fisher to smash everyone up,' Maurice Bowra wrote enthusiastically to Bowen.[33] Whether or not Madame dies 'of talking,' as Leopold fears, her revelation terminates her fictional existence (*HP* 208). The novel concludes with a double embarkation: Ray Forrestier delivers Henrietta, brandishing her pink cockade, to her next escort at the Gare du Nord; afterwards he waits with Leopold for a taxi to transport them to an unknown future. Their wait never ends.

The structure of *The House in Paris* compares to the psychoanalytic concept of 'cryptonomy,' developed by Nicolas Abraham and Maria Torok out of Freud's theory of mourning.[34] In 'Mourning and Melancholia' (1917), Freud argues that the bereaved ego regresses to fantasies of cannibalism, 'incorporating' the lost object in order to deny its death or disappearance. In the normal course of mourning, the incorporated object is eventually expelled; but when mourning intensifies into melancholia, it is the object that swallows up the ego.[35] A lurid example of this process may be found in Hitchcock's *Psycho,* in which the murderer's personality is taken over by the mother whose death he has denied. According to Abraham and Torok, the psychic mechanism of incorporation hollows out a 'crypt' within the ego in which the lost object is buried alive.[36] Through encryptment, Derrida comments, 'a door is silently sealed off like a condemned passageway inside the Self.'[37]

It is important that the secrets sealed up in this passageway belong to the incorporated object, not to the self. Where Abraham and Torok depart most radically from Freud is in insisting that the ego does not suffer from its own repressions but from those of others. The contents of the crypt, unlike those of the Freudian unconscious, never existed in the conscious mind and therefore have never been repressed. What haunts us are 'the gaps left in us by the secrets of others.' Elsewhere Abraham names the agent of this haunting as 'the phantom':

> The phantom is a formation of the unconscious that has never been conscious – for good reason. It passes – in a way yet to be determined – from the parent's unconscious into the child's ... The phantom's periodic and compulsive return lies beyond the scope of symptom-formation in the sense of a return of the repressed; it works like a ventriloquist, like a stranger within the subject's own mental topography.[38]

It is through the phantom that the secrets of the past transport themselves into the present, the dead dictating the behaviour of the living.

In *The House in Paris,* Bowen explores the effects of intergenerational haunting by telling the story from the children's point of view. The adults' story, enveloped in the children's, forms a crypt or 'condemned passageway' within the text in which the secrets of the past are buried alive. Meanwhile Leopold is haunted by the phantom of the former generation, which controls his acts like a ventriloquist, compelling him to re-enact the past. The most striking instance is the scene at the Fishers' mantelpiece, when Leopold sheds his tears on the same hearthstone where his unknown father shed his blood. Thus the phantom passes from the father to the son, but it also strays beyond the family, performing ventriloquy on Henrietta too. At one point, when Henrietta stamps her hands palm-down on the Fishers' polished table and watches 'the misty prints they left disappear,' these prints hark back in time (but forward in the narrative) to the scene at Twickenham, where the 'mark' of Max and Karen's clasped hands disappears into the grass (*HP* 66). Thus the 'mark [their] hands did not leave in the grass' is transported as a phantom into Henrietta's unconscious repetition of the past.

Other recurrent images form chains within the novel, reinforcing the impression of enchainment to the past. While Henrietta is passed along a chain of pink cockades, the reader is passed along a chain of 'violets.' These violets have no fixed meaning but accrue associations from their contexts. The death of Karen's Aunt Violet connects the flower to mortality, recalling Ophelia's plaintive cry: 'I would give you some violets, but they withered all when my father died.'[39] Karen observes that Naomi in mourning looks like someone who has 'lost an aunt,' rather than someone who has 'gained a husband,' because Max has given her no violets to pin to her black 'endy' furs (*HP* 96–8). Once again, violets are associated with a dead aunt and the 'endy' rituals of mourning. Finally Karen prepares for meeting Leopold by pinning violets to her breast, but crushes them when she withdraws into her bed (*HP* 215). In all these contexts, violets are linked to loss and death: loss of aunts ('so many aunts have lately died,' Max comments, with a touch of Wodehouse) and loss of mothers (all the mothers in the novel are missing, dead, or dying) (*HP* 136). But violets are also linked to writing: just before Karen receives the news that her Aunt Violet is dead she happens on a letter from Madame Fisher written in violet ink. Her 'vigorous violet handwriting' suggests that Madame Fisher is the author of all violets, the mother of all losses, the fissure behind all fissures (*HP* 125). Spreading like a rash throughout the text, the violets reveal the ubiquity of her malevolence.

Yet even Madame Fisher is caught up in a process of compulsive repetition that exceeds her authorship. For the violets do not belong to any of the characters but circulate between them, inducing a contagion of identities. In their 'periodic and compulsive return,' these violets correspond to Abraham and Torok's definition of the phantom, which transfers itself from mind to mind, haunting the living with the secrets of the dead. In a similar way, violets float in and out of different stories, implicating all the characters in a nameless crime – perhaps the crime of 'transport' or transference itself. In Freud's discussion of the primal murder in *Moses and Monotheism,* he remarks that 'the difficulty is not in perpetrating the deed, but in getting rid of its traces.'[40] In *The House in Paris,* violets resurface like the traces of this unlaid crime, bearing witness to an immemorial atrocity. Max's suicide could be understood as an attempt to re-enact, and thereby to propitiate, this founding trauma. 'A very melodramatic novel,' as A. S. Byatt has pointed out, *The House in Paris* owes its extraordinary power to a strange imbalance between action and implication – it is not Max's implausible suicide that stirs us, but the depth of its mythological reverberations.[41] Reading the novel, one is haunted by the sense of a primordial violence that exceeds the melodramatic stock-in-trade of betrayal, desertion, sudden death; it is a violence that can only be expressed in terms of the formation of a crypt and the compulsive return of phantom violets.

These violets violate autonomy by trespassing boundaries between selves. Another chain of signifiers that implies the violation of autonomy is poison. The term 'poison' first arises when Karen, returning from Cork to England, has a conversation on the ferry with a vulgar Irish girl identified only by her yellow hat. Joking about taste in men, Yellow Hat says, 'Perhaps *your* poison's not mine,' to which Karen replies, 'I don't know what my poison is' (*HP* 92–3). Later Karen disclaims her love for Max by telling Naomi, 'Your poison's not mine' (*HP* 101). Of course, the statement is not true: Karen does desire Max, and desires him precisely because he is another woman's poison. In this novel, each of the main characters seems to be addicted to someone else's poison, to hanker after someone else's love. Yellow Hat's phrase comes up again when Karen is predicting her family's reaction to her pregnancy: 'They would have to see me as someone poisoned. Only poisons, they think, act on you. If a thing does act on you, it can only be poison, some foreign thing. "Your poison's not mine," she said . . .' (*HP* 154). In each of these examples, the term 'poison' signals the invasion of the self by alien desires. The implication is that desire is 'mimetic': what triggers desire is not an object, but the impulse to identify with the desire of another – to be poisoned by someone else's poison.

René Girard has coined the term 'mimetic desire' to describe the dynamics of erotic triangles, in which the bond between male rivals is often stronger than the bond that draws them both to the beloved female. This structure resembles Freud's anatomy of dirty jokes, discussed in Chapter 3 of this book, in which the impulse to seduce a woman, deflected by the presence of a rival third, transforms itself into the desire to amuse another man. Girard cites many examples from European literature in which the choice of the beloved is determined not by her own charms, but by the fact that she is chosen by a male rival. Thus the woman, ostensibly the object of desire, functions as a conduit for desire between men. Taking up Girard's theory of mimetic desire, Mikkel Borch-Jacobsen argues that there is no 'essential bond between desire and its object': 'the desire for an object is a desire-effect; it is *induced*, or at least secondary, with respect to the imitation – the mimesis - of the desire of others. In other words, desire is mimetic before it is anything else.'[42]

In *The House in Paris*, the mimetic nature of desire means that every love affair involves at least three people, for the bond between lover and beloved depends on the mimetic bond between lover and rival. Max and Karen may have always been in love, but it is Max's engagement to another woman that triggers their disastrous romance. And it is Karen's infidelity with Max that clinches Ray's resolve to marry her. Is Ray in love with Karen, or with Karen's love for Max, or with Max's love for Karen? At the end of the novel Ray and Karen, abstracted into 'HE' and 'SHE,' ponder these questions in a telepathic dialogue:

> SHE: . . . you have changed.
> HE: If I have, it is in loving you more than I did.
> SHE: Because Max loved me?
> HE: That may be.
> SHE: Because I loved Max.
> HE: That may be, too.   (*HP* 216)

Whatever the answer to these questions, it is clear that the marriage depends on the mimesis of a prior love.

In the literary works discussed by Girard, most erotic triangles involve two males bonded in rivalry over a female. But *The House in Paris* overturns this classic triangle, for the bond between the rival females is considerably more compelling than the bond between the males. While Karen functions as a conduit between Max and Ray, Max also functions as a conduit between the women. At one point or another all three witches get a piece of him: Naomi through her engagement, Karen through her affair, and the ogress upstairs through her demonic possession of his soul. By dividing Max between them, like Pentheus between the Bacchae, the female rivals bond together over his shared body. The most important of these female bonds, although also the most understated, is the mimetic rivalry uniting Karen to Madame Fisher. Although they never meet in the same room, theirs is the strongest undercurrent of desire in the novel, theirs the transport to which everyone is sacrificed. Naomi is jilted, Ray betrayed, Leopold abandoned, and Max driven to suicide in order to sustain the bond of opposition between Karen and Madame Fisher – 'that opposition that is love.'

To say that Karen is 'in love' with Madame Fisher, however, would be to mistake a literary character for a real person, and to psychologise the abstract geometry of love that draws these characters into complicity. In Bowen, love is a matter of position rather than psychology; as E. M. Forster proposes, 'there is at times a magic in identity of position . . .'[43] Placed in an identical position to their rivals, lovers are poisoned by identical desires. If desire is mimetic, this implies that lovers are condemned to plagiarise the love of others, substituting themselves for their envied doubles. In this novel Bowen demystifies the 'transports' of the bodice-ripper by taking 'transport' in its locomotive sense – for desire travels in a circuit round this cast of characters, picking up another substitute at every stop. This substitutive movement of desire also orchestrates the action of Bowen's subsequent novel, *The Death of the Heart.*

Notes

1. See Charles H. Gibbs-Smith, *Aviation: An Historical Survey from its Origins to the End of World War II*, p. 186.
2. Quoted in Glendinning, *Elizabeth Bowen*, p. 86.
3. *H* 48, 121; *LG* 150.
4. Henry James, Preface to *Roderick Hudson* (1875; 1908) in *Roderick Hudson*, intro. Tony Tanner (Oxford: Oxford University Press, 1980), p. xli.
5. Walter Benjamin, *The Arcades Project*, p. 152.
6. Elizabeth Bowen, letter to A. E. Coppard, 15 October [1932], HRHRC.
7. Ibid.
8. Cited in Heath, *Elizabeth Bowen*, p. 58.
9. Ford Madox Ford, *The Soul of London: A Survey of a Modern City* (1905), ed. Alan G. Hill (London: Everyman, 1995), p. 15.
10. Gertrude Stein uses the phrase 'daily island life' throughout her essay, 'What is English Literature?' (1935), in *Look at Me Now and Here I Am: Writings and Lectures 1909–45*, ed. Patricia Meyerowitz (Harmondsworth: Penguin, 1984), pp. 31–58.

11. *N* 171, 15, 170, 129, 130.

12. See A. J. Burkart and S. Medlick, *Tourism Past, Present and Future*, pp. 4, 25–33, 167.

13. Lewis Carroll, *Alice in Wonderland*, ed. Roger Lancelyn Green (Oxford: Oxford University Press, 1991), p. 26; quoted in Petra-Utta Rau, *Moving Dangerously*, p. 92.

14. Mary Ellmann, *Thinking about Women*, p. 6.

15. Gustave Flaubert, *Madame Bovary*, trans. Paul de Man (New York: Norton, 1965), pp. 38, 177, 237.

16. Heath, *Elizabeth Bowen*, pp. 60–2.

17. Virginia Woolf, *A Room of One's Own*, in *A Room of One's Own and Three Guineas*, ed. Morag Shiach (Oxford: Oxford University Press, 1992), p. 45.

18. N 117; Compare *HD* 94.

19. Georg Simmel, 'The Metropolis and Mental Life,' in *The Sociology of Georg Simmel*, trans. Kurt H. Wolff (Glencoe, IL: The Free Press, 1950), pp. 413–14.

20. George M. Beard, *American Nervousness* (1881), cited in Daniel J. Czitrom, *Media and the American Mind: From Morse to McLuhan*, p. 19.

21. Bernhard Siegert, *Relays: Literature as an Epoch of the Postal System*, p. 166; Czitrom, *Media and the American Mind*, p. 21.

22. Quoted in Wolfgang Schivelbusch, *The Railway Journey: The Industrialization of Time and Space in the Nineteenth Century*, p. 143.

23. O'Faolain, *The Vanishing Hero*, pp. 180, 173.

24. 'How I write: a discussion between Elizabeth Bowen and Glyn Jones,' 10 May 1950, HRHRC.

25. *H* 97: it should be noted that the word 'effects' is used in its original context to mean 'possessions.'

26. *H* 39–44, 59. See Bennett and Royle's discussion of this episode in *Elizabeth Bowen and the Dissolution of the Novel*, pp. 47–8.

27. Homer, *The Odyssey*, trans. Richard Lattimore (New York: Harper, 1967), bk 19, lines 376–490.

28. Shakespeare, *The Merchant of Venice*, III: ii.104–6, as quoted in Freud, 'The Theme of the Three Caskets,' SE, vol. 12, p. 394. In another reading of the Shakespeare passage, 'paleness' is interpreted as 'plainness.'

29. SE, vol. 12, pp. 295, 294, 301.

30. Michaelis's French translator claimed in 1912 that *The Dangerous Age* was 'the most widely read novel of the present moment' throughout central Europe: *The Dangerous Age: Letters and Fragments from a Woman's Diary*, trans. Marcel Prévost (London: John Lane, The Bodley Head, 1912); introduction by Marcel Prévost, p. 8. Michaelis's novel uses letters and diaries to tell a story of feminine revolt, in which the middle-aged heroine, Elsie Lindtner, flouts convention to leave her loveless marriage and adopt a street arab.

31. 'Présent partout mais visible nulle part': Gustave Flaubert, letter to Mlle Leroyer de Chantepie (1857), trans. Frances Steegmuller, in Richard Ellmann and Charles Feidelson (eds), *The Modern Tradition* (New York: Oxford University Press, 1965), p. 132.

32. Graham Greene, *The End of the Affair* (Harmondsworth: Penguin, 1975), p. 169.

33. Maurice Bowra, letter to Elizabeth Bowen, 7 September [no year], Elizabeth Bowen collection, HRHRC.

34. Bennett and Royle also make this comparison in somewhat different ways in *Elizabeth Bowen and the Dissolution of the Novel*, ch. 3, especially p. 45.

35. Freud, 'Mourning and Melancholia' (1917), SE, vol. 14, p. 249 and pp. 243–58.

36. See Nicolas Abraham and Maria Torok, *The Wolf Man's Magic Word*, and *The Shell and the Kernel*.

37. Derrida, '*Fors*: The Anglish Words of Nicolas Abraham and Maria Torok,' p. xvii.

38. Abraham and Torok, *The Shell and the Kernel*, pp. 171, 173.

39. Shakespeare, *Hamlet*, IV: v. In Oscar Wilde's *The Picture of Dorian Gray* (1891; Harmondsworth: Penguin, 2000) p. 98, Sir Henry Wotton gives a dandyish twist to Ophelia's language of flowers when he says: 'I once wore nothing but violets all through one season, as a form of artistic mourning for a romance that would not die.'

40. Freud, *Moses and Monotheism* (1939), SE, vol. 23, p. 43.

41. A. S. Byatt, Introduction to Bowen, *The House in Paris*, p. 15.

42. See René Girard, *Deceit, Desire and the Novel*; Mikkel Borch-Jacobsen, *The Freudian Subject*, p.26.

43. E. M. Forster, *A Room with a View*, p. 65. See also Nicholas Royle's illuminating discussion of this passage in *E. M. Forster*, p. 42.

5

Furniture: The Death of the Heart, The Heat of the Day, *and* Wartime Stories

The Death of the Heart opens on a winter's day in Regent's Park, when the early morning ice has just begun to break. This ice seems to penetrate the very sentence structure, stiffening the prose into unnatural contortions: 'swans in slow indignation swam.'[1] Nothing human, apart from the sound of footsteps, emerges from the cold until the second paragraph, when a man and woman, leaning on a footbridge, glimmer into view. Yet these figures breathe no warmth into the glacial landscape. Icebound as the lake that they survey, 'their oblivious stillness' makes them 'look like lovers', although this is an illusion soon dispelled. Beneath their feet, their reflections are 'constantly broken up' among the crashing ice floes.

It is the man, St Quentin Miller, who utters the first words: 'You were mad ever to touch the thing.' What is 'the thing'? The with-holding of its name makes the thing loom vast and menacing, as if a sacred object had been violated. 'I wasn't looking for it,' replies the woman, now identified as Anna Quayne. 'I should far rather not know that the thing existed, and till then, you see, I'd had no idea that it did.' This mysterious thing turns out to be a diary that Anna discovered in a secret raid on Portia's room. At this point we do not know who Portia is, only that she makes a mess and *is* a mess, as far as Anna is concerned. Underneath a pile of junk mail, which Anna heaved off Portia's bulging escritoire, the diary fell open at Anna's name. Having scoured it from cover to cover, Anna tried to stash it underneath the avalanche of paper as before, despite being aware that the same muddle cannot be made twice (*DH* 7–10).

Thus the novel opens with a scene of ice, immediately followed by a scene of reading. The juxtaposition hints that reading the diary is Anna's first step towards 'breaking the ice' with Portia, the violent preamble to relationship. But St Quentin, a novelist himself, takes more interest in the style than the content of the diary. 'Style is the thing that's always a bit phony,' he considers,

> and at the same time you cannot write without style. Look how much goes to addressing an envelope – for, after all, it's a matter of set-out. And a diary, after all, is written to please oneself – therefore it's bound to be enormously written up. The obligation to write it is all in one's own eye, and look how one is when it's almost always written – upstairs, late, overwrought, alone . . .

When Anna quotes the first sentence of Portia's diary – '*So I am with them, in London*' – St Quentin particularly relishes the comma after 'them.' 'That's style,' he declares (*DH* 11).[2] He is right: Portia's sentence does show style, however understated – and understatement is itself a style. To take the comma out would weaken the contrast between 'I' and 'them,' diluting the effect of alienation. These faltering monosyllables capture the anguish of a childish waif, transplanted to London and marooned with strangers, a lonely 'I' amidst an unknown 'them.' Yet it is Portia's apparent innocence of style that makes her testimony so disturbing; as Anna says, 'Everything she does to me is unconscious . . .' (*DH* 246). Her diary passes no explicit judgements on Anna and her husband, Thomas Quayne, but constitutes a dossier of their derelictions, recorded with the flattest literalism. 'I don't invent,' Portia protests (*DH* 250).

> When I woke my window was like a brown stone, and I could hardly see the rest of the room. The whole house was just like that, it was not like night but like air being ill . . . Thomas has his breakfast after I have mine, but today he came and said, this must be your first fog . . . Tonight Anna and Thomas stayed at home for dinner. She said that whenever there was a fog she always felt it was something she had done, but she did not seem to mean this seriously. Thomas said he supposed most people felt the same and Anna said she was certain they did not. Then we sat in the drawing-room, and they wished I was not there.
> Tomorrow is Saturday, but nothing will happen.

> (*DH* 114–15)

Every sentence could be read as an indictment, although the diarist presents herself as an impersonal reporter of the facts. Yet there is style, even guile, lurking in this faux-naivety: 'they wished I was not there,' for instance, is an imputation masquerading as a neutral observation.

The Death of the Heart is the story of the Quaynes' ethical awakening: their realisation of responsibility to Portia, to the past, and to the dead. This means that they must come to terms with their ancestral furniture: as Matchett, their Delphic housekeeper, declares, 'Furniture like we've got is too much for some that would rather not have the past' (*DH* 81). But *The Death of the Heart* is also the story of Portia's awakening to the necessity of style – the furniture of prose. H. G. Wells, after reading *To the North*, expressed his admiration with a single reservation: 'In your next book you may have pelmets in one room but you must not notice them in more than one room.'[3] Bowen may have taken his advice about the pelmets in *The Death of the Heart*, but she still makes a 'damn'd fuss about furniture.'

Thomas and Anna Quayne are a well-to-do, stylish couple in their mid-thirties who live at 2 Windsor Terrace, an imposing house on the Outer Circle of Regent's Park, modelled on Bowen's own establishment at 2 Clarence Terrace. 'Queasy and cold,' this house immures the couple from the outside world; callers are 'unheard of,' friends are rarely admitted, and the rooms are connected by internal telephone to deflect unauthorised intrusions. Wife and husband are generally found in separate quarters, Anna entertaining the odd guest in the chilly drawing-room, Thomas retreating to his smoke-filled study. Although isolated from each other, both spouses are unconsciously in league with each other in their determination to sweep away the shadows of the past. In this house, 'all mirrors and polish, there was no place where shadows lodged, no point where feeling could thicken.' Anna is trying to forget her passion for Robert Pidgeon, whose betrayal persuaded her to settle for her present husband; Thomas is trying to forget the family shame that led to Portia's birth. 'Something edited life in the Quaynes' house,' the narrator comments, 'but no one seemed clear quite *what* was being discarded, or whether anything vital was being let slip away. If Matchett were feared, if she seemed to threaten the house, it was because she seemed most likely to put her thumb on the thing' (*DH* 170, 87, 42, 171). Here the portentous term 'the thing' harks back to the first words spoken in the novel, where 'the thing' in question is Portia's diary – 'You were mad ever to touch the thing.' The verbal repetition hints that whatever has been edited from life at Windsor Terrace has come to roost in Portia's diary.

To explain how Portia ended up at Windsor Terrace, Bowen could have used a flashback, as she did in *The House in Paris*. Instead she passes the burden of narration on to Anna, who tells a sardonic version of the story to St Quentin in the freezing park. In this way Anna strives to author Portia in order to retaliate against the diary, in which Portia tries to author Anna. The novel tells the story of their war of style, in which each tries to take possession of the other's narrative.[4] Anna regards Portia as the 'child of an aberration, the child of a panic, the child of an old chap's pitiful sexuality. Conceived amid lost hairpins and snapshots of doggies in a Notting Hill Gate flatlet' (*DH* 246). It seems that Thomas's retired father, although married to an 'implacably nice' woman and apparently content with installing water features in the garden, sank into an adulterous affair with a 'scrap of a widow' called Irene. This pathetic creature had 'a prostrated way of looking up at you, and that fluffy, bird's-nesty hair that hairpins get lost in,' while her 'defective tear-ducts . . . gave her eyes always rather a swimmy look.' The old man 'got knit up with Irene in a sort of a dream wood,' a spell broken only when Irene 'started Portia' (*DH* 16–19). At this point Mr Quayne was forced to confess his infidelity to Mrs Quayne who, determined to do 'right' rather than 'good,' packed up her husband's things and sent him back to Irene on the afternoon train (*DH* 78). Stricken with shame, old Quayne fled to the South of France, where Portia was born. Henceforth the family remained in exile, staying in the back rooms of hotels, or in dark flats in villas with no view, where the old man never got used to the evening chill. Thomas realised that his father 'would die of this, and he did,' effectively murdered by his wife's self-sacrifice (*DH* 21). 'Sacrificers,' Matchett apocalyptically proclaims, 'are not the ones to pity. The ones to pity are those that they sacrifice. Oh, the sacrificers, they get it both ways. A person knows themselves what they're able to do without' (*DH* 74).

Portia was bequeathed to Thomas on his father's deathbed – 'Dying put poor Mr Quayne in a strong position for the first time in his life,' Anna comments wryly (*DH* 13). The old man's last request, dictated to Irene, was that Thomas and his wife should give his misbegotten child a taste of '*normal, cheerful* family life' (*DH* 15). Irene, however, hid this begging letter in her glove-box until she died, when it was discovered by her sister and posted to the Quaynes at Windsor Terrace. In the meantime Irene brought up her child on her own, drifting between out-of-season cheap hotels, where mother and daughter enjoyed the sisterly intimacy that Bowen shared with her own mother during her vagrant childhood in Kent. After Irene's death, Portia was sent to Windsor Terrace, the Quaynes having little choice but to provide the orphan at least with a temporary home. Anna fixes up a pretty room, but Portia makes a mess of it, stuffing every crevice with discarded circulars.[5] 'She gets almost no letters,' Anna complains to St Quentin, 'but she'd been keeping all sorts of things Thomas and I throw away – begging letters, for instance, or quack talks about health' (*DH* 9). In this room full of other people's cast-off letters, Portia writes her diary and engages in long bedtime conversations with Matchett, the only member of the household willing to take notice of the homeless child. Alone together, they talk about the past. 'Talk like that is one climax the whole time,' Anna fulminates. 'It's a trance; it's a vice; it's a sort of complete world' (*DH* 311).

This world breaks apart, however, when Portia falls in love with Eddie, Anna's would-be gigolo. A 'frank *arriviste*' with a chip on his shoulder, Eddie has risen from humble origins to win a place at Oxford, only to be sent down for 'one idiotic act.' Now twenty-three years old and endowed with 'proletarian, animal, quick grace,' he flirts his way into middle-class society. 'Everyone seemed to get a kick out of their relations with Eddie; he was like a bright little cracker that, pulled hard enough, goes off with a loud bang.' Eddie resembles Markie in *To the North*, in that both are monsters of self-pity. But Markie smoulders, whereas Eddie effervesces: his 'cosmic black moods' overflow into hysteria (*DH* 61–2). Addressing everyone as 'Darling,' giggling, pulling faces, sobbing at the least excuse, and impersonating lady-friends who come to tea, Eddie is camp rather than demonic. Protean, he changes shape whenever anyone – especially a woman – tries to pin him down. If Eddie is gay he does not know it; he loves nobody of either sex; his strongest emotion is paranoia, which intensifies into fantasies of penetration. 'In the state he was in, his enemies seemed to have supernatural powers: they could filter through keyholes, stream through hard wood doors' (*DH* 277). Like Milton's Satan, Eddie suffers from a 'sense of injured merit'; convinced he is a victim, he is free to be a cad. Anna says, 'He doesn't have to go far with anybody to fail them: he can let anyone down at any stage' (*DH* 242).

Some months before the beginning of the novel, Eddie's flirtation with Anna ended abruptly when he tried to kiss her – for Anna wanted flattery, not sex. Reluctant to shake him off completely, Anna assumed responsibility for finding him a job – or an '*oubliette*,' as Eddie resentfully describes it – in her husband's advertising firm, Quayne and Merrett (*DH* 61). Anna also offers Eddie a kind of *oubliette* in Portia, at least by turning a blind eye to their relationship. But Portia's love for Eddie escalates into an obsession, on the scale of Emmeline's in *To the North*. She even lets him read her cherished diary. When the Quaynes go off on holiday without her, sending her to Seale-on-Sea in Kent, separation intensifies her passion. In the middle section of the novel, entitled 'The Flesh,' Portia goes to stay with Mrs Heccomb, Anna's former governess, now widowed and living in a seaside villa with the gloriously vulgar name Waikiki. 'Glad to have achieved marriage, not sorry it was over,' the widow shares Waikiki with her grown-up stepchildren, Dickie and Daphne. She blames their brash manners on their mother, who was not, in Mrs Heccomb's view, 'quite-quite' (*DH* 127–8). But Portia finds the rude vigour of this household preferable to the half-frozen world of Windsor Terrace. With its ominous housekeeper, haunting furniture, and festering secrets, Windsor Terrace belongs to the aristocratic world of Gothic fiction, and poses a sharp contrast to the petit bourgeois gusto of Waikiki. At the seaside life is noisy, boisterous, 'unedited':

> The tremble felt through the house when a door banged or someone came hurriedly downstairs, the noises made by the plumbing, Mrs Heccomb's prodigality with half-crowns and shillings, the many sensory hints that Doris [the servant] was human and did not function in a void of her own – all these made Waikiki the fount of spontaneous living. Life here seemed to be at its highest voltage, and Portia stood to marvel at Daphne and Dickie as she might have marvelled at dynamos. At nights, she thought of all the force contained in those single beds in the other rooms.
>
> (*DH* 171)

Portia invites Eddie to visit her at Waikiki, eager to show off her boyfriend to her new-found friends. 'The wish to lead out one's lover must be a tribal feeling; the wish to be seen as loved is part of one's self-respect' (*DH* 178). But Eddie, keeping the besotted girl on tenterhooks, refuses to give her a straight answer, and up to the last minute Portia does not know if he is going to stand her up. In the event he does arrive, but flirts with Daphne. When the young people go off in a gang to see a movie, Eddie humiliates Portia by holding Daphne's hand, for everyone to see, in the chiaroscuro of the cinema:

> Portia sat with eyes fixed on the screen – once or twice, as Eddie changed his position, she felt his knee touch hers. When this made her glance his way, she saw light from the comic [on the screen] flickering on his eyeballs . . . She felt some tense extra presence, here in their row of six.

Wanting to know, she turned to look full at Eddie – who at once countered her look with a bold blank smile glittering from the screen. The smile was diverted to her from someone else . . . The jumping light from Dickie's lighter showed the canyon beyond their row of knees. It caught the chromium clasp of Daphne's handbag, and Wallace's wrist-watch at the end of the row. It rounded the taut blond silk of Daphne's calf and glittered on some tinfoil dropped on the floor . . . The light, with malicious accuracy, ran round a rim of cuff, a steel bangle, and made a thumb-nail flash. Not deep enough in the cleft between their *fauteuils* Eddie and Daphne were, with emphasis, holding hands. Eddie's fingers kept up a kneading movement: her thumb alertly twitched at the joint.

(*DH* 194–5)

The chapter comes to an abrupt halt at this point, suspending Portia's reaction for several pages. Cinematically scripted, the scene of the crime is both hilarious and devastating. Who holds whose hand in the cinema? As Glendinning points out, this is the stuff that fills the pages of teenage magazines, but Bowen 'invests it with the incomprehensible world-shattering outrage which for the person concerned such things have.'[6]

In the passage quoted above, the play of lights and glances enacts the process of displacement that pervades this text, whereby desire ricochets from object to substitutive object. First Portia, looking at Eddie, finds him looking at the actor in the film, his eyeballs twinkling with reflected light. Described by Matchett as 'a little actor,' Eddie seems as insubstantial as the flickering screen, a shadow broken into pieces by the wanton light: here a hand, there an eyeball, there a smile floating like the Cheshire cat's (*DH* 121). With the intentness of a lover, the narrator traces the reflections cast by Dickie's lighter round the curve of Daphne's calf, the rim of a cuff, the circle of a bangle, down to where it dips into 'the cleft' between the seats, exposing Eddie's fingers kneading Daphne's hand, her thumb twitching in response. Yet there is something even more promiscuous about the movement of this light, which also lingers on a piece of tinfoil, flashes on a random wristwatch, and opens up the 'canyon' underneath the row of knees before it homes in on the two hands squirming *in flagrante*. These stray gleams, glancing off a handbag, a silk stocking, or a flashing thumb nail, suggest that the flight path of desire is even more haphazard than Portia fears. We have seen how love affairs in Bowen are haunted by a shadowy third: in the cinema scene, however, the 'extra presence' features as the seventh agent in this row of six, a seventh which is not a shadow but a 'malicious,' prying light that dismembers human beings into part-objects. (This is the single case of septangular desire in Bowen's fiction – even Lacan did not boast that he could teach his students how to count to seven.) While Eddie gropes Daphne, the light gropes him: its faithlessness exceeds his own, and seems to map out his betrayal in advance, guiding his hand, as it guides Portia's eyes, into the dark declivity between the seats.

The third part of the novel, called 'The Devil,' takes us back to Windsor Terrace, returning to the classic manner after the postmodern premonitions of Waikiki. On the street Portia runs into St Quentin, who thoughtlessly asks after her diary. Portia jumps to the correct conclusion that Anna must have read the diary, but also to the wrong conclusion that Eddie has betrayed her secret. In a final showdown, she confronts Eddie in his flat, where the 'hideous rented furniture' bears witness to 'the underlying morality of his class' (*DH* 278). (With her peculiar Anglo-Irish brand of snobbery, Bowen looked down on the morality, rather than the immorality, of the lower orders: she 'disapproved only of disapproval.')[7] Accusing Portia of giving him 'the horrors,' Eddie kicks her out, reluctant even to lend her five shillings for a taxi. Instead of returning to her guardians, however, Portia foists herself on Major Brutt, a pathetic relic of World War I, who has taken to calling at Windsor Terrace, much to the irritation of the stand-offish Quaynes. Portia begs to stay with Major Brutt in his attic-room in the Karachi Hotel, even offering to marry him, but he insists on ringing her relations. The Quaynes, meanwhile, have only just noticed Portia's absence, Matchett having forced it stonily on their attention. After much persuasion Portia allows Major Brutt to make the telephone call, but only on condition that he tell her guardians that she is waiting to see what they will do. The Quaynes come to the conclusion that 'the right thing' is to send Matchett to fetch Portia, and the novel ends with the marmoreal housekeeper opening the giant door of the hotel (*DH* 304).

'But why was she called Portia?' St Quentin asks when Anna finishes her narrative. 'I don't think we ever asked,' Anna replies (*DH* 21). The novel provides no answer to this question either, and Perdita, rather than Portia, seems the obvious name for this lost child. It has been suggested that Bowen's Portia resembles Shakespeare's in that she becomes the agent of justice for the Quaynes.[8] Yet unlike the sophisticated Portia of *The Merchant of Venice*, with her eloquent campaign for mercy, Portia Quayne's innocence is merciless in the extreme. 'Innocence so constantly finds itself in a false position that inwardly innocent people learn to be disingenuous,' Bowen writes.

> They are bound to blunder, then to be told they cheat. In love, the sweetness and violence they have to offer involves a thousand betrayals for the less innocent. Incurable strangers to the world, they never cease to exact a heroic happiness. Their singleness, their ruthlessness, their one continuous wish makes them bound to be cruel, and to suffer cruelty. The innocent are so few that two of them seldom meet – when they do meet, their victims lie strewn all round.

(*DH* 106)

Ostensibly the victimisers, Eddie and Anna are also victims of Portia's inexorable innocence. Characteristically Bowen undercuts moral expectations, making Anna Quayne chic, vain, bored, lazy, cynical, unscrupulous, and 'utterly disabused,' yet also one of the most likeable of all her heroines, with a 'nice fat malign smile.' As Thomas tells her, 'If you were half as heartless as you make out, you would be an appallingly boring woman' (*DH* 310, 241, 242). On the other hand, Eddie has some reason to blurt out that Portia gives him the horrors. For Portia is unsocialised, a noble savage cast adrift in the *beau monde*, who causes as much damage as she suffers. She is constantly depicted as an animal: 'a little crow,' 'a kitten that expects to be drowned,' and even 'a little monster' (*DH* 41, 40, 12). To Major Brutt she looks like 'a wild creature, just old enough to know it must dread humans . . . a bird astray in a room, a bird already stunned by dashing itself against mirrors and panes' (*DH* 287). In Bowen's view, it is Portia's duty to lose her innocence in order to renounce the wilderness, and to come to terms with 'the world, the flesh, and the devil' – the titles of the three parts of *The Death of the Heart.*

It is Anna who calls Portia 'an animal' in the opening scene, when she is telling St Quentin the story of the mess from which the child was engendered (*DH* 8). One reason why Anna is so outraged by Portia's diary is that it proves the animal can speak; the kitten refuses to be drowned in other people's narratives. As Chessman has observed, Portia's story is told three times in *The Death of the Heart*, first by Anna, then by Matchett, but also by Portia's own memories of life with her mother, briefly glimpsed in chapter 2.[9] Anna's discovery of Portia's diary provokes a contest between the older and the younger woman as to who shall be the subject, who the object, of narration. This contest anticipates the battle in *Eva Trout* between Iseult Smith and the eponymous heroine, whose name evokes the primal (Eve) and the inhuman (Trout). This curious name suggests that Eva, like Portia, is also a monster or an animal, an outsider to language who has strayed into the social order from the wilderness before or beyond verbalisation. Iseult introduces Eva into language but abandons her before the work is done, much as Frankenstein abandoned his wordless monster; Eva retaliates by working Iseult into fictions that defy the distinction between life and art. In a similar struggle, Anna tries to script Portia into one version of events, while knowing that Portia is writing Anna into another. 'Her diary's very good,' Anna says, 'you see, she has got us taped. Could I not go on with a book all about ourselves?' (*DH* 304).

But why was she called Portia? Is it because Portia is the 'portion' meted out to the descendants of old Quayne, the fallen father?[10] 'Portion' is defined by the *Oxford English Dictionary* as 'that which is allotted to a person by providence; lot, destiny, fate.' Portia is a portion in the further sense that she is part of a dissected whole, a floating fragment of the past washed up into the present. And Portia is above all portable: she is that which is passed on, from hotel to hotel, from deathbed to deathbed, much as her diary is passed on from reader to reader. Like the junk mail cluttering her escritoire, she is a begging letter, an unsolicited circular that the Quaynes would prefer to disregard. 'Who are we to have her questions brought here?' Anna demands (*DH* 246). Portia resembles Freud's Dora, whose name means 'gift,' in that she functions as an object of exchange within the narrative, creating and dissolving bonds between the other characters.[11] Anna sacrifices Portia to Eddie, thus letting herself off the hook while sustaining her relationship with him vicariously; Eddie, on the other hand, uses Portia as a substitute for Anna but also as the vehicle of his revenge against the woman who has passed him on. The chain of substitutions does not stop here, however, but reaches back into the past. Anna also uses Eddie as a surrogate for her faithless lover, Robert Pidgeon, a veteran of World War I.[12] By letting Eddie loose on Portia, Anna re-enacts by proxy her own betrayal at the hands of Pidgeon.

Another surrogate for Pidgeon is Major Brutt, once Pidgeon's comrade-in-arms, who runs into the Quayne family at a Marx Brothers movie that nobody finds funny.[13] Major Brutt is 'the sort of thoroughly decent fellow who never, for some reason, gets on in the world' (*DH* 257). Eight years previously, when Anna and Pidgeon were lovers, Brutt spent an evening in their company and has idolised the memory ever since: 'There is no fidelity like the fidelity of the vicarious lover who has once seen a kiss' (*DH* 91). A 'born third,' redundant to the lovers, redundant to the novel, redundant to peacetime Britain, Brutt is a leftover, a 'ghost with no beat,' a loose end *at* a loose end (*DH* 45). His brand of manhood is defunct: 'Makes of men date, like makes of cars; Major Brutt was a 1914–18 model: there was now no market for that make. In fact, only his steadfast persistence in living made it a pity that he could not be scrapped . . .' (*DH* 90). Once the manager of a rubber plantation in Malay, now lodged at the Karachi Hotel, Brutt is associated with imperialism as well as with World War I. No wonder his contemporaries in the 1930s would prefer to forget that he exists. 'And why Brutt? Where does he come in?' Thomas Quayne demands (*DH* 304). One of Bowen's funniest but also most pathetic characters, Major Eric E. J. Brutt resembles the famous loose end in Joyce's *Ulysses*, the unidentified 'man in the mackintosh,' who drops into the plot repeatedly without excuse or explanation. These visitations seem to represent the element of chance that subverts the teleology of realist narrative. Similarly, Major Brutt takes to dropping in at Windsor Terrace, disrupting the Quaynes' plotted lives, and functioning for them as a needling reminder of a chance encounter; for us, of the indelibility of chance in narrative.

Major Brutt is another unwelcome 'portion' of the past that the Quaynes would prefer to cast aside. Anna describes him as 'the appendix to the finished story of Robert . . . legated to her by Robert' (*DH* 261). Portia, also the appendix to a finished story, legated by old Quayne to his reluctant heirs, recognises her affinity to Major Brutt: 'You and I are the same,' she tells him (*DH* 288). Major Brutt resists this identification, but shows unconscious understanding of her plight by giving Portia jigsaw puzzles. Her attempts to piece together these fragmented pictures mirror her efforts to puzzle out her past, to answer that tormenting question posed by Leopold in *The House in Paris*: 'Why am I? What made me be?' (*HP* 67). Portia never finishes the second puzzle; her infatuation with Eddie intervenes; and 'the unfinished puzzle' lingers on like 'a thing left from another age' (*DH* 190). Portia and Major Brutt themselves are unfinished puzzles left over from another age – puzzled, puzzling reminders of an expurgated past.

Yet ironically it is Portia, the only Quayne to form a bond with Major Brutt, who delivers the most devastating blow to the 'old boy' who 'took it on the Somme' (*DH* 260, 47). At the end of the novel, doubly betrayed by Anna and Eddie, Portia seeks refuge with Major

Brutt. But this is the last thing the 'old buffer' wants – he fears this messy girl will mess up his relations with her guardians (*DH* 89).

> 'When you come here and tell me you're running off, you put me in a pretty awful position with your people, who are my very good friends. When a man's a bit on his own, like I've been lately, and is marking time, and feels a bit out of touch, a place like their place, where one can drop in any time and always get a warm welcome, means quite a lot, you know. Seeing you there, so part of it all and happy, has been half the best of it. But I think the world of them, too. You wouldn't mess that up for me, Portia, would you?'
>
> (*DH* 288)

'There's nothing to mess,' is Portia's blood-curdling reply. 'You are the other person that Anna laughs at . . . Anna's always laughing at you. She says you are quite pathetic . . . And Thomas always thinks you must be after something. Whatever you do, even send me a puzzle, he thinks that more, and she laughs more. They groan at each other when you have gone away. You and I are the same' (*DH* 288). This must be one of the most mortifying moments in English fiction, rivalling Emma Woodhouse's humiliation of Miss Bates, or the most excruciating scenes in Patrick Hamilton. The voice-over observes: 'Illusions are art, for the feeling person, and it is by art that we live, if we do' (*DH* 91). Portia's cruelty, unwitting though it is, strips Major Brutt of his illusions, shattering the art of his existence, and leaving him a 'discard' with 'no context, no function, no outlet' (*DH* 90).

But the narrator does not allow us to discard him; instead she forces us to recognise ourselves in Major Brutt's position as the looker-on. It is not just he, but we, who leech our thrills from other people's lives. Bowen's magisterial first-person plural implicates us in Major Brutt's voyeurism, and even grants a kind of gallantry to his fixation: 'Not for nothing do we invest so much of ourselves in other people's lives – or even in momentary pictures of people we do not know . . . It is the emotion to which we remain faithful, after all: we are taught to recover it in some other place' (*DH* 91). Recovering emotion in another place could be described as the prime motor of *The Death of the Heart*. As 'vicarious lover,' Major Brutt exemplifies the common predicament of Bowen's characters, each of whom is reliving experience by proxy; for 'experience means nothing till it repeats itself,' as Anna says – twice (*DH* 245, 11). Desire is vicarious or substitutional in essence: Eddie is Anna's substitute for Pidgeon, Portia is Eddie's substitute for Anna, while the Quaynes are Major Brutt's substitute for the idealised dyad of Pidgeon and Anna. In this vortex of emotional displacement, everyone seems out of place, obliged to play the part of someone else. Portia's brother is a surrogate father, Portia a surrogate daughter, taking the place of the two children that Anna miscarried before the book begins. Major Brutt is a surrogate for Pidgeon, a wandering appendix legated to Anna by her faithless lover. And Portia's diary – perhaps the ultimate protagonist – strikes Anna as a 'distorted and distorting' substitute for life, which threatens to devour every other version of the truth (*DH* 10).

Freud argues that the finding of an object of desire is always a 'refinding' of an object previously lost.[14] *The Death of the Heart* exemplifies this logic, for the object of desire is always a replacement for a lost ideal, an 'appendix' to a vanished imaginary plenitude. In this world of proxies, where every emotion is 'recovered in another place,' and 'experience means nothing till it repeats itself,' even the desiring subject is a plagiary. This is the mortifying lesson Portia learns from Eddie: that lovers can never be original. 'But after all, Eddie,' she protests, 'anything that happens has never happened before. What I mean is, you and I are the first people who have ever been us.' 'That's what's the devil,' Eddie cries. 'You don't know what to expect' (*DH* 281). Knowing what to expect demands experience, and 'experience means nothing till it repeats itself.' 'In fact, till it does that, it hardly *is* experience,' Anna insists (*DH* 11). What Portia has to learn is that love is not unique but necessarily vicarious, legated, secondhand; that neither lover nor beloved is primogenital; that a feeling can 'spring straight from the heart, be imperative, without being original.' Here the narrator inserts a humbling parenthesis:

> (But if love were original, if it were the unique device of two unique spirits, its importance would not be granted; it could not make a great common law felt. The strongest compulsions we feel throughout life are no more than compulsions to repeat a pattern: the pattern is not of our own device.)

> (*DH* 169)

To fall in love is to succumb to this compulsion to repeat. Portia learns the hard way (which is the only way) that every spontaneous endearment or caress belongs to a script passed down by countless generations. This is the death of the heart, but it is also Portia's debut into history, her recognition of the power of the past. To fail to love is to deny the past, and to deny the ghosts of bygone lovers clamouring for encores of their tragedies. It is to live as if one had inherited no furniture.

We have seen how characters constantly change places in this novel, standing in for one another and ghosting for the dead or disappeared. These displacements could be understood as repetitions of the primal displacement of old Quayne. For the father's folly left a house without a head, and scrambled the relations of the family, making the brother (Thomas) father to the sister (Portia), the daughter (Portia) sister to the wife (Irene). In this sense Quayne resembles Sophocles's Oedipus, who blames his unintended crime of incest for 'a monstrous commingling of fathers, brothers, sons; of brides, wives, and mothers!'[15] Being brother to his offspring, son to his wife, lover to his mother, father to his siblings, Oedipus has sinned against the name. Similarly, old Quayne's primeval crime (for such is the stigma accorded to his peccadillo) has resulted in a 'monstrous commingling' of kinship terms, leaving Portia an insoluble puzzle over names. 'I mean, if Thomas's mother was – what would I call her? There wouldn't be any name,' she laments (*DH* 74). This nominal confusion, compounded with the shame attached to Quayne's crepuscular affair – shame that far exceeds its cause – suggests that his transgression goes beyond adultery. A whiff of incest hovers over his debacle. This is not to say that Quayne literally committed incest, but that he sinned in being sexual at all, unthinkable behaviour in a father from a child's unconscious point of view. Besides, in the 'atmosphere of ancient fable' that pervades this novel, a-bit-on-the-side is enough to summon up the Furies.[16] Claude Lévi-Strauss describes incest as bad grammar in the language of kinship, and it is telling that the two characters primarily associated with bad grammar in Bowen's work – Portia Quayne and Eva Trout – both have dead fathers shamed for sexual delinquency.[17] Ostracised, addicted to self-punishment, Portia's father turns into a parody of Oedipus: Anna imagines all those dawns in Notting Hill Gate, 'with Irene leaking tears and looking for hairpins, and Mr Quayne sitting up denouncing himself' (*DH* 18).

The only figure to remain outside the circuit of displacement is Matchett, as if her 'stony apron' weighed her down against the winds of mutability. Only she remains in her predestined place – beside the furniture (*DH* 312).[18] We are told that she was moved to Windsor Terrace 'with the furniture that had always been her charge' (*DH* 23). 'When they made a place for it,' she explains, 'they made a place for me' (*DH* 82). The sentence structure here suggests the interchangeability of it and me, of it-ness and me-ness, in a world where things and people, like the living and the dead, are constantly encroaching on each other's territory. Matchett herself is presented as a household fixture: a 'living arch,' a 'wall,' a 'caryatid,' her creased and padded body seems upholstered rather than enfleshed, her 'vein-marbled eyelids' petrified (*DH* 77, 79, 312, 23). While Matchett turns into a piece of furniture, the furniture itself becomes the silent witness of the house of Quayne – for household objects 'seem to watch you the whole time' in Bowen's world.[19] Matchett scrubs and polishes the furniture incessantly in order to protect herself from its unblinking scrutiny: 'If I just had to look at it and have it looking at me, I'd go jumpy,' she declares (*DH* 81). Yet Matchett also praises the vigilance of furniture as evidence of its 'moral superiority.'[20] 'Unnatural living runs in a family, and the furniture knows it, you be sure. Good furniture knows what's what . . . it's made for a purpose, and it respects itself – when I say *you're* made for a purpose,' she rebukes Portia, 'you start off crying' (*DH* 81).

The purpose of furniture is to remember: 'furniture like we've got is too much for some that would rather not have the past' (*DH* 81). Furniture is a survival that betokens the resurgence of the past within the present, and in this sense it corresponds to Portia and Major Brutt, those human relics 'left over from another age.' In her book *On Longing*, Susan Stewart distinguishes the relic from the souvenir: both are objects impregnated with the past, but the souvenir marks the transformation of matter into meaning – a paperweight purchased at the seaside evokes the vanished holiday – whereas the relic marks the transformation of meaning into matter – the holiness of Christ is condensed into a hair, a rag, a tooth.[21] Given this distinction, Bowen's furniture represents a relic, rather than a souvenir, because its meaning is condensed in matter, sense in substance. To put it another way, furniture operates as a synecdoche, rather than a metaphor, of time gone by, partaking of the very substance of the past. But furniture also haunts its owners with the future – that is, with the past they are compelled to re-enact: 'It all has to come back,' as Matchett says. This is a law that the Quaynes have neglected at their peril: 'They'd rather no past – not have the past,' Matchett chides. 'No wonder they don't rightly know what they're doing. Those without memories don't know what is what.' Anna's memory is 'all blurs and seams' (*DH* 80, 45). Matchett, on the contrary, is 'not a forgetter.' While the other inhabitants of Windsor Terrace struggle to erase the past – Anna to forget Pidgeon, Thomas to forget his father's shame – only Matchett, the spirit of the furniture, helps Portia to reconstruct the puzzle of her history. In their nocturnal tête-à-têtes,

Matchett tells the young girl more about the past than she can bear. 'I just asked about the day I was born,' Portia weeps. 'Well, the one thing leads to the other,' Matchett ruthlessly replies (*DH* 80).

Chessman has proposed that objects loom large in Bowen's world because of their resistance to narration.[22] But furniture differs from other objects insofar as it conveys the past into the present, thus ensuring that 'the one thing leads to the other,' which is the basis of the continuity of narrative. Far from resisting narrative, furniture therefore embodies narrative in solid form, impacted into metal, fabric, wood, and stone. If Matchett distrusts Eddie, it is not just because he toys with Portia's feelings, but because he represents a threat to furniture. An upstart, he has broken with the past, much as the cinema with which he is associated has exploded the continuity of narrative into thousands of imperceptible divisions. Alan Clark once said snobbishly that Michael Heseltine was the kind of man who 'bought all his own furniture'; but Eddie is the kind who has to rent it.[23] In this sense he defies the principle that the one thing leads to the other – there is no way of knowing where his furniture has been. His horrid flat, with its 'hideous hired furniture,' and its buff walls impervious to any 'trace' of previous lives, stands for the erasure of tradition (*DH* 278).

When Portia challenges Eddie about his treachery with Daphne at the movies, he retorts: 'People have to get off when they can't get on' (*DH* 205). Goronwy Rees, thought to be the prototype of Eddie, got off with Rosamond Lehmann under Bowen's nose when both lovers were visitors at Bowen's Court in 1936. At this time Rees was assistant editor of *The Spectator,* although Bowen met him five years earlier when he was awarded a fellowship at All Souls College in Oxford. Ten years younger than Bowen, clever, sexy, irresponsible, Rees fascinated his hostess at Bowen's Court. Yet when he neglected her for the beautiful Lehmann, Bowen characteristically resented the insult to the house more keenly that the insult to herself. Writing to Isaiah Berlin, who had witnessed the intrigue, Bowen ranted: 'This is no house to go creeping about at nights.'

> What I cannot understand is that anyone who was happy in the house qua house as these two people were or said they were should have so little sense of its character and of the character of our life here as to feel it was the place for amorous visits – or for the prosecution of a love affair so ruthless that it crashed across the sensibility and dignity of everyone in else here; a sensibility and dignity which is nothing to do with *me*, which this house creates and imposes on me as it does on everyone else.

When Bowen confronted Rees about the escapade, he out-Eddied Eddie, exploding into wild hysterics:

> he started the most awful nerve-storm, wept, screamed, threw himself about the room, said that I had an unholy power over him, that my point of view of things was killing him or sending him mad; that he would go mad, he knew, and that something terrible in my attitude had made him become a "beautiful shell of horror".

'Does he always cry so much?' she wonders.[24] If Eddie was indeed based on Goronwy Rees, Bowen clearly had to tone down the original – no one would believe such histrionics in a novel.

St Quentin remarks, 'To write is always to rave a little' (*DH* 10). In *The Death of the Heart*, Bowen went on raving about Rees, and he recognised himself in the volatile Eddie. Gratified at first, Rees told Rosamond Lehmann that the book was brilliant. On second thought, however, he took offence and threatened to sue Bowen for libel, but was dissuaded by her friends, notably by E. M. Forster. This episode may explain Bowen's subsequent dissatisfaction with *The Death of the Heart*, which most critics regard as her masterpiece. It was a Book Society Choice, and made her enough money to install electricity and a telephone in Bowen's Court. But Bowen felt the novel should have been condensed into a story, implying that the writing – or the raving – had got out of hand.[25] But writing necessarily gets out of hand – this is the central insight of *The Death of the Heart*. There are three writers in this novel: St Quentin the novelist, Portia the diarist, and Eddie himself, the author of a forgotten satirical novel, who 'worked off his sense of insult' in its 'savage glitter' (*DH* 62, 67). In addition, Anna, Matchett, and Portia herself compete for possession of Portia's story, each striving to become the author, rather than the butt, of the narration. Portia's room, stuffed with junk mail, compares to the workshop of filthy creation in *Finnegans Wake*, that famous mess in which the writer, Shem the Penman, forges new literature out of the litter of other people's letters, recycling 'quashed quotatoes' and 'messes of mottage.'[26]

St Quentin warns Portia that it is 'madness to write things down.' When Portia protests that she merely records what happens – 'I don't invent' – he tells her that she puts 'constructions on things,' setting 'traps' that 'ruin our free will.' What is more, 'nothing like that stops with oneself.' 'Suppose somebody read it?' he demands (*DH* 248–50). At this point Portia realises that somebody already has. Writing never stops with the author, but lives on, just as Portia lives on, pestering the present with the past; and just as poor old Major Brutt lives on, a haunting reminder of the bloodbath at the outset of the modern century. Portia is both a writer and a form of writing: she assumes the role of family historian, as Bowen did in *Bowen's Court*, but she also functions – like the furniture – as history incarnate. If 'something edited life at the Quaynes' house,' Portia is the portion expurgated from the text. Posted to Windsor Terrace as a sequel to the post-humous letter from old Quayne, she represents the 'steadfast persis-tence' of the writing of the past. Both writing and written, Portia has to learn that writing never stops with oneself, nor is it possible to write without putting constructions on things, or pinning people down – 'she's got us taped,' as Anna says. When St Quentin insists that 'you cannot write without style,' it is worth remembering that the word 'style' derives from the Latin *stilus,* meaning stake or pale, and refers to a pointed instrument used for cutting letters or for stabbing flesh. If you cannot write without style, you cannot write without impaling those you write about, or staking them under the stiletto of your pen.[27] The death of the heart is Portia's initiation to the violence of style.

On Wednesday, 16 October 1940 Virginia Woolf's flat at 52 Tavistock Square was completely destroyed by a bomb. Three months later Bowen wrote: 'When your flat went did that mean all the things in it too? All my life I have said, "Whatever happens there will always be tables and chairs" – and what a mistake.'[28] Bowen's wartime fiction struggles to make sense of a world suddenly stripped bare of furni-ture. If the past inheres in furniture, the loss of tables and chairs implies the destruction of memory, and as Matchett warns, 'Those without memories don't know what is what.' Deprived of solid objects to bind the living to the past, there is little to bind them to the present.[29] In *The Heat of the Day*, Stella Rodney, having stored her possessions in 'limbo' and moved into a rented flat, finds her relations with her son Roderick sorely strained by 'the absence of every inanimate thing they had had in common.' The flat expresses her 'unexceptionably but wrongly'; so Harrison, her stalker, discovers to his cost when he compliments her taste in ornaments, only to be told that they are not her own (*HD* 49, 55, 24). This is reminiscent of a Jewish joke discussed by Freud, in which a marriage-broker invites the prospective groom to examine the rich possessions of the family of the bride.

'But,' asks the suspicious young man, 'mightn't it be possible that these fine things were only collected for the occasion – that they were borrowed to give an impression of wealth?' 'What an idea!' answered the broker protestingly. 'Who do you think would lend these people anything?'[30]

Who is Stella without her furniture? Does her identity belong to her belongings? Marooned in the 'effects' of other people, does she remain herself or turn into another person, like an actress in a stage set, her 'fine things' timed to vanish on the stroke of midnight? In *The Death of the Heart*, published two years before bombs began to fall on London, Bowen comments that 'the destruction of buildings and furniture is more palpably dreadful to the spirit that the destruction of human life,' for 'these things are what we mean when we speak of civilisation' (*DH* 207). Eleven years later, *The Heat of the Day* examines how the bonds of passion, kinship, history, custom, class, heredity, and nationality are torn apart by the destruction of buildings and furniture. At the same time, the furniture of realism is shattered by the violence of Bowen's style: the author told Jocelyn Brooke that she intended the structure of the novel to resemble 'the convulsive shaking of a kaleidoscope, a kaleidoscope also of which the inside reflector was cracked.'[31]

Although Bowen began writing *The Heat of the Day* in 1944, the novel came out only in 1949, eleven years after the success of *The Death of the Heart*. Given that Bowen published no fewer than four novels during the 1930s, three of which are masterpieces, the 1940s were the longest gap in her career as a novelist (the second longest silence came in 1955–64, after the death of Alan Cameron). But she found the short story better suited than the novel to her experience of war, an experience of negative capability in which she

> lived, both as a civilian and as a writer, with every pore open; I lived so many lives, and, still more, lived among the packed repercussions of so many thousands of other lives, all under stress, that I now see it would have been impossible to have been writing only one book.

She describes her short stories as fall-out from the blasts: 'sparks,' 'disjected snapshots,' 'flying particles of something enormous.' A fragmented world required a fragmentary artform. In her 1945 Postscript to her wartime stories, *The Demon Lover*, Bowen remembers how 'people whose homes had been blown up went to infinite lengths to assemble bits of themselves – broken ornaments, old shoes, torn scraps of the curtains that had hung in a room – from the wreckage' (*MT* 95–9). Similarly, Bowen's wartime fiction, with its meticulous inventories of household objects, each depicted with surreal intensity, strives to rescue treasures from destruction.

In her powerful story 'Ivy Gripped the Steps' (1945), Bowen returns to the coast of Kent to salvage fragments of her childhood (*CS* 686–711). The story is set in 1944, when the official ban on visitors to Southstone, a seaside town, has just been lifted. Gavin Doddington, on leave from the Ministry, takes his earliest opportunity to visit the Southstone villa where he spent the most vivid moments of his early years. 'The ban had so acted on his reluctance that, when the one was removed, the other came away with it – as a scab, adhering, comes off with a wad of lint' (*CS* 688). This disturbing metaphor suggests that the wound beneath the scab has now reopened, letting forth a haemorrhage of memories. Gavin finds the villa he remembers abandoned and entombed, its windows sealed with metal sheets, rendering them 'sightless' though 'in sight.' The ivy that grips the steps, stretching its voracious suckers over brick and stone, is now in fruit, as if it were 'feeding on something inside the house.' The narrator comments: 'The process of strangulation could be felt: one wondered how many more years of war would be necessary for this to complete itself' (*CS* 686).

The house is all that remains of Lilian Nicholson, its widowed former owner and the object of Gavin's childhood passion. The story began before his birth, when Lilian spent a 'finishing year' with Gavin's mother Edith in Dresden (*CS* 689). Soon afterwards Lilian married Jimmie Nicholson, a wealthy businessman, whereas Edith married an impoverished landowner, with a bloodsucking mansion to maintain. Bowen locates the Doddingtons' estate in the Midlands, but it bears a telling resemblance to the Big Houses in Ireland, whose owners struggled for generations to maintain 'the illusion that prestige, power and permanence attach to bulk and weight' (*MT* 95). Like the Anglo-Irish, the Doddingtons have long since passed their sell-by date: 'Had the Doddingtons been told that their kind would die out, they would have expressed little more than surprise that such complicated troubles could end so simply' (*CS* 692). In the light of Bowen's own life story, it is probable that downtrodden Mrs Doddington and fun-loving Mrs Nicholson represent two sides of the same mother: the oppressed Mrs Bowen of Bowen's Court, drained by the inheritance that drove her husband mad, and the liberated Florence of Bowen's childhood in Kent. The two characters even wear the same clothes, although the hand-me-down dresses that look so glamorous on Lilian flutter loose on Edith's wasted form. Yet the little boy caresses these mousselines and satins with an erotic absorption that alarms his mother, 'for fetishism is still to be apprehended by these for whom it has never had any name' (*CS* 697).[32]

A delicate child, Gavin is sent for holidays to Southstone, where he falls in love with Mrs Nicholson. Using the technique that Henry James employs in *What Maisie Knew*, Bowen presents the adult's life entirely from the child's point of view. What Gavin knows, or does not know, is that his charming guardian is having an affair with Admiral Concannon. Yet because the child is too young to understand the adults' words and gestures, they linger in his mind like stubborn stains. Through his half-blinkered vision, we infer that the Admiral, married to a hypochondriac, takes no risks with his respectability: he is a sanctimonious version of the mother's lover whom Bowen later recreates in the romantic form of Major Burkin-Jones in *The Little Girls*. The turning-point of Gavin's life occurs when he is climbing up the cliff path from the beach and catches sight of Mrs Nicholson, who fails to meet his eye.

> The heat of midday, the glare from the flowered cliff beat up Gavin into a sort of fever. As though a dropped plummet had struck him between the eyes he looked up, to see Mrs Nicholson's face above him against the blue. The face, its colour rendered transparent by the transparent silk of a parasol, was inclined forward: he had the experience of seeing straight up into eyes that did not see him. Her look was pitched into space: she was not only not seeing him, she was seeing nothing. She was listening, but not attending, while someone talked.
>
> Gavin, gripping the handrail, bracing his spine against it, leaned out backwards over the handrail into the void, in the hopes of intercepting her line of view. But in vain. He tore off clumps of sea pinks and cast the too-light flowers outwards into the air, but her pupils never once flickered down. Despair, the idea that his doom must be never, never to reach her, not only now but ever, gripped him and gripped his limbs as he took the rest of the path – the two more bends and few more steps to the top. He clawed his way up the rail, which shook in its socket.

(*CS* 694)

'In sight' but 'sightless,' like her coffined villa decades later, Mrs Nicholson stares 'at nothing' with the unseeing eyes of a corpse. The 'experience of seeing straight up into eyes that did not see him' is Gavin's first confrontation with death. The despair that 'grips' the child on this feverish ascent anticipates the ivy that 'grips' the steps to the forsaken house, and commences the 'process of strangulation' of his heart. The crisis is temporarily relieved when Gavin finally reaches Mrs Nicholson, interrupting her conversation with Admiral Concannon, who is prophesying war with Germany. Mrs Nicholson makes fun of these forebodings with shameless complacency and chauvinism. Why would anyone want to upset things now that history has turned out so well? 'Civilised countries are polite to each other, just as you and I are to the people we know, and uncivilised countries are put down – but, if one thinks, there are beautifully few of those. Even savages really prefer wearing hats and coats.' As for Germany, Mrs Nicholson remembers only her glorious girlhood in Dresden: 'I have never been happier anywhere' (*CS* 696). This conversation takes place in 1907; Mrs Nicholson, destined to die in 1912 (the same year as Bowen's mother), is never to find out how wrong she was about the war. She may have been right, however, to anticipate the argument of Woolf's *Three Guineas* (1938) that Admiral Concannon needs a war to prove his masculinity. 'That's why he's so anxious to have that war,' she tells Gavin. 'One would have thought a man could just be a man' (*CS* 702). Ever afterwards Gavin has thought of World War I as Major Concannon's war.

Gavin, by contrast, might as well have been a woman. Too young to fight in World War I, too old in World War II, he is the same age as his author and her century, and likewise restricted to the Home Front. Two World Wars after Lilian laughed history away, her beloved Dresden soon to be reduced to ruins, Gavin returns to Southstone, still searching for an answering gaze in those unseeing eyes.[33] Lilian having died when 'he was still only at the first chapter of the mystery of the house,' Gavin has become a casual 'amorist,' a wolfish 'preyer' with 'a whole stopped mechanism for feeling' (*CS* 706, 689, 711). Rebuffed by the blind and strangled villa, Gavin pays a nostalgic visit to Admiral Concannon's former house, now requisitioned for the war effort. Peering voyeuristically through the window, he spies an ATS girl, 'abrupt with youth,' sitting at the table. But she remains unconscious of his gaze, and 'for the second time in his life, he saw straight up into the eyes that did not see him' (*CS* 710). Gavin waits for the girl to leave her post and then pursues her down the street, entreating her to look around. When she finally turns, it is she who finds herself looking into the eyes of a corpse: 'She had seen the face of somebody dead who was still there.' Alarmed, she hurries off to meet her date, leaving Gavin to his 'tour of annihilation' (*CS* 711, 708).

This enigmatic story, although much admired, has been little understood, its critics trying to insert a moral framework that Bowen pointedly omits. Phyllis Lassner, for example, completely overlooks the love triangle to focus on the self-deceptions of the middle class, satirised in Lilian's pooh-poohing of the threat of war.[34] More perceptively, Harold Bloom recognises that Gavin is in love with Mrs Nicholson, but tries to pin the blame for Gavin's frozen heart on Lilian's emotional predation.[35] In effect Bloom takes the part of Admiral Concannon, the moral bully, who accuses Lilian of making 'a ninnie of that unfortunate boy,' when it is clear that the Admiral's real gripe is that she cares for someone other than himself (*CS* 707). But this is not a story about child abuse: Lilian betrays Gavin on the parapet merely by looking 'at nothing' rather than at him, by giving herself up to nothing and leaving him stranded in a world evacuated by the only look that ever mattered. Her death has turned him into a pervert, condemning him to seek the vacant gaze of a dead woman in every living woman's eyes. Lilian is an abuser only insofar as it is an abuse to die.

The beach, the steep ascent, the faraway woman, the military lover, and the threat of war – all these recur in the central flashback of Bowen's later novel, *The Little Girls* (1964).[36] But in the novel, the child Dinah witnesses the tender parting of her mother and the Major on the beach, whereas Gavin witnesses a very different showdown of the lovers in the drawing-room. Despite such variations, it is hard not to suspect that Bowen is rewriting her mother's love affair in Kent, giving new constructions to impressions stored in childhood – beach, soldier, ghostwoman, precipice, war – much as one might reinterpret the figments of a dream. If the story has a moral, it is not that Lilian is a bad parent, or that her views are politically incorrect, but that no adult experience of love can equal the intensity of childhood passion. In Gavin's case, this is a passion for the house, as much as for its owner, an agonising lust for secret chambers he has always longed to penetrate: 'Their still only partial familiarity, their fullness with objects that, in the half light coming in from the landing, he could only half perceive and did not yet dare touch, made him feel he was still only at the first chapter of the mystery of the house' (*CS* 706). In spite of all his subsequent amours, Gavin has never reached the second chapter, nor touched the secret furniture of love.

Bowen's passion for her own house found expression in her family history, *Bowen's Court*, also written during the war years. Like many of her other writings of this period, *Bowen's Court* turns back to her Irish past – not to drag it up, she protests, but to 'lay it' (*BC* 453–4). Of her ten published stories set in Ireland, five were written during World

War II; one of these, 'Sunday Afternoon,' is discussed at the conclusion of this chapter. But Bowen also had a secret mission to perform in Ireland. In a letter of 1 July 1940, she told Virginia Woolf that she had volunteered her services to the British Ministry of Information. What she did not divulge was her assignment: to spy on political and civic life in Ireland, and particularly to gauge public opinion of Irish neutrality. Her well-observed reports on politics as well as shopping, rationing, black-marketing, and travelling in wartime Ireland earned her the commendation of Lord Cranborne, Head of the Dominions office, who sent her report of November 1940 to the Foreign Office for Halifax's personal attention. Bowen had written:

> The childishness and obtuseness of this country cannot fail to be irritating to the English mind. In a war of this size and this desperate gravity Britain may well feel that Irish susceptibilities should go to the wall. But it must be seen (and no doubt is seen) that any hint of a violation of Eire may well be used to implement enemy propaganda and weaken the British case.

Despite her commitment to the British war effort, Bowen lamented the presence of 'anti-Irish feeling' in England, and insisted that Ireland's neutrality – its 'first *free* self-assertion' – was 'positive, not merely negative': 'She has invested her self-respect in it. It is typical of her intense and narrow view of herself that she cannot see that her attitude must appear to England an affair of blindness, egotism, escapism or sheer funk.'[37]

Just after Churchill had spoken in the House of Commons of the 'heavy and grievous burden' imposed on Britain by the loss of the Treaty ports, Bowen warned that a British take-over of Irish ports would be disastrous for both countries.[38] Yet she also pointed out that the 'virtual closing of the Irish Channel' had exacerbated 'claustrophobia and restlessness' in Dublin, breeding parochialism as well as a potentially fascistic cult of '*Heimkunst.*'[39]

Two years later, Bowen's experience of wartime London had eroded her sympathy for Irish isolationism. Unimpressed by the general standard of political debate in Ireland, she deplored its crypto-fascist element.[40] Yet her secret memoranda paint a vivid portrait of the Fine Gael politician James Dillon, whom she admired despite his fascist leanings. It is possible that Dillon – well-off, unmarried, contemptuous of 'society,' his nature 'concentrated,' his intellect 'powerful and precise' – may have given Bowen some ideas for the fascist double-agent Robert Kelway in *The Heat of the Day*.

151

But Dillon, unlike Robert, was no oil painting; he showed an 'almost morbid interest in Hitler's personality,' combined with a 'religious fanaticism of the purest kind I have ever met.'[41] Dillon had no idea that Bowen had reported their private conversations to the British government until 1979, when the historian Robert Fisk showed him her reports. Although offended by her abuse of his hospitality, he merely pitied her repugnance to his religiosity: 'Poor woman – you can see her unhappy agnosticism.'[42]

In *The Heat of the Day*, Stella Rodney discovers that she has been practicing neutrality involuntarily. Knowingly, she has been working for the Allied cause through an organisation known as XYD (perhaps a parody of the proliferating acronyms of wartime); unknowingly, she has been sleeping with a Nazi spy. Together the lovers have retreated into a 'hermetic world,' like the 'claustrophobic' world of neutral Ireland, creating a kind of *Heimkunst* (home-art) to resist the global holocaust.[43] Yet this secluded world of love cannot seal off all its ports against the world at war; no island can remain immune to history, or to horror. In a crucial passage, already quoted in this study, Bowen writes:

> No, there is no such thing as being alone together. Daylight moves round the walls; night rings the changes of its intensity; everything is on its way to somewhere else – there is the presence of movement, that third presence, however still, however unheeding in their trance two may try to stay. Unceasingly something is at its work.

> (*HD* 195)

In this instance the third presence represents the voice-over itself, which bombs into the lovers' intimacy, shattering the illusion of realism like a Brechtian alienation-effect. In this cinematic scene it is as if the camera, following the daylight round the walls and tracking the intensities of night, had suddenly turned the lens upon itself. Arriving 'out of nowhere,' the narrative voice imposes its ghostly presence on the lovers, who are trying – like the neutral Irish – to remain alone together.[44] (It is worth noting that *sinn fein* is usually translated as 'ourselves alone.') We have seen how the third presence in Bowen's early fiction functions as a catalyst, but also as an obstacle to love. In *The Heat of the Day*, however, the third presence stands for the incursion of history into private life: 'Their time sat in the third place at their table' (*HD* 194).

At this point in the novel, the time is 1942, two years after the Blitz, when Londoners, no longer traumatised by nightly raids, were

152

growing acclimatised to ruin. It was during the Blitz (we later learn) that Stella Rodney and Robert Kelway fell in love, their first words silenced by the din of aerial bombardment: 'the cataracting roar of a split building: direct hit, somewhere else' (*HD* 96). Deprived of a beginning, their love affair is also robbed of its conclusion, when Robert, exposed as a fascist spy, falls to his death from the roof of Stella's flat. Was it an accident, a murder, or a suicide? We never know, and the 'unfinished haunts,' as Stella says (*HD* 321). So does the unbegun: the beginning of this romance, 'from having been lost,' has acquired 'the significance of a lost clue' (*HD* 96). Bowen also deprives the reader of beginnings: the novel opens in an afterworld, the first Sunday of September 1942, when the 'great globular roses' in Regent's Park have reached 'the height of their second blooming,' and the deathlike 'trance' of love has already been eroded by the time that it strives to hold at bay (*HD* 17).

Noise obliterated the beginning of the lovers' story, and noise is the form in which the time asserts itself throughout this novel: the shriek of sirens, the crash of bombs, the 'sting' of telephones, the striking of clocks, the peal of victory bells, and most memorable of all, the 'icelike tinkle of broken glass . . . swept up among the crisping leaves' (*HD* 93). These noises burst through bolted doors and blacked-out windows, penetrating all enclosures in which lovers try to be alone together. This is a novel about leaks, about the porousness of architectural and psychic space, about the failure to keep secrets in, intruders out. Bowen herself remembers living 'with every pore open' during the War: 'Sometimes I hardly knew where I stopped and somebody else began . . . Walls went down ̦. . .' (*MT* 95). This porousness creates the perfect climate for romance – for love, like war, breaks down the boundaries between solid objects: 'War at present worked as a thinning of the membrane between the this and the that, it was a becoming apparent – but then what else is love?' (*HD* 195). Robert Kelway is a 'leak' in human form who peddles secrets to the enemy (*HD* 35). In this sense he embodies the osmosis that pervades the narrative from the beginning. The novel's opening scene, an outdoor concert in Regent's Park, seethes with images of leakage and effluvia: the 'smell' of evening steals out of the thickets, 'blades of sunset' flicker through the crowd, and hints of music escaping from the 'muffled hollow' of the orchestra enter 'senses, nerves, and fancies' 'drop by drop' (*HD* 7–13).

This general invasion of the senses sets the scene for local, personal invasions, which follow in a chain reaction – for Bowen's narrative, like a Racinian tragedy, is driven by serial sexual harassment. First Louie Lewis (Bowen's rather patronising portrait of the 'factory girl'), discarded by her latest pick-up, intrudes on Harrison, a stranger she encounters at the concert, interrupting his theatrical display of 'thinking in public' (*HD* 14). Harrison is brooding about Stella Rodney, or rather, his mind has been invaded by the thought of her – for Bowen's characters do not exactly think, in the masterful Cartesian sense; their minds are passive vessels blitzed by thought. Next Harrison intrudes on Stella, 'forcing his way back' into her home – although Bowen makes a point of itemising every door that Stella has left open for him: 'she had left the street door unlatched and the door of her flat, at the head of the stairs, ajar . . .' (*HD* 22–3). Having invaded her flat (a space that grows and shrinks with disconcerting elasticity), Harrison proceeds to invade Stella's mind with knowledge about Robert's treachery. Robert (she is told) is spying for the 'enemy,' but he is also being spied upon by the authorities at home, and thus revealing secrets to both sides. He is a leak that spills in both directions.

Stella is placed in a diabolical dilemma. Either she dumps Robert and prostitutes herself to Harrison, in return for Robert's temporary safety, thus admitting Robert's culpability; or else she interrogates her lover, knowing that his knowing that other people know will drive him to betray himself, should he be guilty. As Harrison puts it: 'I've never yet known a man not change his behaviour once he's known he's watched: it's exactly changes like that that are being watched for' (*HD* 37). Caught in these (Jamesian) wheels of surveillance – watching the watched watch the watchers – Stella has no choice but to become a spy herself. But she tries to comprehend the present by investigating Robert's past, in a secret effort to fathom his 'case-history' (*HD* 103). In the same period that psychoanalysts such as Ernest Jones were tracing 'the psychology of Quislingism' back to infantile sexuality, Stella seeks the roots of Robert's alleged treason at Holme Dene, his garden-gnome-infested childhood home.[45]

Harrison's accusation, whether true or false, forces Stella to conceal a secret from her lover, thus destroying the illusion that the couple had ever been alone together. When Robert discovers the deception, he imagines Stella's secret as a monstrous pregnancy: 'With you, the story takes – seeds itself in some crack that you felt between us . . . We have not then been really alone together for the last two months. You're two months gone with this' (*HD* 190–1). Yet if Robert is himself a double-dealer, the lovers could never have been merely two. Robert the fifth column is also the 'third presence,' the foreign body at the heart of love, the enemy within.[46] In the closing pages of the novel Harrison divulges that his own first name is Robert too, thus reinforcing the suspicion that the lover and the third presence are one and the same. And Stella's doubt about her lover's innocence, whether justified or not, splits her in two. In an essay called 'Disloyalties' (1950), Bowen agrees with Graham Greene that writers are duty-bound to be disloyal; in *The Heat of the Day*, as in her wartime espionage in Ireland, she created situations in which one-sided loyalty became impossible (*MT* 60).

The Heat of the Day, together with *Bowen's Court*, is Bowen's most strenuous attempt to show how the political is implicated in the personal; how the 'third presence' of history seeds itself into the cracks of private life. This was a task, she told Charles Ritchie, which presented 'every possible problem in the world.'[47] The difficulty was to squeeze the panorama of an international conspiracy into Stella's fold-up flat in Weymouth Street, so that everything that happens outside the 'intense and narrow' world of love is acknowledged only by its impact on the inside. In Stella's flat, 'rooms had no names; there being only two, whichever you were not in was "the other room." ' There is 'no one right place to put a tray'; and the hired sofa, which doubles as a bed, 'might have been some derelict piece of furniture exposed on a pavement after an air raid or washed up by a flood on some unknown shore' (*HD* 51, 52, 55). The collapse of the partitions of familial space implies a breakdown of the sexual taboos of kinship. In this world where rooms have no names, and men's names are disconcertingly alike, personal identities dissolve into incestuous proximity – there is 'so little space left' between them (*HD* 46). Two Roberts figure in this novel, plus two Victors, one dead (Stella's husband), the other newborn (Louie's lovechild); 'Roderick Rodney' is virtually the same name stammered twice, like the curiously androgynous name 'Louie Lewis.' Through the power of the name, twos become ones; but at the same time, ones split into twos – individuals divide into opposing halves. Harrison is distinguished by his strange duality of vision – 'his ununified way of regarding you simultaneously out of each eye' – which gives Louie Lewis 'the feeling of being looked at twice – being viewed then checked over again in the same moment' (*HD* 75). Harrison's 'inequality' of gaze finds its counterpart in Robert's 'inequality' of gait – his limp, which Stella puts down at first to 'the general rocking of London and one's own mind' (*HD* 12, 90). Robert's legs, like Harrison's eyes, move at cross-purposes, somatic symptoms of psychological duplicity. Yet in spite of their divided bodies and divided loyalties, both characters merge into one 'Robert' at the end. Dividuals rather than individuals, both are two-in-one and one-in-two.

Stella's son Roderick also has a double, his friend Fred, whom he quotes admiringly at every opportunity:

> as Fred says, it comes to seem fishy when one *is* told anything. Go by what you find out for yourself, he says. If a thing's true, you find it sticks out a mile once you come to look. Whereas if anybody goes out of his way to tell you something, Fred says you can take it he's got an axe to grind.
>
> (*HD* 64)

In these absurd self-contradictory clichés, Fred advises Roderick not to be advised – advice that Roderick ignores by quoting it. Like 'Mrs Harris,' Mrs Gamp's imaginary fan in *Martin Chuzzlewit*, Fred never appears: 'Where's Fred gone?' (*HD* 294). Fred is the funniest of many absent characters who haunt this novel, impugning the supremacy of presence: 'Fred asks to be remembered' (*HD* 202).[48] Absentees include Louie's husband Tom, drafted abroad and destined never to return; Robert's sister Amabelle, trapped in India for the duration of the war, whose unlovely children have been sent for safety to Holme Dene; Roderick's father Victor, doubly erased by his divorce from Stella and his death; and Francis Morris, Victor's cousin, who dropped dead before the book begins, bequeathing his Big House in Ireland to Roderick, Victor's son.

Roderick, as well as being twinned with Fred, tends to dissolve into the force called 'Robert' that threatens to engulf all men into one name (it is worth remembering that Bowen herself, had she been born the boy her parents were expecting, would have been named Robert). For instance, Roderick looks 'more like [him]self' when he is wearing Robert's dressing-gown in Stella's flat (*HD* 47). The scene that follows bristles with double entendre. Roderick reaches his hand into his mother's lover's 'slippery pocket,' and comes upon '*something* . . . pulped by age in its folds, limp from being in silk near a body's warmth.' This is not what it sounds like, but a piece of paper 'long ago folded' and possibly harbouring a secret message. Having 'twiddled it round and round,' Roderick yields the object to his mother who, holding its 'dynamite . . . between her fingers and thumbs,' undergoes a sharp moral crisis as to whether to unfold it or to tear it up. Finally she succumbs to her suspicions, peeks inside and finds 'nothing at all' – nothing, that is, that she is willing to divulge to

Roderick (*HD* 62–4). The reader, placed in the same position as Roderick, never discovers whether any message was actually secreted in those warm limp folds. It is not what this paper says that matters, but what it does – the way it circulates between the mother, son, and absent third, implicating everyone (including the reader, the fourth party to this guilty transaction) in a conspiracy of secrecy, desire, and betrayal.

While the lovers strive to make one little room an everywhere, Bowen compresses everywhere into a little room, or more precisely into six carceral spaces. Her camera jump-cuts between Stella's flat in Weymouth Street, Louie's boarding-house in Chilcombe Street, and Robert's family house Holme Dene, taking excursions to Mount Morris – the Irish estate bequeathed to Roderick by cousin Francis – and to Wistaria Lodge, the asylum where Francis's wife Nettie, driven crazy by Mount Morris, has retreated to save her insanity. The sixth enclosure is another makeshift flat where Harrison finds Stella at the end, navigating someone else's rented furniture. Even the few scenes that take place outside these domestic chambers – such as the outdoor concert in Regent's Park, or the restaurant where Stella, Harrison, and Louie collide in chapter 12 – feel constricted, over-crowded, and shut in. Contrasted to the claustrophobia of London under siege is the 'uncontainable' idea of global war; the narrator observes that there were 'too many theatres of war' for Londoners to grasp (*HD* 308). Yet the 'windowless rooms' that provide the setting for the 'indoor-plotted' action of the novel also seem theatrical: Robert describes his family home, perpetually for sale, as a stage set with 'touring scenery' (*HD* 142, 121). The novel, with its cramped spaces, overwrought tête-à-têtes, and meticulous attention to lighting, props, and choreography, resembles a low-budget television melo-drama, shot almost entirely in studio.

It is Harrison who links the stories taking place within these separate confines. When Stella first lays eyes on him, Harrison is 'stepping cranelike over the graves' at Cousin Francis's funeral; and Harrison's aesthetic function is to step cranelike over the interiors in which the rival narratives are staged (*HD* 66). In this sense Harrison, the shadowy third, mimes the work of the narrator herself, who splices the divergent plots together, often by deliberately intrusive means. Harrison's mysterious appearance at the funeral, where he falls implausibly in love with Stella, links the spy plot to the story of Mount Morris; his accidental brush with Louie Lewis in the Park brings her story into contiguity with Stella's; and it is Harrison, again by accident, who brings the two women together in the phantasma-goric restaurant of chapter 12. Although connecting all the dwelling-places in the novel, Harrison himself has no address: like a 'ghost or actor,' he goes 'into abeyance . . . between appearances.' When Stella asks him where he lives, he replies: 'There are always two or three places where I can turn in.' 'But . . . where do you keep your razor?' she persists. 'I have two or three razors.' Harrison mirrors the narrator insofar as he intrudes into the theatres of the novel but does not inhabit them. He is therefore 'by the rules of fiction, with which life to be credible must comply . . . a character "impossible." ' Each time he foists himself on Stella, he shows 'no shred or trace of having been continuous since they last met' (*HD* 140–1).

But the other men in Stella's life also lack a fixed abode. Her son Roderick is constantly in transit, even though Mount Morris, 'standing outside war,' beckons him to a 'historic future' (*HD* 50). Robert Kelway alternates between Holme Dene and Stella's flat, but he has other 'haunts' that he reputedly frequents between appearances; he also has a secret 'beat' that he retraces like a restless ghost, closely shadowed by his doppelganger Robert Harrison (*HD* 37). For Bowen, who believed that landed property protected her ancestors from the worst excesses of the will to power, Robert's rootlessness is ominous. 'We have everything to dread from the dispossessed,' she writes in *Bowen's Court.* 'While property lasted the dangerous power-idea stayed, like a sword in its scabbard, fairly safely at rest' (*BC* 455). In *The Heat of the Day*, Bowen suggests that the dangerous power-idea, unrestrained by property, can boil over into fascism.[49] Nor is it enough to purchase property, as the Kelways bought Holme Dene, for property must be inherited in order to impose a 'sense of limitations' (Bowen told Charles Ritchie that the sense of guilt was specific to the middle-class – 'not enough humility and sense of limitations.')[50] Built to 'please and appease middle-class ladies,' Holme Dene has been effectively usurped by Robert's bossy sister and castrating mother, leaving Robert dispossessed and vaga-bond (*HD* 257).

Of the men in the novel, only Cousin Francis has ever been the master of his own estate, but he is dead before the book begins, and it is telling that his line is dying out. Having no descendants he was forced 'to go out looking for a son' (*HD* 209). It is women who dominate domestic space, most toxically in the 'blackly furnished' mazes of Holme Dene (*HD* 107). In her scathing portrait of the Kelway ménage, Bowen lets forth all her Yeatsian abhorrence of the middle-class, laced with a strong dose of misogyny. Even to call the Kelways middle-class makes Stella wonder, 'middle of what? She saw the Kelways suspended in the middle of nothing' (*HD* 114). Their house is 'planned with a kind of playful circumlocution,' its 'swastika-arms of passage leading to nothing' (*HD* 256, 258). 'Flock-packed with . . . repressions, doubts, fears, subterfuges, and fibs,' this is a house that forces its inmates into play-acting: 'Their private hours, it could be taken, were spent in nerving themselves for inevitable family confrontations such as meal-times, and in working on to their faces the required expression of having nothing to hide' (*HD* 256). The extravagances of the architecture belie the stinginess of its inhabitants; at tea-time no one offers any butter to the guests, the family members hoarding their respective rations. Robert's hearty sister Ernestine shows spontaneous feeling only when she speaks of her dead dog: 'I often think that if Hitler could have looked into that dog's eyes, the story might have been very different' (124). (In point of fact Hitler was even soppier than Ernestine towards animals.) Holme Dene has been for sale since it was purchased, but when someone finally offers to buy it, the Kelway women refuse to budge. It is as if they can appreciate their monstrous mansion only by destroying other people's hopes of owning it.

Presiding over this 'man-eating house' is Mrs Kelway, whose offspring address her by the nauseating (and suspiciously Teutonic) pet name 'Muttikins' (*HD* 257, 107). Robert's father, long since dead, was treated like a wind-up toy, programmed to perform the part of manliness yet stripped of the power attendant on the role. 'Lockshorn,' his 'sex had . . . lost caste' (*HD* 257). Deprived of a convincing model of masculinity, Robert feels he was 'born wounded; my father's son.' Robert's limp, caused by a wound inflicted at Dunkirk, intensifies in the presence of his family; and Robert regards the fiasco of Dunkirk as proof of the impotence of British manhood: 'Dunkirk was waiting there in us – what a race!' (*HD* 272). The women of Holme Dene have decorated Robert's bedroom walls with photos of himself at every age, playing tennis, flaunting trophies, or standing arm-in-arm with Decima, his former fiancée. The whole gallery of imitation moments amounts to a burlesque of masculinity. Whenever Robert enters this excruciating shrine, he is 'hit in the face' by the sensation that he does not exist – 'that I not only am not but never have been.' Stella exclaims, 'they've . . . made this room as though you were dead' (*HD* 117–18). In this collage of spurious identities, there is no authentic self for Robert to betray. Readers have objected that

Robert's character is unconvincing, a woman's idea of a man, but this is precisely Bowen's point: Robert has no character, being nothing but a jumble of projections – those 'fictions of boyishness' inflicted on him by the gorgons of Holme Dene (*HD* 116). This is why he is 'a character "impossible"' – like Harrison – devoid of depth, consistency, and motivation; why it is hard to tell where Robert Kelway ends, and Robert Harrison begins; and why spy-catcher and spy are both condensed into a single name, a single culpability. If Robert hankers for the law and order he perceives in fascism, even at the price of infamy, it is in a desperate effort to cement a self out of his swirling images.

When Robert finally confesses his fascism to Stella, he says, 'you'll have to re-read me backwards,' which is precisely what a psychoanalyst would do (*HD* 270). By tracing Robert's treason back to a powerless father, Bowen endorses the current psychoanalytic view of Quislingism, which Ernest Jones described in 1941 as the 'peculiar inability to face, or even to recognize, an enemy.' Jones attributes Quislingism to a crisis of masculinity, brought about by a failure to resolve the Oedipus complex, either by establishing independence from the father or by reconciling conflictual impulses towards the mother. 'Treachery, by allying oneself with the conquering enemy, would seem to be an attempt sadistically to overcome the incest taboo by raping the mother instead of loving her.'[51] In view of Robert's handicap, it is worth noting that Oedipus means 'he who limps.' Bowen differs from the psychoanalysts, however, in insisting on the architectural determinants of treason. Robert's crime is imputed to his father's impotence, his mother's wickedness, his sister's brassiness, her labrador's subservience; to the unearthed materialism of the middle-class; to the Kelways' contempt for language, evident in loathsome baby-talk like 'Muttikins,' 'teeny weeny,' and 'uncomfy'; but above all to the house itself, with its twisting corridors, obstructive furniture, and garden kitsch (*HD* 251, 111). A crooked house creates a crooked mind.

Contrasted to Holme Dene is the traditional sanctity and loveliness of Mount Morris. It was in this house that Roderick was conceived. But soon after his birth his father, Victor Rodney, who was wounded in action in World War I, demanded a divorce from Stella to marry his nurse. When he died of complications shortly afterwards, Victor's family blamed Stella for the breakdown of the marriage. Preferring to be thought a monster than a victim, she made no effort to clear her name. Victor's Cousin Francis, having no heir, bequeathed Mount

Morris to Roderick, *'In the hope that he may care in his own way to carry on the old tradition'* (*HD* 87). Robert is appalled to learn that Mount Morris has been left to Roderick: 'To unload the past on a boy like that – fantastic!' (*HD* 160). But Roderick is determined to fulfil the destiny that Cousin Francis has 'decided' for him, even though he finds the terms of the bequest ambiguous: is he to care in his own way, or to carry on the old tradition in his own way? '*Why* must lawyers always take out commas?' he complains (*HD* 213, 87). (It is interesting that Roger Casement's trial for treason hinged on the omission of such commas.) Since 'the house, non-human' has become the hub of Roderick's imaginary life, Stella feels obliged to keep an eye on the estate until the War is over, and her son can be demobbed. Halfway through the novel she travels to Mount Morris, where she encounters the 'ageless, wifeless' Donovan, its chthonic caretaker, and his 'two surprisingly young' daughters (*HD* 165). Stella is surprised to find that neutral Ireland is suffering from shortages as harsh as Britain's: the candles that she burns during her visit are the last the Donovans have saved up for the winter. In Mount Morris no voices are raised for Irish neutrality. Cousin Francis, exasperated with his country's isolationism, had died in England on a clandestine mission to offer his services to the British War Office; and Donovan tells Stella that an Englishman with a strange 'discord between his two eyes' had also visited Mount Morris for midnight talks with Cousin Francis (*HD* 170). We never learn what Harrison and Francis plotted, but it was probably involved with counter-espionage. Stella's visit coincides with Montgomery's victory in El Alamein, which Donovan broadcasts with jubilation: 'Montgomery's through! . . . We bred a very fast General' (*HD* 178).

But Stella feels she has betrayed Mount Morris, having broken faith with the silent communion of her foremothers, whose portraits gaze across the halls at one another, indifferent to the living tenants of the house. 'It had been Stella, her generation, who had broken the link – what else could this be but its broken edges that she felt grating inside her soul?' Stella hopes that Roderick's accession to Mount Morris will restore 'the fatal connexion between the past and future,' but the novel conveys a strong impression that the culture of the Big House is defunct (*HD* 176). 'All that's a thing of the past,' says Colonel Pole, a relative of Cousin Francis who attends his funeral. The new generation, Pole insists, will want to 'travel light.' He advises Stella to tell 'Robert' (a symptomatic slip for Roderick) to get rid of the 'white elephant' as soon as he can: 'One thing he should do at once is take the roof off the house, or they'll be popping nuns in before you can say knife' (*HD* 82). Comic though he is, Colonel Pole may well be right to see Mount Morris as a poisoned gift, destined to ruin its possessor. The house has already driven Nettie mad, like Bowen's own father; the flipside of Mount Morris is Wistaria Lodge.

Of all Bowen's Anglo-Irish sleepwalkers, Nettie Morris comes the closest to achieving living death. Securely netted in her plush asylum, with 'nothing to trouble her but the possibility of being within reach,' she has dropped out of the narrative of the ascendancy, a narrative enshrined in the galleries of ghostly ladies at Mount Morris (*HD* 215). Not only has she opted out of Cousin Francis's scenario, refusing the roles of wife and mother, but she repudiates the very concept of a story. When Roderick visits her in chapter 11, she laments that 'there should have to be any stories. We might have been happy as we were.' 'Something has got to become of everybody, I suppose, Cousin Nettie.' 'No, I don't see why,' she counters. 'Nothing has become of me: here I am and you can't make any more stories out of that' (*HD* 214). In this novel everyone seems trapped in someone else's story: Nettie is co-opted into Cousin Francis's fantasy of marriage, Roderick into his romance of fatherhood; Stella, misrepresented as a *femme fatale* in her in-laws' story of her marriage, is also blackmailed by Harrison into the inconclusive story of his lust; Robert is scripted into 'fictions of boyishness' cooked up by his sister and his mother; while Louie Lewis is flattered into ready-made identities spewed out by the daily press. 'Was she not a worker, a soldier's lonely wife, a war orphan, a pedestrian, a Londoner, a home- and animal-lover, a thinking democrat, a movie-goer, a woman of Britain, a letter-writer, a fuel-saver, and a housewife?' (*HD* 152).

As far as Nettie is concerned, however, all stories are over. Like Beckett's Murphy, another refugee from the 'descendancy,' she dreams of nothing more enticing than a padded cell; like Mr Endon, Murphy's lunatic chess partner, who manoeuvres all his pieces back to their original position on the board, Nettie represents the end of history, the terminus of narrative. Yet, as Chessman has pointed out, Nettie's 'resistance to story' puts her in a paradoxical position in the novel. 'Like all characters, Nettie literally owes her existence entirely to her author; she inhabits a story whether she wants to or not. One could say that her author gives her asylum . . .'[52] Nettie occupies a position in Wistaria Lodge similar to that which Mrs Kelway occupies in Holme Dene: both exemplify the insight, expressed by Lou in 'Look at All Those Roses,' that 'people who stay still generate power.'

Both are fates (Mrs Kelway comes equipped with knitting-needles, Nettie with embroidery); each ensconces herself in the interior, locked in 'the self-contained mystery of herself,' while exercising power by remote control. The difference is that Nettie turns her back against the window, whereas Mrs Kelway commands the view from all three windows of the drawing-room (*HD* 108–9). Watching, waiting, plotting, Mrs Kelway still belongs to the teleology of narrative, whereas Nettie rejects the very notion of a story. Yet in spite of herself, Nettie continues to influence the action from her hideout; in particular, she tells Roderick that it was his father who betrayed his mother, rather than the other way around, thus demolishing the master-fiction of his childhood.

The other woman in the novel to resist narration is Louie Lewis. In the first place Louie has no sense of time, whereas narrative implies duration, sequence, continuity. Harrison, by contrast, resembles the narrator, both in his ability to straddle the enclosures of the novel, and in his fanatic punctuality: 'wheeling in on the quiver of the appointed hour as though attached to the very works of the clock' (*HD* 22). Louie also resists narration in the sense that she has no command of words. Her mouth resembles a wound or a vagina, rather than a speaking organ:

> it was big; it was caked round the edges, the edges only, with what was left of lipstick inside which clumsy falsified outline the lips turned outwards, exposed themselves – full, intimate, woundably thin-skinned, tenderly brown pink as the underside of a new mushroom . . . Halted and voluble, this could but be a mouth that blurted rather than spoke, a mouth incontinent and at the same time artless.
>
> (*HD* 11)

Louie hails from the coast of Kent, where her elderly parents were blown up in the Battle of Britain. With her soldier husband stationed abroad, Louie has taken a job in a factory, returning in the evenings to the marital tenement in Chilcombe Street, where she dozes heavily beside 'the hollow left by Tom's body' (*HD* 17). At other times she wanders through the streets and parks of London, hungering for crowds to relieve her of the exercise of will. The occasional fling alleviates her loneliness, and also brings her closer, in her own imagination, to her husband – any man is more like Tom than no man. Her life improves when Connie, her new neighbour, falls upstairs, and Louie helps to gather up her scattered groceries. Butch, hard-boiled Connie is an ARP warden with a postbox mouth (a detail borrowed from the physiognomy of Wemmick in *Great Expectations*), which makes a comic contrast to Louie's vulnerable orifice. Although Connie has the courage to be 'a saviour of the human race,' she also has 'a tongue like a file, so that you could not take her to be the race's lover' (*HD* 148). Connie introduces Louie to newspapers, which provide the orphan with a smörgåsbord of pre-packed selves, analogous to the fictions of boyishness plastered over Robert's walls. Living like her author 'with every pore open,' Louie soaks up propaganda like a sponge; in fact, Connie bosses her to watch her pores because she lacks 'a London skin' (*HD* 243).

Louie's subplot coincides with the main plot in chapter 12, when she bumps into Harrison and Stella at a restaurant 'which had no air of having existed before tonight' (*HD* 225). In this surreal environment, Stella's eyes are finally opened to her lover's treachery, and accordingly the visibility of objects becomes overpowering. In particular, Harrison's eyeballs are subjected to microscopic scrutiny, as Stella searches for the source of their strange discord in their reddened rims, feathering veins, 'whitish whites,' and eyelashes surprisingly unsinged by cigarettes. Wherever Stella turns her gaze, detail takes on 'an uncanny salience.' So exhaustive is the inventory that the author even breaks her usual silence about food, scouring the remains of Harrison and Stella's half-eaten lobster mayonnaise with sickening exactitude. In this cruel light – crueller than the naked bulbs account for – 'there survived . . . not one shadow: every one had been ferreted out and killed.' With its garish lighting and its air of transience, the restaurant resembles an interrogation chamber: 'What a lie-detecting place this is,' Stella exclaims (*HD* 225–7). Over the neglected lobster Harrison informs her that he knows exactly when she tipped off Robert, because her lover changed his beat the following day. 'So now,' Harrison corkscrews, 'you know I know' (*HD* 232). At this point Louie blunders into the fray, under the flimsy pretext of retrieving her dog, which she hastily names 'Spot' although it has no spots and actually belongs to someone else (*HD* 235). Stella has just decided to purchase Robert's safety by giving in to Harrison's sexual demands. Yet unaccountably, Harrison rejects her offer, and shoos both women out into the night.

'Elizabeth came to see me in the morning and brought me a cyclamen,' Charles Ritchie writes on 11 January 1942.

> She talked about women's friendships, apropos of Virginia Woolf and her niece and Jane Austen and her niece, Fanny Knight. She says that every

young woman has such friendships and that the older woman puts into them all the lyrical, poetic side of her nature and that she lives her youth again. The girl finds so much pleasure in being seen through the eyes of love and admiration that she may have a flirtation with a man simply for the pleasure of telling the other woman about it. This is all quite apart from Lesbianism.[53]

It has been noted already in this study that Bowen persistently pairs off girls with women – Emmeline with the experienced Cecilia, Sydney with Mrs Kerr, Portia with Anna, Eva Trout with Iseult Smith – but these relations are often more antagonistic than the author intimates (whether they are 'quite apart from Lesbianism' is also a matter of dispute). In these pairings, the younger woman tends to be verbally handicapped, the older gifted with articulacy, and their relation takes the form of a struggle for narration, the older woman striving to be author of the younger, the younger resisting this authority through silence or through counter-narratives. Chessman makes the intriguing suggestion that these doubled female figures represent Bowen's impulse towards a breaking of narrative form, but also her efforts to contain this impulse.[54]

In *The Heat of the Day,* these opposing impulses flesh themselves out in the form of Louie and Stella. Scabbed with lipstick, Louie's mouth is made for blurting, bleeding, or 'incontinence,' but not for speaking – 'I have no words.' Nonetheless the young girl feels 'crowded to death' by the unarticulated feelings trapped inside her. Stella, by contrast, speaks 'beautifully' (*HD* 245). When both women are cast out by Harrison, the tongue-tied and the eloquent move towards interpenetration in the darkness:

> Louie felt herself entered by what was foreign. She exclaimed in thought, "Oh no, I wouldn't be *her*!" at the moment when she most nearly was. Think, now, what the air was charged with night and day – ununderstandable languages, music you did not care for, sickness, germs! You did not know what you might not be tuning in to, you could not say what you might not be picking up: affected, infected you were at every turn. Receiver, conductor, carrier – which was Louie, what was she doomed to be?

> (*HD* 247–8)

In the event, Louie is 'doomed,' or blessed, to be the 'carrier' of the next generation, when she is impregnated by an unknown soldier. Yet the pregnancy is convolutedly attributed to Stella, specifically to Louie's being 'affected, infected' by the misreported story of Stella's role in Robert's death. At the inquest Stella protects her lover from disgrace by sacrificing her good name, and allows the newspapers to paint her as a tramp, the same story formerly promulgated by her in-laws. Louie, initially disillusioned in her idol, comes to think of Stella's fall from grace as permission to imitate her promiscuity. In this circuitous sense, the pregnancy stems from the accidental union of the women in the night, and from Louie's need to find an author for her own existence, a story to provide her with a role.

We have seen how Bowen evades the traditional marriage-plot, often by killing off the would-be groom; in this novel she also kills off the prospective father.[55] Just before Connie plans to break the news of Louie's pregnancy to Tom, a telegram arrives with the message that the young man has been killed in action. The last time we see Louie, she is proudly wheeling her baby, Thomas Victor, in a second-hand pram: 'every day she saw him growing more like Tom' (*HD* 330). In a sense this baby, born of the porosity of war, is Tom's son as much he is anyone's – he is a product of the breakdown of the walls of consciousness, the leakage and contagion of identities.[56] From an-other perspective the baby is the product of the verbal intercourse between the older and the younger woman, for Louie is 'entered' by Stella's beautiful speech, much as the Virgin Mary is entered by the word of God. The baby, like the novel, is created by the confluence of the divided impulses the women represent – the union of eloquence and inarticulacy – a union strained to breaking-point throughout the text in Bowen's notoriously twisted syntax, which spares no effort to avoid a 'direct hit.' When her editor questioned some of the con-tortions, Bowen replied: 'I'd rather keep the jars, "jingles" and awkwardnesses – e.g. "seemed unseemly", "felt to falter". They do to my mind express something. In some cases I *want* the rhythm to jerk or jar – to an extent, even, which may displease the reader.'[57]

The only eligible man to survive Bowen's massacre of husbands, lovers, and fathers is Harrison. Why does Harrison turn Stella down? Even when she offers herself freely after Robert's death, Harrison rejects the overture. It is hard to understand why Stella, now be-trothed to an Anglo-Irish cousin, should wish to bed a man that she supposedly detests – unless she has fallen for her sexual blackmailer (like the heroine of Middleton's *The Changeling*), or feels the need to be the author, rather than the victim, of his plot. But it is even harder to explain the vicissitudes of Harrison's desire. In their final interview, Stella describes Harrison as 'love's necessary missing part,' the shadowy third that both abetted and destroyed her trance with Robert. Were Harrison's desire to be satisfied, he would cease to represent the lack that drives the narrative, the absence that sustains its central love affair. Conversely, Stella comes to realise that Robert played the 'necessary missing part' in her inconclusive dance with Harrison. Without Robert, she tells Harrison, 'you and I are no longer two of three. From between us some pin has been drawn out: we're apart' (*HD* 320). Unpinned by a third presence, twosomes fall asunder.

Although the two Roberts change places at the end, it is Harrison who usually takes the role of shadowy third. This is why he is 'a character "impossible"' – for he functions as an algebraic variable rather than a personality. As the other within, he is persistently associated with the telephone: Stella says he rings up 'like the Gestapo' (*HD* 33). Harrison is telepathic (literally 'far-feeling'), in that he always seems to know what Stella has divulged to others, but he is also telephonic – far-speaking and far-listening. Throughout the novel, the telephone intrudes into domestic space as a supplementary, incalculable third, both fetishised and feared. The fetishism is apparent when Stella fondles the receiver in the dark:

> with the unfumbling sureness of one who habitually answers a telephone at any, even the deepest, hour of the night. Her hand would have reached its mark before her eyes opened; before her brain stirred her ear would be ready, so that the first word she heard, even the first she spoke, would be misted over by some unfinished dream.
>
> (*HD* 44)

With telephones like that, who needs lovers? (although in this case she is speaking to her son). Much of the contact between lovers takes place over the telephone, but its 'demoniac ringing' also precipitates the traitor's death (*HD* 264). At the end of the novel Robert, dragooned by his family to Holme Dene to discuss the offer on the house, realises the authorities have found him out when he hears a telephone he never answers. It seems that the summons is itself the message: the ring alone reveals that he has been tracked down and singled out for execution. Nor is there any question that the call could be for someone else – he never asks for whom the bell tolls. This is odd because most callers to Holme Dene ask for Ernestine, whose telephone manner consists of 'a series of groans, warning hisses, and hydrophobic laughs' (*HD* 251). When Robert's call comes, his gassy sister surprisingly freezes to the spot. Yet Robert also fails to answer. By refusing to be hailed and subjected to the law, he steals a little time to die, as he has lived, equivocally.[58]

When the telephone rings, the outer world irrupts into the inner sanctum of the home. For this reason Bowen associates the telephone with the shadowy third: the outside that lurks within the inside, rendering autonomy impossible. Yet a ringing telephone demands an answer without conferring identity on either the caller or the called. Until the receiver is picked up, both parties to the dialogue remain unnamed, unknown: 'You did not know what you might not be tuning in to, you could not say what you might not be picking up . . .' What the ring represents is not a call to subjectivity, nor an invitation to exchange, but a summons to sheer exteriority, beyond the subject and beyond the reciprocity of human intercourse. This is why the telephone is linked to death, although it is also linked to the erotic. Bowen's characters are called to love as they are called to death, and the call comes not from the heart but from 'sheer "otherness,"' embodied in the telephone's peremptory, inhuman summons – 'the telephone stung an intact silence.'[59]

Bernhard Siegert has observed that 'telephone systems demand a third person, in whom first and second persons are grounded – namely, the exchange office . . .'[60] Harrison plays the part of this 'third person,' the operator who connects the first and second persons into networks of exchange. He is 'a character "impossible"' because he represents a switchboard rather than a personality, a link to a vast invisible bureaucracy. Similarly Robert is impossible because he represents a spy-ring rather than a single spy. Both spy-catcher and spy are merely functions of the global labyrinth of espionage; in futuristic terms, both are hooked into a worldwide web. Long-legged Harrison is the spider who can surf this web; lame-legged Robert is the fly who gets entrammeled in it. Yet by giving them the same first name, Bowen intimates a profound identity between the traitor and the spy: both are implicated in a system that renders individualities of character irrelevant.

When her flat was bombed in London, Virginia Woolf spoke of the 'exhilaration of losing possessions.'[61] How different this seems from Bowen's blind faith in the perseverance of tables and chairs. Yet Bowen's wartime fiction reveals a fierce division in her attitude towards furniture: on the one hand, a piety for solid things; on the other, an intoxicated dream of weightlessness. 'The violent destruction of solid things, the explosion of the illusion that prestige, power and permanence attach to bulk and weight, left all of us, equally, heady and disembodied' (*MT* 95). In *The Heat of the Day*, this 'freedom in nothing' is contrasted to Mount Morris, where Roderick is destined to be master of the furniture (*HD* 175). But Bowen makes it clear that the Big House, and the way of life enshrined in its magnificence, is dying out: 'all that's a thing of the past.' The reader never learns if it was wise to carry on the old tradition or to travel light.

Another wartime story that addresses this dilemma is 'Sunday Afternoon.' Henry Russel has taken a break from bomb-ravaged London to visit the Veseys in their ancestral house in neutral Ireland. The aging entourage, sitting on the 'sheltered edge of the lawn,' tacitly conspire to ignore the growing chill. They are dismayed to hear that Henry's flat and all his 'beautiful things' have been wiped out in the Blitz. A guest wonders 'how much of you *has* been blown to blazes.' Henry says he has no way of knowing: 'You may feel . . . that I should have preferred, at my age, to go into eternity with some pieces of glass and jade and a dozen pictures. But, in fact, I am very glad to remain. To exist.' Only Maria, 'young and savage,' can rejoice in the idea of living without furniture. She yearns for the excitement of a world at war, but Henry refuses to be party to her getaway. When he calls her attitude 'destructive,' she is surprised that he should mind: it was he, after all, who defended bare forked life against her elders' reverence for furniture. 'I still want the past,' he retorts. Yet suddenly he finds himself flooded by desire, both for the past and for the future, for the 'grace of the thing done over again' and for the charm of this young woman brutishly shaking off tradition. 'Your whole existence has been in contradistinction,' he warns her; in London she will have a number rather than a name, and experience atrocities for which there is 'no language' and 'no literature.' He insists on calling her Miranda, presumably because she is compelled to leave the magic island and to confront a brave new world of fire and blood (*CS* 616–22).

'It is a fact that in Britain, and especially in London, in wartime many people had strange deep intense dreams,' Bowen wrote in the Postscript to the American edition of her wartime stories. Such dreams were 'an unconscious, instinctive, saving resort' at a time when 'life, mechanised by the controls of wartime, and emotionally impoverished by changes, had to complete itself in *some* way' (*MT* 96). Bowen's famous story 'The Happy Autumn Fields' explores these compensatory dreams of plenitude. The narrative consists of two disrupted sequences, one set in the ruins of bombarded London, the other in the fields of the idealised past. The story begins with a family walking-party, the older daughters in long dresses and the sons in black, following their father in dynastic procession through his lands. The action is perceived through Sarah's adolescent consciousness: she is the far-feeling narrator, helplessly porous to the triumphs and tribulations of the group. Judging by the styles of apparel and address, the period is late Victorian, while autumn is the season Bowen usually elects for her fictional excursions into Anglo-Ireland. Here the cornfields have been stripped to stubble, and everything is falling – the foliage, the setting sun; the children 'go down like a pack of ninepins' when Emily stoops down to tie her boot, while the young boys, pretending to be shooting birds, rejoice 'in the imaginary fall of so many rooks.' Persistent references to rooks, to falling, to the stubble underfoot, and to the silence that closes in behind the company suggests that these are the Elysian fields traversed by a procession of the dead. At the rear of the cortege, Sarah and her younger sister Henrietta, 'still ankle-free,' long to be alone together, looking forward to tomorrow when their brothers will return to school. The sisters break file when two horsemen, like those of the apocalypse, thunder out of the distance. These are Fitzgeorge, heir to the estate, and Eugene, Sarah's suitor, who dismounts when he arrives, leading his horse between the sisters. Barred from the lovers by the horse, Henrietta begins to sing, and 'her pain, like a scientific ray, passed through the horse and Eugene to penetrate Sarah's heart.'

At this point a pain shoots through an outflung hand, and Mary wakes up to her bombed-out house, having struck a table with her knuckles in her sleep. Before she lapsed into her coma, she had disinterred a box out of the rubble, which contained the letters, yellow photographs, and diaries of a vanished family. These memorabilia, we are given to infer, conjured up the idyll of her dream. Yet the story never settles whether Mary is the dreamer or the dreamed. 'Saddled with Mary's body,' which she regards as someone else's, she is shocked to see a photograph of Sarah from the outside, since she knows her only from the inside. All sense of 'proprioception,' of owning and belonging to one's body, has been transferred from Mary into Sarah. Desperate to find out what happened to the sisters, Mary longs to stay asleep, while her fiancé Travis urges her to leave the house before its walls collapse around her. But Mary insists on seizing two more hours in the past; Travis retaliates by whisking off the 'dangerous box.' When the dream reopens, the family has retired to the drawing-room. Here every object seems to 'quiver' on the brink of falling, as if the merest breath, let alone a bomb, would bring down these possessions like a pack of ninepins: 'Sofas, whatnots, armchairs, occasional tables . . . all stood on tottering little feet.' Yet precarious as they seem, the 'towering vases,' high-perched ornaments, and piled albums 'all had, like the alabaster Leaning Tower of Pisa, an equilibrium of their own.' In this room, the narrator insists, nothing will ever fall or change, for everything is 'muted, weighted, pivoted by Mamma.' The dream breaks off with Eugene on the point of sending for his horse, his love still undeclared and Sarah speechless with foreboding.

Another explosion rocks the house in London, snowing plaster dust over the sleeping woman. Waking up, Mary realises that her survival has ensured the obliteration of the past: 'The one way back to the fields was barred by Mary's surviving the fall of ceiling.' When Travis returns with a taxi, Mary mourns the lost intensity of that-which-was, for that-which-is seems nothing but a paltry imitation of her dream: we 'know inconvenience now, not sorrow. Everything pulverizes so easily because it is rot-dry; one can only wonder that it makes so much noise . . . All we can do is imitate love or sorrow.' She has been left with 'a fragment torn out of a day,' yet a fragment so replete with feeling that it discredits her existence in the present. The dead are more alive than she is; the living world, enshrouded in white dust, is ghostlier than the reanimated past. While Mary was asleep, however, Travis perused the contents of the box and found out how the story ended. He now knows that Mary cannot be descended, as she longs to be, from Sarah, for the symbiotic sisters both remained unmarried and probably died young. A letter from the eldest son Fitzgeorge refers to a young friend, presumably Eugene, who was thrown from his horse and killed, riding back from a visit to the family's house. 'Fitzgeorge wonders, and says he will always wonder, what made the horse shy in those empty fields.'

What made the horse shy? Was it the 'ray' that Henrietta shot through horse and horseman to her sister walking by the other flank? 'No one will ever be quite alone with Sarah,' Henrietta later warns Eugene – there will always be a third walking beside them. 'Whatever tries to come between Sarah and me becomes nothing' (*CS* 671–85). In the event Eugene never came between them, and neither sister was obliged to abandon the other for a man. The happy autumn fields represent not only the historic past but the idealised world of child-hood, unravaged by the blitz of sexuality. 'Childhood is the kingdom where nobody dies,' wrote Edna St Vincent Millay; in childhood, the

171

sky does not fall down, and the maternal gaze holds every tottering object in its place. But the horse that comes between the sisters on their walk betokens the incursion of a principle of separation, associated both with sexuality and death, specifically with death by falling. Moreover, the horse's narrative function is to separate the dreamer from her vision: the first instalment of the dream dissolves with the arrival, the second with the merest mention of the horse. Like a Lawrentian stallion, the horse stands for the forces of desire and aggression that overturn the world of innocence, toppling the furniture of childhood.

Caught in the ruins of the present, Mary projects on to the past her fantasies of plenitude and equipoise; yet the dark horse indicates that paradise has already begun to fall. The horse that throws its rider in the empty field proves that terror can rise up without a bomb. Yet this rebellious horse is also reminiscent of Pegasus, the winged horse of poetry: it stands for the creative force that smashes the traditional furniture of narrative, engendering a violent new style. In this story, past and present blast into one another, shattering the unity of either scene, and tearing down the walls of personal identity. The aging company in 'Sunday Afternoon' agree that the bombing has no place in human experience: 'It will have no literature' (*CS* 618). 'The Happy Autumn Fields' proves this verdict wrong. Yet the story's splintered form suggests that the literature of such a cataclysm can no longer rely on the old certainties of time or place, nor on the continuity of consciousness. A literature of bombing has to bomb itself into existence, demolishing the rot-dry fabric of the past. As Pepita says in 'Mysterious Kor', 'If you can blow whole places out of existence, you can blow whole places into it' (*CS* 730).

Notes

1. Charles Ritchie remembers Bowen using this phrase to describe the swans in Regent's Park in his diary entry of 2 June 1942, in *The Siren Years*, p. 143.
2. In a previous version of the novel, entitled *Anna*, the eponymous heroine has a crush on a heterosexual St Quentin, who gives her a lecture on style similar to that which the gay St Quentin delivers to Portia in *The Death of the Heart*. The earlier St Quentin's most memorable advice concerns the treatment of sex: ' "Another point" said St Quentin, turning her way and raising his voice austerely "don't try and

debunk sex. If it doesn't fuss you, it ought to. What has been good enough for a lot of right-feeling people ought to be good enough for you. What do you know about it, anyway?" ' In revising the novel Bowen seems to have split the original St Quentin into the two figures of St Quentin and Eddie, both of whom are novelists and sexually ambiguous, while splitting the original figure of Anna into Anna and Portia (Fragment of a novel *Anna*, ch. 4, HRHRC).

3. Cited in Glendinning, *Elizabeth Bowen*, p. 85.
4. Harriet S. Chessman, 'Women and Language in the Fiction of Elizabeth Bowen,' pp. 78–80. I refer to the original version of this essay because Harold Bloom has unhelpfully removed the scholarly apparatus in his reprint in *Elizabeth Bowen*.
5. David Trotter discusses Portia's mess in *Cooking with Mud: The Idea of Mess in Nineteenth-Century Art and Fiction*, pp. 6–7.
6. Glendinning, *Elizabeth Bowen*, p. 124.
7. Ibid., p. 50.
8. Ann Ashworth, ' "But Why Was She Called Portia?" Judgment and Feeling in Bowen's *The Death of the Heart*,' pp. 159–66.
9. Chessman, 'Women and Language,' p. 78.
10. See Ashworth, ' "But Why Was She Called Portia?" ', p. 160.
11. Freud, *Fragment of an Analysis of a Case of Hysteria* (1905), SE, vol. 7, pp. 3–122.
12. Although described by Major Brutt as 'a rare bird,' Pidgeon's name suggests the commonest of flying vermin. On the other hand, carrier-pigeons were used to send messages in the trenches during World War I, which links Pidgeon to the theme of circulation.
13. The following discussion is indebted to the 'Major Brutt Special' issue of Bennett and Royle (eds), *The Bowen Newsletter* 1: 2 (1992) pp. 4–6.
14. Freud, *Three Essays on the Theory of Sexuality* (1905), SE, vol. 7, p. 222.
15. See René Girard, *Violence and the Sacred*, p. 75.
16. O'Faolain, *The Vanishing Hero*, p. 173.
17. See Claude Lévi-Strauss, *The Elementary Structures of Kinship* (1949; revised edition 1967), trans. James Harle Bell and John R. von Sturmer, ed. Rodney Needham (Boston: Beacon Press, 1969).
18. The following discussion is indebted to the 'Furniture Special' issue of *The Bowen Newsletter* 2: 1 (1993).
19. Bowen, 'Pink May' (1944), *CS* 712.
20. Andrew Bennett, 'Movables: Across *The Death of the Heart*,' *Bowen Newletter* 2: 1 (1993) p. 4.
21. See Susan Stewart, *On Longing: Narratives of the Miniature, the Gigantic, the Souvenir, the Collection*.
22. Chessman, 'Women and Language,' p. 78.
23. Alan Clark, quoting Michael Jopling, in *Diaries* (1993; London: Phoenix, 1994), p. 350.

24. Bowen, letter to Isaiah Berlin, Thursday, 23 September [1936] in Berlin Archive, Wolfson College Oxford.
25. Glendinning, *Elizabeth Bowen*, pp. 122, 125.
26. James Joyce, *Finnegans Wake* (1939; New York: Viking, 1967), p. 183.
27. Jacques Derrida makes great play with the polyvalency of the word 'style' in *Spurs: Nietzsche's Styles*.
28. Elizabeth Bowen, letter to Virginia Woolf, 5 January [1941], *MT* 216–17.
29. In Graham Green's Blitz novel *The Ministry of Fear* (1943), bombing is also associated with loss of memory. When a bomb-blast shocks the hero Arthur Rowe into amnesia, he enjoys a few months' respite from the tormenting recollection of his mercy-killing of his wife.
30. Freud, *Jokes and their Relation to the Unconscious* (1905), SE, vol. 8, pp. 64–5.
31. Broadcast interview with Jocelyn Brooke, 3 October 1950, HRHRC; cited in R. F. Foster, *Paddy and Mr Punch*, p. 103.
32. This splitting of the mother-figure resembles the fantasy described by Freud as the 'family romance,' which resurfaces in many fairy-tales and myths, whereby the true parents are replaced by richer or nobler alternatives. With the advent of sexual knowledge, when the child learns that maternity is certain whereas paternity is always hypothetical, 'the family romance undergoes a curious curtailment: it contents itself with exalting the child's father, but no longer casts any doubts on his maternal origin, which is regarded as something unalterable.' Instead the mother is projected into 'situations of secret infidelity and into secret love-affairs.' If 'Ivy Grips the Stairs' shows traces of the family romance, it also challenges the patriarchal bias of Freud's theory, for fathers scarcely feature in Bowen's story: instead, the mother is exalted in the form of Lilian, while she is also scripted into an illicit love-affair (Freud, 'Family Romances' (1909), SE, vol. 9, p. 239).
33. 14 February 1945 was the date of Bomber Harris's infamous 'Thunderclap' raid in which Dresden was destroyed in a firestorm.
34. Phyllis Lassner, *Elizabeth Bowen: A Study of the Short Fiction*, pp. 92–3.
35. Harold Bloom, Introduction to *Elizabeth Bowen*, ed. Harold Bloom, pp. 7–11.
36. In the later novel, the cliff-face of 'Ivy Gripped the Stairs' is replaced by the sea-wall, over which Mumbo disappears into the future.
37. Elizabeth Bowen, 'Notes on Eire,' FO 800/310, pp. 252, 255, 253. As mentioned in Chapter 1, p. 35, note 7, an ill-edited version of this report may be found in *'Notes on Eire': Espionage Reports to Winston Churchill, 1940–2*, ed. Jack Lane and Brendan Clifford. For an accurate transcription of extensive passages from Bowen's reports see Robert Fisk, *In Time of War: Ireland, Ulster and the Price of Neutrality 1939–45*.
38. Winston S. Churchill, speech to the House of Commons, 5 November

1940, cited in Fisk, *In Time of War*, p. 287; Bowen, 'Notes on Eire,' FO 800/310, pp. 257, 262.

39. Bowen, 'Notes on Eire,' pp. 265, 264.
40. See Foster, *Paddy and Mr Punch*, p. 103.
41. Bowen, 'Notes on Eire,' pp. 265, 264.
42. Fisk, *In Time of War*, p. 366n.
43. *HD* 90. This argument about the correspondence between the lovers' isolationism and Irish neutrality is indebted to Adam Piette's brilliant analysis of *The Heat of the Day* in *Imagination at War: British Fiction and Poetry 1939–1945*, pp. 171–2.
44. Robert L. Caserio, '*The Heat of the Day*: Modernism and Narrative in Paul de Man and Elizabeth Bowen,' p. 270.
45. Ernest Jones, 'The Psychology of Quislingism,' pp. 1–6.
46. Evelyn Waugh comments in his war novel *Put Out More Flags* (1942; Harmondsworth: Penguin, 2000) that the phrase 'fifth column' was 'just coming into vogue' (p. 120). The phrase, which came to mean a hostile infiltrator or an enemy within, referred originally to a group of Falangist sympathisers in Madrid during the Spanish Civil War who were prepared to join the four columns of insurgents marching on the city.
47. Elizabeth Bowen, letter to Charles Ritchie, March 1945; quoted in Glendinning, *Elizabeth Bowen*, p. 150.
48. See Gill Plain, *Women's Fiction of the Second World War: Gender, Power and Resistance*, pp. 176, 181.
49. See Karen Schneider, *Loving Arms: British Women Writing the Second World War*, pp. 78–9.
50. Ritchie, *The Siren Years*, p. 120 (entry of 22 October 1941).
51. Jones, 'The Psychology of Quislingism,' pp. 2, 6.
52. Chessman, 'Women and Language,' p. 69.
53. Ritchie, *The Siren Years*, p. 131.
54. Chessman, 'Women and Language,' p. 75.
55. Smith, *Lesbian Panic*, p. 79.
56. It is worth noting that Roderick also feels he has 'three fathers – the defeated Victor, the determining Cousin Francis, the unadmitted stepfather Robert: there was a confluence in him . . . of the unequal three' (*HD* 312).
57. Letter to Daniel George, 2 June 1948, HRHRC.
58. Louis Althusser argues that ideology constitutes subjects through '*interpellation* or hailing': see 'Ideology and Ideological State Apparatuses,' in *Lenin and Philosophy and Other Essays*, trans. Ben Brewster (New York: Monthly Review Press, 1971), p. 174.
59. *HD* 318; *FR* 45.
60. Bernhard Siegert, 'Switchboards and Sex: The Nut(t) Case,' p. 81.
61. Virginia Woolf, *A Writer's Diary*, ed. Leonard Woolf (New York: Harcourt Brace Jovanovich, 1982), p. 343 (20 October 1940).

6

Incubism: A World of Love
and The Little Girls

In Bowen's World War II story, 'The Demon Lover' (1941), Kathleen Drover returns to her shut-up house in London and finds an unstamped envelope waiting for her in the hall. Inside is a letter signed only with a 'K,' the initial of her own first name. Yet Mrs Drover instantly identifies the sender as her former fiancé, who had terrorised her into an engagement before he disappeared in World War I: 'She could not have plighted a more sinister troth.' Now he has come back in World War II to remind her of her promise to meet him 'at the hour arranged.' Desperate to avoid this revenant from her past, Mrs Drover jumps into a taxi. But at the stroke of seven o'clock, the driver brakes, and Mrs Drover, jolted forward, meets his eye. She starts to scream, while the taxi whirls her through the hinterland of deserted streets, 'accelerating without mercy' (*CS* 661–6).

In Bowen's postwar novels *A World of Love* and *The Little Girls*, the characters also find themselves driven by demons from the years preceding World War I. Both these novels excavate the world of Bowen's childhood, before the wars mowed down two generations: *A World of Love* is set in County Cork, while the central section of *The Little Girls* returns to the Kentish seaside. Yet both novels take place largely in the present day: their theme is not the past itself, but the anguish of calling it to mind. In *A World of Love*, a cache of letters is discovered in the attic; in *The Little Girls*, an empty coffer is discovered in the ground. Both discoveries invalidate the memories on which the characters have founded their identities, breaking down the comforting but paralysing fictions of their lives. Bowen writes in an essay of 1950, 'The Bend Back': 'the past is veiled from us by illusion – our own illusion. It is that which we seek. It is not the past but the idea of the past which draws us' (*MT* 58).

The strange title of the present chapter is borrowed from Joyce, who gave the term 'incubism' to the style (or 'technic') of the 'Hades' episode of *Ulysses,* in which a Dublin drunk is buried in Glasnevin Cemetery.[1] Joyce never divulged what he meant by the coinage 'incubism,' which has yet to gain admission to the *Oxford English Dictionary,* but the word breaks down into several parts, each of which captures an important element of Bowen's later fiction. To 'incube,' an obsolete nonce-word, is to infix like a cube, to box in; the term could therefore be extended to encompass Abraham and Torok's notion of 'encryptment,' in which the lost object is boxed into the ego, entombed alive as in Poe's horror stories.[2] Technically, to 'incubate' is to sit on eggs; hence the term has come to mean to 'brood,' in the cogitative as well as the procreative sense. The obsolete word 'incubo,' stemming from the Latin term for a spirit that lies on a treasure to guard it, means a covetous man who broods over or jealously guards his wealth. But an 'incubus,' derived from a late Latin term for 'nightmare,' is a feigned evil spirit or demon, originating in personifications of the nightmare, which was supposed to descend on sleepers, and especially to seek carnal intercourse with women. An incubus can also refer to a feeling of weight or oppression on the chest or stomach during sleep – that is, to the weight without the thrill of the night visitor. The word 'incubism' therefore brings together ideas of sleep, death, and sexuality. It has to do with incubating that which is incubed, or reinvigorating that which is encoffined, as well as with the dreams gestating in the womb of sleep.

A World of Love and *The Little Girls* both explore the psychic consequences of 'incubing,' as opposed to burying, the dead: a process that results in an inability to come to terms with loss. Incubed, the lost object proceeds to incubate, hatching nightmares to oppress the living. In *A World of Love,* the characters are relics of the ascendancy, caught up in a sexual delirium about Guy Danby, the heir to their Big House, who died in World War I. Each of his survivors guards his memory like a miser squatting on a casket full of treasure. The women seem to be trying to remain asleep in the hope of being ravished by Guy's incubus; instead they find themselves oppressed by his dead weight, while burning with desire for their demon lover. In *The Little Girls,* the dead mother is incubed in the central flashback, a structure that harks back to *The House in Paris,* in which 'The Past' is boxed into the coffin of 'The Present.' Both *A*

177

World of Love and *The Little Girls* show that the lost object must be disincubed in order to be laid to rest: the work of mourning can begin only when the crypt is shattered and its secrets are released. Abraham and Torok claim that 'what haunts are the gaps left in us by the secrets of others.'[3] The central action of both these postwar novels consists of disentombing the secrets of the dead.

A World of Love returns to County Cork to pay a final valediction to the Big House and its vanished way of living. In *The Last September*, published twenty-six years earlier, the ascendancy had still displayed frenetic signs of life (or afterlife), the Big House buzzing with rumours, intrigues, and flirtations. Even the Troubles, by forcing the inhabitants of Danielstown into retreat, had intensified their 'centripetal life' (*BC* 20). In *A World of Love*, by contrast, whatever vitality remained in the Big House has long since been snuffed out. Montefort, the crumbling mansion that provides the setting for the novel, has grown so isolated that neighbours are amazed to discover it is still inhabited: 'No idea there was anyone living here,' marvels a local. At the bottom of its 'extinct avenue,' Montefort seems 'waiting, perhaps for ever, for its dismantlement to be complete.' Indoors, 'air had died,' while objects disappear behind the thickening dust; shreds of butterflies cling to the cornices, 'out of reach of the mop' (*WL* 30–1).

From the first sentence onwards, an oppressive feeling of belatedness descends over the scene: 'The sun rose on a landscape still pale with the heat of the day before' (*WL* 9). After the ascendancy, after the Troubles, after the World Wars, after 'the heat of the day' . . . the coded reference to Bowen's previous novel suggests that *A World of Love* represents an afterword, a postscript, even an epitaph to Bowen's former works, borrowing its 'heat' from the decomposition of past narratives. Not just the setting but the themes of former fictions reappear. As Hermione Lee has pointed out, there is a hint of self-parody about the way that Bowen pulls out her old tricks.[4] The first tableau, featuring a dilapidated house, a beautiful young woman dressed in a trailing Edwardian muslin gown, reading a letter as she leans against an obelisk, suggests the author has been rummaging around the attic of her own imagination – just as the character herself, Jane Danby, has dredged her 'anachronistic' dress out of a coffer in the eaves (*WL* 10). One is reminded of the opening of Beckett's *Murphy*: 'The sun shone, having no alternative, on the nothing new.'[5] In Bowen as in Beckett, everything has been done, worn, felt, shone upon, and written about before. Even Bowen's fresh untried young heroine is dressed in some forerunner's yellowing clothes.

The opening scene conveys the impression that the novel is set in the past, specifically in the 1920s, when Lois Farquar made her first appearance in *The Last September* costumed in a frilly white berib-boned dress. But Jane Danby, although dressed in Lois's clothes, is a creature of the modern age, soon to abandon Montefort to its ruins. Her uncanny beauty mystifies her family – where did it come from? Neither of her parents, Fred or Lilia, seems equal to the miracle. Their marriage was a shady deal, cooked up by Antonia, the owner of Montefort. In her youth, before Antonia became the bitter, hard-drinking, heavy-smoking, yet surprisingly appealing cynic that we meet, she had fallen in love with her first cousin Guy, the heir to Montefort. Guy was killed in action in World War I, leaving a broken-hearted fiancée called Lilia, a 'wonderful golden willow of a girl' (*WL* 14). Guy having left no will, Antonia felt duty-bound to find a niche for Lilia, but the querulous girl, her early beauty faded, could not make a go of anything. At her wit's end, Antonia decided to offer Montefort to her illegitimate cousin Fred Danby on the three con-ditions that he marry Lilia, maintain the house, and allow Antonia free access to its finest quarters. Surprisingly, Fred accepted the bribe. Unknown to Antonia, he discerned, or fancied he discerned, the girl that Guy loved in the flaccid ravages of Lilia. His passion for her just outlasted the birth of their first child Jane. Now husband and wife sleep at opposite ends of the house, Lilia constantly complaining of fatigues and worries, and Fred forever bowing out, leaving the house in the command of women. In the interim a second child has been born, the eccentric Maud, a budding religious maniac who calls down vengeance on the house and deplores her father's abdication of the role of patriarch. The remaining members of this household are invisible, but absence merely intensifies their influence. Guy is dead, although 'a little thing like that wouldn't bother him' (as Robert Kelway says of Cousin Francis's death in *The Heat of the Day* (*HD* 160)). Maud has an imaginary adversary called Gay David, described by her family as a witch's 'elemental' or 'familiar' (*WL* 143, 41). Her scuffles with this 'dream companion' bring to the surface her family's un-conscious battle of attrition with the dead (*WL* 94).

This peculiar set-up at Montefort has lasted twenty-one years, trapping the characters, both absent and present, into a suffocating mutual dependency. Lilia wilts under the life in Montefort, but has 'ceased to more than dream of escape' (*WL* 14). It is difficult to tell who holds the power or the purse strings: Fred and Lilia dangle on Antonia's caprices, yet every year their patroness drifts further into their debt. The consequence is paralysis for all concerned. When the novel opens, the closeness of the household is exaggerated by a heatwave; everyone droops, mopes, faints under the sweltering atmosphere. It is not just the weather that oppresses them, however, but uncompleted mourning for the dead. Guy is not yet dead enough to let the household live; his 'unlived life' consumes the energy of his survivors. 'The living were living his lifetime' (*WL* 45).

Virginia Woolf, in her autobiographical fragment 'A Sketch of the Past,' describes herself as 'held in place' by the unseen forces of the dead: 'it is by such invisible presences that "the subject of this memoir" is tugged this way and that every day of his life; it is they that keep him in position.'[6] Similarly, it is the dead that keep the living in position in *A World of Love*, indeed the word 'guy' means a rope, chain, or rod used 'to secure or steady anything liable to shift its position or to be carried away' (*OED*).[7] In *A World of Love*, however, all the characters are mis-positioned; Guy's death resembles old Quayne's downfall in *The Death of the Heart* insofar as it reshuffles his survivors like 'a pack of cards' (*WL* 61). Fred has taken Guy's place as Lilia's husband and master of Montefort, however unconvincing his performance of these roles. Antonia, having inherited Montefort in Guy's place and assumed his responsibility for Lilia, has now unloaded these burdens on to Fred, reducing him into the proxy of a proxy. Fred, in his short-lived passion for Lilia, attempted to assume Guy's place by emulating his desire: 'Thought there ought to be something in Guy's girl,' he says (*WL* 104). Maud's imaginary sidekick Gay David also takes the place of Guy, as indicated by the echo of the names; in fact a telling misprint conflates the two into 'Guy David.'[8] And Antonia entertains the fantasy that Fred and Lilia are merely surrogates for Jane's true parents, Guy and Antonia herself: '*Our* blood, [Guy's] and mine . . . roundabout by way of the byblow Fred' (*WL* 80).

This cooped-up family, with its criss-crossing desires, suggests that the taboo against incest is at risk: a danger made explicit in Fred's festering passion for his daughter Jane, and somewhat less explicit in the miasma stifling the house – the same atmospheric symptom that descended on Thebes in retribution for Oedipus's crime. Bowen, like Lacan, imputes the weakening of the taboo to the dereliction of the father: the death of Guy seems to mean that no one else can be a full-fledged 'guy,' or accede to the position of the patriarch. 'I was never Guy,' Fred confesses (*WL* 103). Fred is treated by the family much as Joseph is treated in Renaissance Nativity paintings, where everything is set up to dispel the notion that he could really be the father. 'Now you tell me this: who's your father?' a new acquaintance demands of Jane – but her answer is never divulged (*WL* 64). This is the same question that Athena puts to Telemachus in *The Odyssey*; his reply is that he cannot say, for no one knows for certain who his father is.[9] In *A World of Love*, however, these haunting doubts about paternity are bound up with the love letters incubating in the attic.

In the opening scene of the novel, when Jane makes her dazzling appearance by the obelisk, the letter she is reading comes from Guy. To whom this letter was originally addressed is another question, never satisfactorily answered: 'And now these letters. To whom, why?' (*WL* 96) Poking round the attic, Jane discovered a packet of Guy's love letters incubed in the same trunk as the muslin gown. These letters, 'headed by the day-names only – "Tuesday," "Saturday," and so on,' had been removed from their envelopes, making it impossible to trace their sender or their addressee: 'nothing showed where they had been written or when posted' (*WL* 33). Yet Jane felt entitled to read them. If she discovered the dress, the letters discovered her; indeed, she is convinced that they demanded to be liberated. 'She gloried in having set free the dress. But the letters – had they not insisted on forcing their own way out?' (*WL* 35). A glimpse of the word 'obelisk' caused her to snap the band holding the package together, so that the letters spilled out 'showering' around her (this image alludes to Antonia's idea that Jane was conceived in 'a shower of gold') (*WL* 34, 81). Having fallen 'in love with a love letter,' Jane dreams that she herself is Guy's intended audience, and that his 'letter had been no more than delayed on its way to her' (*WL* 39, 48).

The whole household seems transfixed in the time-lag between the posting and delivery of Guy's love letters. None of the clocks at Montefort works, and no one cares what time it is, with the exception of Maud, who insists on listening to Big Ben strike the hour on the radio, presumably as a confirmation of all things phallic, patriarchal, 'absolute' (*WL* 129). When Jane says, 'Maud needs another battery,' it is momentarily unclear which needs to be recharged, the radio or Maud herself, in her aspirations for robotic authoritarianism (*WL* 84). Yet if Maud needs a new battery, her family also needs refuelling, arrested as they are in suspended animation until Guy's 'dead letters' have returned to circulation. The exhumation of the letters frees

Guy's ghost, who seduces Jane in everything but body. Given Antonia's view that Jane should have been Guy's daughter, one could say that Jane falls in love with her ideal father, ousting her mother as the presumed addressee of Guy's desire.

Bowen wrote a number of ghost stories, including 'The Demon Lover,' but *A World of Love* is the closest that she came to writing a ghost novel. Despite her penchant for the supernatural, the realist tradition of the novel operated as a kind of ghostbuster, debarring visitations from beyond. Yet even in *A World of Love* the ghost of Guy walks only once: he gatecrashes a dinner-party hosted by the Danbys' new neighbour, Lady Vesta Latterly, at the same time that he barges through the bounds of realism. As her name suggests, Lady Latterly has only lately come into a fortune, but 'better late than never,' as Antonia sagely observes (*WL* 57). This glamorous arriviste has taken possession of an 'unusually banal' Irish castle, long empty owing to disrepair: 'no one has stayed here long,' Jane says ominously (*WL* 57, 61). In the castle's better days, Guy had visited it frequently; tonight, invoked by Jane's utterance of his name, he assumes the empty place laid at the dinner-table for an absent guest. The assembled company, forming a 'circle of the displaced rich,' take part in a séance without knowing it, for the 'current [making] circuit' through these 'apt conductors' raises the young soldier from the dead (*WL* 67). 'Visible, and visible all at once, were the variations and contradictions, the lights and shades of the arrested torrent of an existence' (*WL* 68–9). Yet Guy materialises only when the others do not look at him directly: 'dominator of the margin of vision,' he vanishes when Jane looks straight across the table at his empty place (*W* 69). Moreover, he makes his appearance only when the dinner guests are drunk. W. J. McCormack links Bowen's Guy to Sheridan Le Fanu's Guy Deverell, and suggests that the return of Guy in *A World of Love* stands for the resurgence of Irish Gothic. Certainly the cobwebbed mansion, crumbling castle, hidden letters, and inquisitive young beauty of *A World of Love* derive from the classic repertoire of Gothic romance. But Bowen also mocks her Irish heritage by adding drink to the pastiche, substituting alcoholic bleariness for Celtic twilight.[10]

Nonetheless, Guy is a very literary ghost: incubated in the Gothic fictional tradition, he finally hatches out of a letter, reanimated by the act of reading. 'To whom does a letter belong?'[11] This teaser, posed by Jacques Lacan in his seminar on Poe's story 'The Purloined Letter,' also perplexes the characters of Bowen's novel. Do the rediscovered letters belong to their author? If so, their authorship remains disputable, for they are 'signed with a squirl,' rather than a name, and Jane marvels that 'one could tie up a "G" into such a knot' (*WL* 41–2). Guy, of course, is the 'knot' or 'not' that binds the characters to Montefort (like Mr Knott, the master of the house in Beckett's *Watt*), squirling them into each other's dreams. Do the letters belong to their recipient? Their addressee is even more uncertain than their sender. Or do these cinders of burnt-out passion belong to Antonia, because she owns the house and all its contents, despite the fact that she shrugs the letters off: 'Who said they were mine?' 'Everything in this house belongs to you,' Maud retorts (*WL* 107). No one knows who stored the letters in the attic: could their preserver have been Guy himself? If so, why did he save the letters that he wrote, rather than the letters he received? Perhaps because it is better to 'recall how it felt to love; to have been loved means a little less', as the narrator observes from the margins. Were these letters ever posted? Were they even intended to be sent? Perhaps they never had addresses, but were left 'lightly hidden' to ambush dozing princesses to come (*WL* 141).

Whatever their origins, the letters remain in Jane's possession only briefly before they start to circulate among the other characters; we soon learn that Guy himself was equally promiscuous. First Maud steals the letters from Jane's hiding-place (if ownerless objects can be stolen) and tries to flog them to her father for ten shillings. Fred reacts with unprecedented violence, shaking the child and restoring the letters to his wife, to whom, he supposes, they rightfully belong. But Lilia is not so sure: 'How could I ever bear to read them again; even if I did ever read them before?' she cries. 'What d'you want to know – whether they *are* to me? How am *I* to know after all these years, or indeed care? . . . What he's saying here well might not make sense to me any longer, whether it *was* to me or to who knows else' (*WL* 101). It turns out that Lilia has always known that Guy betrayed her; the last time she said goodbye to him, at the railway station, she caught him looking out for someone else. Antonia, who arrived at the station moments after Lilia made her shamefaced getaway, inter- cepted the same faithless glance. Thus both women separately dis- covered that Guy's gaze, like his letters, was always directed somewhere else, beyond the subject, beyond the fiction of reciprocal desire. There was always one look too many – like the look that Lilian Nicholson directs 'at nothing' in 'Ivy Gripped the Stairs.' Guy's roving glance, like his roving letters, intimates that desire is inevitably forwarded or posted on. Bowen's epigraph from Traherne expresses this insight in religious terms, suggesting that the characters' nostalgia for lost passion represents a longing for a world of love beyond the grave: 'there is in us a world of Love to somewhat, though we know not what in the world that should be . . .'

Guy's letters are addressed 'to somewhat', not to any known or recognisable beloved. These letters 'have no beginnings'; they 'simply begin,' without a salutation. Apart from the islanded word 'obelisk,' we learn almost nothing of their contents. Only one sentence is quoted in full: ' "*I thought*," he wrote, "*if only YOU had been here!*" ' (*WL* 48). This 'YOU' could be anyone or no one: the most we know is that its referent could not be 'here' or present at the scene of writing. The 'YOU' is a trap for narcissism: Jane, Lilia, Antonia would each like to believe that it is addressed to her alone. 'But here I am,' Jane protests, 'Oh, here I *am*!' (*WL* 48). In Bowen's fiction, however, love always bypasses the second person, reaching out to a shadowy third presence. There is always one guest too many at love's table.

If no one is strictly entitled to the letters, Maud still believes her father should take command of them. 'Father needed them more,' she tells Antonia. 'Whatever for?' Antonia demands. 'To put a stop to their being around.' Maud correctly perceives the circulation of the letters as a threat to patriarchal authority. Already dwarfed by Antonia's ownership of Montefort, Fred has now been further belittled by a cruising ghost. Maud explains:

> 'I have done my best; I have never not treated him as my father. I did my duty to him, and now you see. I've done all in my power to set him up as ruler over his own house, even when it's been your house, Cousin Antonia. His word ought to have been law, so I have very often obeyed him . . . I've been to a lot of trouble, honouring him. But in spite of all, there he went about, this last day or two, looking small. Why should I put up with that?'

Antonia cuts this conversation short, realising that 'to invite or to allow any more from Maud would be to get in irretrievably deep with the Old Testament.' But she reflects that Maud has 'put into power, one might say forced into being, a father-figure.' This is paradoxical because Maud behaves like 'a bandit,' constantly 'knocking other people about.' At school she has figured out 'not only how to begin but how to beget fights', although to her credit she leaves Catholics alone and confines her assaults to her co-religionists. Nonetheless she is 'the purest authoritarian.' If she is an outlaw, it is 'not out of contempt for law but out of contempt for its missingness from

Montefort' (*WL* 108–12). ('Yes. Yes,' Alfred Coppard wrote to Bowen. 'You *are* fond of mad little girls.')[12] In her championship of patriarchy, Maud seems to parody the Lacanian idea that the father stands for the law against incest, a law that assigns a name and position to members of the family and determines their possibilities of combination. Without this law, there is nothing to confine them to their places in the web of kinship, or 'to put a stop to their being around.' Guy's letters, 'being around,' at large and out of place, also jeopardise the sexual taboos of Montefort, implicating all the characters in an unconscious orgy with the dead.

When Fred restores the letters to Lilia, Jane catches sight of her warring parents briefly united in contemplation of the booty. Furious with envy, like a child spying on the primal scene, Jane feels she has been robbed of both her mother's lovers, Guy and Fred, in one fell swoop: 'She had lost her father . . . Yes, and in that comprehensive view through the arch she'd not only blundered upon a man and woman but perceived the packet upon her mother's wanton lap. Guy too, then, had finished his course here' (*WL* 119). Jane is wrong, however: Guy's course does not finish on her mother's lap, for his letters have several further circuits to complete. When Lilia rejects the letters, Fred deposits them in the hall, and Antonia is the next person in the chain to pick them up. She in turn leaves them in the kitchen for 'whoever's next' (*WL* 123). The last we hear is that the letters have been burnt, apparently at Antonia's request. But Kathie, the servant entrusted with their cremation, grew frightened when she 'found a name in them,' and passed them on to Jane. Thus Jane discovered the identity of the mysterious Beloved before she flung the letters to the flames. She reveals the name to Antonia, demanding that she pass it on to Lilia. But Antonia refuges to divulge it, informing Lilia instead that Jane has burned 'those letters from Guy to you' (*WL* 139). This evasion compares to the climactic lie in Joseph Conrad's *Heart of Darkness,* when Marlow tells the nameless 'Intended' that the last word Kurtz uttered was her name, whereas the cry he actually repeated was 'The horror! The horror!' Similarly, Antonia suppresses the horror of Guy's betrayal in order to protect Lilia's illusions, pretending that the last word detected in the letters was her name. 'If not the Beloved, what was Lilia? Nothing. Nothing was left to be' (*WL* 96).

Should Antonia's lie be regarded as a kindness or a cruelty? Antonia herself points out that Lilia has wasted her whole life playing the part of Guy's Beloved, a part both women have always known to be fraudulent. It is only when they both admit that Guy was 'untrue' that either can come back to life (*WL* 125). In their spellbound state, frozen to the dead yet also overheated by frustrated love, 'the transfixed women' resemble Bowen's preposterous description of the chimney-piece: 'Marble like a temple in a fever-swamp it stood, chilled off and haunted by the miasma' (*WL* 41; 117). Both jilted women have to touch Guy's letters and to pass them on in order for the chill to thaw, the heat to lift, the marble to return to motion. The circulation of the letters, although analogous to the transmission of a curse or a disease, also has a strangely curative effect: everyone who handles them is freed, to some degree, from the 'knot' that rivets them to Montefort. By the end, an exorcism has occurred. Antonia realises that Guy 'came back, through Jane, to be let go. It was high time' (*WL* 135). Lilia decides to take a trip to London, preceded by a visit to the hairdresser, which represents a seismic shift for this 'snow-woman,' formerly immobilised with gloom (*WL* 18). The novel concludes with a car drive to Shannon airport, where the Danbys pick up Lady Latterly's discarded boyfriend, Richard Priam, newly landed from his flight. When Richard first sees Jane, she is looking 'at nothing' – an ominous sign in Bowen's fiction – her 'collar up as though she expected the skies to fall.' But as soon as their eyes meet, they fall in love (*WL* 149). Thus the sleeping princess, awakened by a letter from beyond the grave, eventually rejects her mother's lovers, both dead and alive, and finds her destiny beyond the walls of Montefort. Her young lover (brand-new to Jane if 'latterly' a little used) falls from the sky like golden rain.

There are many ways in which the dead may suffocate the living, through the 'triumphant displacement of their air' (*WL* 65). But Bowen hints that those who die before their time remain alive at the expense of their survivors. Guy's life-in-death condemns posterity to 'death-in-life' (*WL* 78). *A World of Love* is a work of mourning – mourning not for one man only, nor even for one civilisation, but for the numberless young men who died before their time in two World Wars. In a painfully sad aside, Bowen tries to calculate the effect upon the living of these torn-off lives:

> it is hard . . . to see a young death in battle as in any way the fruition of a destiny, hard not to sense the continuation of the apparently cut-off life, hard not to ask, but *was* dissolution possible so abruptly, unmeaningly and soon? And if not dissolution, instead, what? This had been so, so far, for Antonia in the case of her cousin Guy: yes, though a generation was

mown down his death seemed to her an invented story. Not that it was
unlike him to be killed . . . but that it was unlike him to be dead . . .
death, yes, why not? – but deadness, no . . . It would be long before Guy
was done with life . . . these years she went on living belonged to him, his
lease upon them not having run out yet. The living were living his
lifetime; and of this his contemporaries – herself, Lilia, Fred – never
were unaware. They were incomplete . . . Meantime, another war had
peopled the world with another generation of the not-dead, overlapping
and crowding the living's senses still more with that sense of unlived lives.

(WL 44–5)

In one sense Guy was just a guy, a nameless casualty among the
decimated millions: 'Guy was Guy' (*WL* 82). In another sense he
functions as a guy or effigy, a symbol of his slaughtered generation; by
burning his letters, Jane burns an effigy in effigy. To Fred and Lilia,
Guy represents the 'third presence' that brought them together yet
also haunts their marriage with the unattainable illusion of a greater
love, much as the memory of Michael Furey haunts the married
couple in Joyce's 'The Dead.' Like Gabriel and Gretta Conroy in
Joyce's story, or Stella and Robert in *The Heat of the Day*, Fred and Lilia
can never be alone together: another guy is always hovering around
the 'margin of vision.' One way or another, everyone at Montefort has
been turned to stone by 'the annihilating need left behind by Guy'
(*WL* 76). Maud, batty though she is, gives expression to this need
more clearly than the others. By inventing 'non-dimensional Gay
David,' she conjures up an effigy of lack that she can persecute into
submission; the battle constantly renews itself, but Maud always
comes out 'on top' (*WL* 142–3). Maud's struggles with this phantom
correspond to Freud's account of the struggles of the ego to overcome bereavement, briefly discussed above in Chapter 4. According
to Freud, the ego initially refuses to acknowledge loss, but regresses to
infantile fantasies of cannibalism in an effort to devour or 'incorpo-
rate' the absent object. Yet the object, once devoured, preys upon the
ego in return, until the latter is 'totally impoverished.' In the normal
course of mourning, the ego disgorges the incorporated object, but
when mourning mushrooms into melancholia, the object over-
whelms the ego, driving it to self-destruction.

The symptoms of melancholia, as Freud describe them, exactly
match the psychic atmosphere of Montefort: 'a profoundly painful
dejection, cessation of interest in the outside world, loss of the
capacity of love, inhibition of all activity, and a lowering of the
self-regarding feelings to a degree that finds utterance in self-re-

proaches and self-revilings.'[13] Yet underneath this ennui burns a secret rapture. Anita Sokolsky observes of melancholia:

> The disconsolate and preoccupied mood that amounts at times to a kind of indolent stupor conceals an exultant sense that the seemingly vanished object persists . . . the melancholic refuses to accept a devastating loss even while seeming to grieve for it, sustaining the lost object in inchoate and mobile internal dramas that belie his or her mute and static posture . . . Because these subterranean narratives are scarcely registered, the melancholic seems indolent, whereas in fact he or she is living on a hectic if inaccessible level.[14]

Similarly, Montefort's inmates present themselves as hectic and indolent, heated and 'chilled,' fevered and marmoreal at the same time. Their lassitude conceals their exultation: if they seem dead, it is because they are preoccupied with keeping Guy alive.

In Maud, this subterranean narrative rises to the surface, the inside literally erupting on the outside when she breaks out in a rash of hives. Meanwhile her tussles with Gay David externalise the psychic tug-of-war of melancholia. During the final car drive to the airport:

> Maud's duality as a passenger became oppressive . . . Each time the child slid down on the seat she'd seemed to be dragging with her another entity, whom she kept down with her in a grapple; and each time she'd reared herself up again she'd done so with an oblique bullying hoist, forcing whatever it might be to sit still more erect, take still more furious notice than she had decided to do herself. She and her familiar would have been matched but that Maud just always came out on top. This preoccupation with Gay David, whose chastening if mind-broadening outing the afternoon evidently was, had relieved the others of much of Maud, at least up to now; but it had rattled Harris [the driver], particularly up here in the mountains . . . unnatural occupancy of his van he had not foreseen, nor would he stand for it.
>
> (*WL* 143)

In this claustrophobic space, emblematic of the psychic terrain of Bowen's fiction, 'the hard law of present-or-absent [is] suspended' (*DH* 148). Both there and not there, Gay David enables Maud to stage her family's fiercely divided feelings towards the dead. If Maud always comes out on top, it is because she has created a symbolic substitute for lack, whereas her family is stuck in the tautology: 'Guy was Guy.' Yet the name of Maud's familiar, 'Gay' David, insinuates that Guy – on the contrary – was gay. The dead man's letters to a nameless correspondent, suggestive of the love that dare not speak its name, together with his final wayward glance, hint that Guy's desire was addressed elsewhere: perhaps to guys. Whatever the object of his roving eye, Guy was 'untrue,' not only to his women but more importantly to their idea of him. Guy was not Guy, not the guy they took him for, and their recognition of his otherness enables them to live, and him to die.

Psychoanalysts have argued that Holocaust survivors can come to terms with their experience only by recreating it in a symbolic form.[15] When the symbolic function is impaired, the literal event seems nothing more than 'an invented story' (*WL* 44). In *A World of Love,* the circulation of Guy's letters reactivates this process of symbolisation. As the letters pass along the chain of Guy's survivors, they restore what Lacan calls the 'signifying chain'; that is, the capacity for substitution and exchange.[16] The frozen postures of this household – the Beloved, the Male Rival, and the Jilted Third – finally break down, allowing genuine relationships to re-emerge. Speaking of Lilia's love affair with Guy, Jane asks, 'Couldn't it be a destiny to be someone something had once happened to?' 'But more has happened to me than that,' her mother replies. 'For one thing, there was your father' (*WL* 92). After a lifetime of playing the 'Beloved' that she never was, Lilia finally recognises what she has and is. If her marriage survives, its future will belong to the living rather than the dead.

As a work of mourning, *A World of Love* grieves not only for its absent hero and his murdered generation, but also for the kind of novel that Bowen will never write again. The narrative itself, like the melancholy world of Montefort, seems frozen and febrile at the same time. There is a strong impression that Bowen's story lines have petrified, whereas her syntax has overheated to the point of breakdown, producing such contortions as 'Mush for the chickens, if nothing else, was never not in the course of cooking . . .' (*WL* 21). We have seen how Bowen describes the apparent choices of the artist as the 'enforced return' of glorified addictions (*MT* 53). In *A World of Love,* however, these addictions have begun to atrophy into strangulating mannerisms. The exorcism of Guy gives thematic form to Bowen's need to exorcise the ghost of her past works, a ghost that asserts itself as early as the opening sentence of the novel: 'The sun rose on a landscape still pale with the heat of the day before.' Familiar figures from her former novels rise again: the kid and the cad return as Jane and Guy, while the wicked older woman, epitomised by Madame Fisher in *The House in Paris,* re-emerges as the battle-scarred Antonia. To exorcise these spectres, Bowen takes mercy on them.

Jane survives her encounter with the cad, her heart awakened rather than destroyed. Fred and Lilia survive Antonia's manipulations, re-united without blackmail in the aftermath of passion, their marriage still aglow with 'the heat of the day before.' Antonia survives Guy by re-directing the letters to Lilia, even though they were written by anyone for anyone. Only by giving them a signature and an address can she 'put a stop to their being around,' or condense the omni-present influence of Guy to human size, reducing him from a miasma to a man.

Guy may have been a three-timer or four-timer, a closet homo-sexual, a liar and a cheat, but his betrayal opens up a world of love unbounded by a subject or an object. It is such a world that Bowen evokes in the first scene of the novel, in which heat, light, bodies, faces, rocks, and buildings melt into one another, dissolving the distinctions between human and inhuman, mind and matter, life and death: 'The half-asleep face of Montefort was at this hour drowned in early light.' This light breaks down the boundaries between solid objects, casting its 'coppery burnish' wantonly over 'flowing fields, rocks, the face of the one house and the cliff of limestone over-hanging the river.'[17] Its pervasiveness suggests that love is not a letter addressed by a single 'I' to a single 'YOU,' but 'a thinning of the membrane between the this and the that.' If Guy was not Guy, then neither was Antonia Antonia, nor Lilia Lilia: the novel hints that such identities are narcissistic traps that incube the movement of desire. The 'transfixed women' come to recognise that lovers come and go, but that a world of love remains within them and around them: 'a new world – painted, expectant, empty, intense' (*WL* 9–10). While love inevitably flees, abandoning both lover and beloved, it translates itself into another intensity. This is the solace Yeats offers to the aging beauty in 'When You Are Old':

> When you are old and grey and full of sleep . . .
> Murmur, a little sadly, how love fled,
> And paced upon the mountains overhead
> And hid his face amid a crowd of stars.

After the publication of *A World of Love* in 1955, it was nine years before Bowen completed her next novel, *The Little Girls*. In the interim the only full-length book she published was *A Time in Rome*, a travelogue recounting her second visit to the city. On a subsequent tour, accompanied by a friend, Bowen insisted on using *A Time in Rome* as their guidebook, but the work would scarcely reassure the apprehensive tourist. Far from offering a streetwise navigation of the city, Bowen's memoir conveys an overwhelming sense of being lost. The first chapter, entitled 'The Confusion,' opens with a poignant image of the widowed novelist's discomfort, dining solo in a restaurant and wondering if it is impolite to read. The following pages record her struggles with the map, blown 'blindingly' into her face by gusts of cold spring wind; her inability to find her way, whichever guidebook she consulted; and her feeling of being 'a born stranger.' Most disturbing is her sense that memory has tricked her, for the city is not as she recalls. Many days elapse before the reality of Rome dislodges her stubborn recollections of its scenes.

> Ingrained pictures refused to be broken up; I had lived with them, lived on them . . . they had been "Rome" for me. What I recollected could not be found again: it had not existed. There came points when I wondered, where was my sanity? Memory must be patchy; what is more alarming is its face-savingness. Something in one shrinks from catching it out – unique to oneself, one's own, one's claim to identity, it implicates one's identity in its fibbing. Proust remarks, creative wrong-memory is a source of art. Good: but when it deceives one about a city this trickiness is a plague and the very devil. It succeeded in tying up Rome for me into unnecessary, dismaying knots.[18]

It is this 'wrong-memory' – at once 'the very devil' and the fount of creativity – that becomes the central theme of *The Little Girls.*

John Carey recently described Bowen as 'James with sex,' but this soundbite does both novelists injustice, since James is sexier, and Bowen less Jamesian, than Carey acknowledges.[19] To vary the formula, however, 'Proust without sex' more or less sums up *The Little Girls.* Yet the idea of a novel without sex verges on self-contradiction. Novels run on sex, their plot lines driven by desire: the reader's quest to know what happens next is both excited by and mirrored in the lover's quest for the beloved. Youth, with its desires and frustrations, galvanises narrative; the traditional hero of the European novel is the adolescent, cut loose from the stability of childhood and thrust into an undetermined future. In *The Little Girls,* however, Bowen defies this convention. Her protagonists – emphatically in the plural – are three women in late middle-age, whose affairs of the heart, such as they were, belong to the distant past. 'No one of the three of them – I think – is specifically to be termed "our heroine," ' Bowen wrote in her notes for a public reading of *The Little Girls*; indeed there are passages in which it is impossible to distinguish them from one another.[20] Dinah Delacroix, née Piggott, is an eccentric widow whose love-life is over, apart from a low-key attachment to her neighbour Frank Wilkins, a retired Major handy for odd jobs. Sheila Artworth, née Beaker, is married to a dull estate agent, the great clandestine passion of her youth having ended in her lover's death. Clare Burkin-Jones, briefly married to Mr Wrong, now runs a chain of gift shops called Mopsie Pye. Memory, rather than desire, stokes the action of *The Little Girls*; the force that motivates the narrative is the urge to recover the forgotten past, rather than to couple men and women in the future. The novel intimates that the deepest affections of our lives take root, not in the pangs of youthful passion, but in the careless sociability of childhood. Sex, Dinah declares, is just 'a put-up job,' the 'one great centre of the prefabricated feeling racket' (*LG* 168). There is perhaps an echo here of E. M. Forster's *A Passage to India*, where Mrs Moore despairs of sex: 'centuries of carnal embracement, yet man is no nearer to understanding man.'[21]

'Proust without sex' is one way to describe *The Little Girls*; another way is 'Proust burlesqued.' The novel opens with a Proustian scene so contrived as to smack of parody. Dinah's latest craze is to bury tokens of *le temps perdu* in 'a sort of bear-pit . . . either a shallow cave or a deep recess – or, possibly, unadorned grotto?' (*LG* 9). This quotation typifies Bowen's late style, in which 'little questions flutter (like eyelashes?) across the text,' as Mary Ellmann has observed. These questions lend the prose a provisional, indeterminate air; and in this case the narrator's uncertainty suggests that this bizarre enclosure, reminiscent of Kafka's burrow, cannot be defined in language.[22] Dinah's cave, like the Freudian dream, is a place where words regress to things, and objects take the place of thoughts and feelings. Here Dinah secretes articles that people 'have obsessions about: keep on wearing or using, or fuss when they lose, or can't go to sleep without.' Among these objects are a pair of nail-scissors with the tip broken, a silver pencil with tooth-marks, and other apparently valueless mementoes. Dinah's whimsical plan is to incube these trifles as 'clues' or 'posers' for posterity, so that their contributors will be remembered as the oddballs that they were, not 'as a *race*' or 'stuck together in one lump.' Dinah explains: 'You know, a person's only a *person* when they have some really raging peculiarity' (*LG* 11, 14–15). It is worth remembering that these are Dinah's views, not Bowen's, whose contempt for 'Personal Life' remained the cornerstone of her conservatism. She informed Charles Ritchie in 'a dry voice': ' "Take it from one of the best living novelists that people's personalities are not interesting . . . except," she added, "when you are in love with them." '[23]

In *The Little Girls*, a neighbour's innocent question about Dinah's cave, 'Who's going to seal it up?' plunges its proprietor into Proustian recall (*LG* 16). All in a flash Dinah remembers her schooldays at St Agatha's, when the little girls Dinah (nicknamed 'Dicey'), Clare ('Mumbo'), and Sheila ('Sheikie') buried a coffer full of secrets in the school grounds. This involuntary rush of memory inspires Dinah first to dig up her old chums and later to enlist their help in digging up the long-forgotten coffer. 'Dinah, don't be fey!' Frank Wilkins begs; alas, his caution is ignored (*LG* 24). By advertising in the personal columns in the newspapers, Dinah succeeds in conjuring up her childhood companions, but 'in a way which *is* likely to annoy,' as Bowen later commented.[24] In the final section of the novel the three women, jokingly compared to the three witches in *Macbeth*, disinter the coffer, now buried in the grounds of a private house called the Blue Grotto. The coffer is empty.

For Dinah, this revelation triggers a breakdown. Returning home, she slips on the steps of her cave and suffers a concussion, as a consequence of which she loses interest in everything but loss itself: 'Nothing's real any more' (*LG* 163). One by one her resurrected friends, gathering around her sickbed, disincube the tragic compromises of their lives. Sheila, once a talented but ill-taught dancer, had 'too much to unlearn' to embark on a professional career (*LG* 172). Mumbo, once a child of promising intelligence, now sells knick-knacks, and never re-experienced the adoration that she felt for Dicey's mother, Mrs Piggott. Only Dinah seems to have avoided tragedy: the late Mr Delacroix is scarcely mentioned, and widowhood has merely granted greater license to her whims. It is telling that she has not aged; she and Frank, in their passionless camaraderie, are both described as overgrown children, 'a pair of ageless delinquents, whose random beauty was one of the most placid of their effronteries, or cheats: a cheating of Time. Nobody of their ages, it might be said, had any business to look as those two still did' (*LG* 12). Bowen commented: 'we are dealing with the remorseless simplicities of childhood – childhood at any age.'[25] But the blow that Dinah suffers, both physically and sentimentally, precipitates her into old age. In the last scene of the novel, she awakens from her lifelong spell, and insists for the first time on calling Mumbo 'Clare', a sign of resignation to maturity. Clare, meanwhile, acknowledges the humbling truth that 'we do not choose our company' (in the words of *The Death of the Heart*). Dinah may drive her crazy, but the little girls 'were entrusted to one another, in the days which mattered . . . Entrusted to one another by chance, not choice. Chance, and its agents time and place. Chance is better than choice; it is more lordly' (*LG* 236–7).

In her notes for a public reading of *The Little Girls*, Bowen played down the significance of the burial and exhumation of the coffer:

> The 'box' theme – *which I do hope may not be taken as* too *symbolic* is *far from being the whole of The Little Girls*
> It is, in fact, little more than the *spine* of the plot
> This is a story about identity.
> It is about the *involuntary* element in behaviour: 'Chance, not choice.'
> [. . .] Above all, it is a comedy – though, from time to time, possibilities of disaster come into view.

'A novel in terms of two times,' *The Little Girls* divides into three parts, the opening and closing sections taking place within the present, the middle section reverting to the past.[26] At the end of the first section, the news that St Agatha's, long since emptied of little girls, was bombed 'into thin air' during World War II prompts a flashback to the eve of World War I (*LG* 63). Here Bowen returns to the scenes of her childhood in Kent, specifically to 'Southstone,' the imaginary seaside town where schoolgirls once recited poetry, took swimming lessons, spent their pocket money on the High Street, and travelled free on buses (thanks to their school hats). This idealised picture of the past is a little 'claggy', to borrow Bowen's term of condemnation for anything she saw as sentimental, mawkish, or maudlin ('squashy' was another damning epithet).[27] In contrast to Bowen's former *enfantes terribles*, such as Theodora Thirdman or Maud Danby, the eponymous little girls are perilously cute. Yet the novel contains moments of great poignancy, particularly at the picnic that concludes the flashback, when the children meet for the last time before the War divides them for half a century. The little girls do not sense the oncoming catastrophe, but their elders do, and the mismatch between adult and childish perception is handled with great delicacy.

Especially touching is the scene where Dicey's enchanting, absent-minded mother bids farewell to Mumbo's father, Major Burkin-Jones (a scene presented in a different light in 'Ivy Gripped the Stairs,' when Admiral Concannon, the Dickensian humbug, dismisses Lilian with a lecture). The Major is leaving for the battlefields in which he will be killed; Dicey and her mother are moving to Cumberland for safety, where Mrs Piggott will perish of the Spanish flu that wiped out many survivors of the War. Present at the lovers' parting, Dicey witnesses a series of looks, gestures, and unfinished sentences whose import eludes her childish grasp:

> Still not far away from them he had stopped, turned and was standing. They saw him. He saw them, calmly and with great clarity. Was there more he wanted, could there be anything else? Mrs Piggott, though moving no more than he did, may have sent some wordless inquiry. He said: 'Just good-bye.' His eyes rested on their alike faces. 'God bless you,' he said to them – turned, and this time was gone.
>
> 'Mother?'
> 'Yes?'
> 'Why did he say that? He said – '
> 'I know, darling.'
> 'What made him? He – '
> 'I don't know, darling.'
> 'He never – '
> 'Oh, Dicey – *Dicey*!'
>
> So the child fell silent, sometimes rubbing her cheek slowly against the tussore of the coat sleeve, sometimes rolling her face round against it and breathing into it, with a low loving continuous snuffling sound. Where the warmth of the breath made its way through the stuff moisture remained.
>
> (*LG* 132)

Dicey is too young to understand these adult cues, but as Bennett and Royle have observed, 'her body registers the force of this intimate exchange.' Rubbing, rolling, snuffling, nuzzling, warming herself in her own moist breath, she acts out the unspoken desire of the adults.[28] The last glimpse we catch of the vanished world of 1914 is of Mumbo disappearing over the sea wall.

'Dinah, don't be fey!' Although many scenes are masterfully scripted, *The Little Girls* suffers from its story-teller's uncharacteristic inclination to be fey. In particular, the leading lady is so whimsical, her schemes so corny, that it is embarrassing to think that Bowen sympathises, let alone identifies, with Dinah. But the externality of the narration makes it hard to know where Bowen stands. Rejecting personality as a 'claggy' thing, Bowen strives to present her trio of heroines entirely from the outside, revealing nothing of their 'inner weather.' Evelyn Waugh once told Bowen he had no idea what his characters were thinking: 'I merely see them and show them.'[29] Showing without telling – this is what Bowen tries to do in *The Little Girls*, which she described as 'a story told in plain terms, without adumbrations or analysis.'[30] But this aloofness grates against her natural artistic tendencies. She even abandons the authorial commentary inherited from her great nineteenth-century predecessors, which culminated in the piercing wisdom of *The Death of the Heart.* The reader, stranded by the author, finds it difficult to know which side to take. Are we supposed to like Dinah, to enter with delight into her girlish pranks, or to dismiss her as a harmless if exasperating crackpot? No voice-over resolves the quandary. Like the aging little girls unearthing their coffer, the reader is obliged to dig for meaning in unrecognisable terrain, where familiar routes and landmarks have been overlaid by recent incongruous developments, the literary equivalents of the Blue Grotto – Waugh's archness, Pinter's spareness, or Compton-Burnett's use of dialogue, in which the voice of the narrator disappears.

At the time of writing *The Little Girls,* Bowen was reviewing contemporary fiction in a weekly column in *The Tatler,* in the 1950s a high-toned gossip magazine for the British upper class, where the bulk of articles on debutantes and polo were interspersed with improving updates on 'the arts.' A notorious soft touch as a reviewer, Bowen wrote on a wide range of fiction, usually giving her generous endorsement to works as far afield as Ivy Compton-Burnett's 'icy-sharp' studies of 'blood-relationship and its attendant psychological maladies,' Kingsley Amis's 'brash, bumptious and biting' satires, Eudora Welty's 'pungent, at times bloodcurdling but delicious comedy of America's spectacular Deep South,' James Joyce's 'giant, not always intelligible books,' and Ian Fleming's James Bond novels, the best of which in Bowen's view was *From Russia with Love.*[31] She also wrote admiringly of Rosamond Lehmann, Evelyn Waugh, Iris Murdoch, Rebecca West, and L. P. Hartley; while Georges Simenon and Margery Allingham ranked among her favourite detective novelists. In a review of Welty's *The Ponder Heart* in 1954, Bowen reflects on the paradox that the most innovative writers of the century have emerged from backward societies, including Ireland, still-feudal Russia, and provincial France, while Faulkner and Welty – 'two of the most outstanding writers of our times' – have arisen from the hinterland of the American South.[32] One of the few works of fiction that Bowen was snooty about was Storm Jameson's *A Cup of Tea for Mr Thorgell,* as a Tory, Bowen recoiled from its Marxism, and particularly from its savage satire of Oxford, which struck her as bad publicity for British institutions.[33]

While devouring the work of her contemporaries, Bowen was also attempting to modernise herself, relinquishing the Jamesian intricacies of her earlier work in favour of a leaner style, purged of melodrama: 'It's been too hot, you'll admit,' as Lilia says (*WL* 131). Facts are made to speak instead of feelings; lists of objects take the place of arpeggios of emotion. The pared-down world of *The Little Girls* leaves no room for tragedy, and spares the reader little of the unremarkable. Indeed the dialogue is sometimes ruthlessly banal. When Frank visits Dinah's sickbed, for example, he hears a murmur from her pillow:

> 'What?' he asked, furrowing his forehead.
> 'I said, "There you are." '
> 'I thought I would just look in,' he explained. 'How are you?'
> 'How are you?' she wanted to know.
> 'What's that pot of jam doing over there, Dinah?'
> 'Jelly. Mrs Coral. Where have you been?'
> Crying out inwardly 'Where have *you* been? – where are you now?' he went over to verify the Coral jelly, before answering: 'Oh, I've been about, you know. Round about.'
> 'Keeping an eye on things?'
> 'You might say so – yes'.
>
> (*LG* 225)

Words, words, words. Yet the very flatness of this conversation evokes the immensity of the unsayable. Bowen, unlike Waugh, cannot rid her characters of depth: we learn what Frank is 'crying out inwardly,' as well as what he says out loud. Frank and Dinah's lifeless blah suggests that conversation is itself a form of burial, where unasked questions are entombed in dusty answers to await an exhumation that never occurs. If Dinah strives to confer value on the everyday by incubing gewgaws in her cave, Bowen tries to do the same by incubing platitudes in prose. Her remorseless naturalism in *The Little Girls* intimates that survival is the opposite of heroism. Life is not an affair of passion, nor of obstacles and dangers overcome, but of endurance in the face of triviality. If memories of childhood seem to offer an escape route from the boredom of the present, the novel's denouement implies that the idealised past is nothing but an empty coffer. Nostalgia is the most prefabricated feeling of them all: whole industries, like Mopsie Pye, are dedicated to sustaining its false memory.

Yet Bowen's fascination with incubing objects goes beyond nostalgia; it verges on the passionate hoarding that Freud associates with anal eroticism. In Dinah's catalogues of keepsakes, Bowen parodies her own compulsive lists and inventories.[34] These lists include the contents of Dinah's garden, 'the miscellany of objects' in her cave, the china of Mrs Piggott's drawing-room, the merchandise in a

197

secondhand shop called Curios, the free samples collected by Sheila, the knickknacks for sale in Mopsie Pye, and the missing treasures in the coffer.[35] Bowen had already revealed an addiction to such lists in *The Heat of the Day*, with its obsessive breakdown of the spoils of Mount Morris:

> colourless billiard balls, padlocks, thermometers, a dog collar, keyless key-rings, a lily bulb, an ivory puzzle, a Shakespeare calendar for 1927, the cured but unmounted claw of a greater eagle, a Lincoln Imp knocker, an odd spur, lumps of quartz, a tangle of tipless tiny pencils on frayed silk cords . . . So much for the past . . .
>
> (*HD* 163)

In *Seven Winters* Bowen observes that 'it is things and places rather than people that detach themselves from the stuff of my dream' (*SW* 10). Nowhere is this mania for things more evident than in *The Little Girls*. Nor are these things valued only as mementoes, for the very process of collecting them destroys what Walter Benjamin would call the 'aura' emanating from their origin in place and time.[36] In Bowen's collections, the preservation of the past provides a flimsy pretext for the *jouissance* of sheer accumulation ('so much for the past . . .'). It is significant that only two of the 'extra-secret objects' incubating in the coffer ever had a bearing on the past: Mumbo's copy of Shelley, a poet she had 'given up,' and Sheikie's sixth toe, severed at birth (*LG* 188, 234). The other objects look forward to the future: a letter, written in blood in an 'Unknown Language,' antici-pates a reader yet to come; while a revolver awaits a murderee, destined to emerge in *Eva Trout* (*LG* 156, 115).[37] Yet even objects as dramatic as revolvers and amputated toes are reduced to junk in Bowen's lists. Like the miscellany, the list has a strangely levelling effect, undermining any hierarchy of significance.[38] Objects, although fetishised, are stripped of meaning: only the process of encrypting them, in coffers or in prose, transforms them into 'par-ticles of sadness.'[39]

As we saw in Chapter 4, the term 'encryptment', with its double meaning of entombing and encoding, has been adopted by the psychoanalytic theorists Abraham and Torok to reinterpret Freud's conception of mourning and melancholia. Where Freud argues that the ego deals with bereavement by internalising its lost objects, Abraham and Torok insist that there are good and bad ways of taking things in. The good way is through 'introjection,' whereby the ego articulates its loss in language, creating a verbal substitute for the lost object. The bad way is through 'incorporation,' in which the ego denies loss, devouring the object in fantasy rather than replacing it with words. According to Abraham and Torok, incorporation occurs when '*words* fail to fill the subject's void and hence an imaginary thing is inserted into the mouth in their place.'[40] Dinah externalises this process of incorporation by inserting relics into her cave, filling up its mouth with objects rather than expelling them in words. According to Abraham and Torok, incorporation is characterised by muteness: to open one's mouth, to speak the loss, would be to let the object go. To seal one's lips, by contrast, is to trap the lost object in the self, as suggested by the rude imperative 'shut your trap.' In this context, it is worth noting that Bowen refused ever to speak about her mother's death; her famous stammer, which began with her father's mental illness, consistently balked on the word 'mother.' This muteness could be understood as an attempt to keep the lost mother encrypted or incubed within the self. 'One is mute because preoccupied,' Sokolsky comments, 'occupied in advance, as it were, by the very figure whose loss one seems to mourn.'[41]

This account of incorporation goes some way towards explaining Dinah's 'predisposition to bury things,' and Bowen's curious decision to write a novel about it (*LG* 22). For these burials re-stage the process of psychic incubism or encryptment in which the lost object is entombed alive within the ego. The structure of *The Little Girls* reflects this process: the first and final sections form a crypt around the middle, in which the dead mother, in the form of Mrs Piggott, is restored to life. Her daughter Dinah, unable or unwilling to acknowledge loss, fossilises any object that might ward it off, with the result that she has fossilised herself. If she does not age, it is because she has remained embalmed within the past. The delusion of incorporation – 'fantasmatic, unmediated, instantaneous, magical, sometimes hallucinatory' – prevents the ego from engaging in the work of introjection – 'gradual, slow, laborious, mediated, effective' – that would free it from the clutches of the dead.[42] In *The Little Girls*, the work of introjection begins with Dinah's breakdown, when she discovers that the coffer is empty. Only with this recognition can she begin to articulate the loss disavowed throughout her life: 'Nothing's left, out of going on fifty years' (*LG* 163). Realising that the object has long since disappeared, despite her frantic work of preservation, Dinah finally relinquishes her childhood, casting off her 'self-protective infantilism.'[43] She begins to live – which is also to begin to die.

'*Should* one let sleeping dogs lie?' Bowen asked her audience at the end of her public reading of *The Little Girls*. 'That's for YOU to say.'[44]

In *A World of Love* and *The Little Girls*, Bowen struggles to break free from her past manner, just as her characters struggle to break free from the dead. The novelist attacks the themes and methods of her former works, taking drastic measures to write against her own addictions. If Antonia never fulfils her intention to clear out the attic, Bowen accomplishes this task in her own imagination, burning the letters and emptying the coffers of the past. In *The Little Girls*, Dinah wonders if it 'might be better to have no pictures of places which are gone. Let them go completely' (*LG* 169). It is clear that Bowen had to let go of her past style in order to move into the futuristic universe of *Eva Trout*.

Notes

1. Incubism is the technic designated for the 'Hades' episode in the so-called Gilbert scheme, first circulated in 1921; see Appendix to James Joyce, *Ulysses*, ed. Jeri Johnson (Oxford: Oxford University Press, 1993), p. 734.
2. See above, ch. 3, n. 35.
3. Abraham and Torok, *The Shell and the Kernel*, p. 171.
4. Lee, *Elizabeth Bowen*, p. 184.
5. Beckett, *Murphy* (1938; London: Picador, 1973), p. 5.
6. Virginia Woolf, "A Sketch of the Past" (1939–40), in Woolf, *Moments of Being*, ed. Jeanne Schulkind (London: Hogarth Press, 1985), p. 80.
7. See Bennett and Royle, *Elizabeth Bowen and the Dissolution of the Novel*, p. 119.
8. 'Guy David's Hole,' *WL* 46; see Andrew Bennett, 'Maud Danby's Character,' *The Bowen Newsletter*, 'Maud Danby Special,' 1: 3 (Autumn 1992) p. 4.
9. Homer, *The Odyssey*, trans. Richard Lattimore (New York: Harper, 1967), bk 1, lines 215–16.
10. W. J. McCormack, *Dissolute Characters: Irish Literary History through Balzac, Sheridan Le Fanu, Yeats and Bowen*, p. 209.
11. Lacan, 'Seminar on "The Purloined Letter"' (1955/1966), trans. Jeffrey Mehlman, in Muller and Richardson, *The Purloined Poe: Lacan, Derrida and Psychoanalytic Reading*, p. 41.
12. Letter from A. E. Coppard to Bowen, 31 July 1934, HRHRC.
13. Freud, 'Mourning and Melancholia,' SE, vol. 14, pp. 249–50, 253, 244.
14. Anita Sokolsky, 'The Melancholy Persuasion,' in Maud Ellmann (ed.), *Psychoanalytic Literary Criticism* (London: Longman, 1994), p. 130.

15. See Jacqueline Rose, 'Daddy,' in Maud Ellmann (ed.), *Psychoanalytic Literary Criticism*, p. 229.
16. See, for example, Lacan, *Ecrits: A Selection*, trans. Alan Sheridan (London: Tavistock, 1977), p. 153.
17. I am indebted here to Clare Hanson's Deleuzian reading of *A World of Love* in 'Little Girls and Large Women,' pp. 189–90.
18. Bowen, *A Time in Rome* (London: Longman, 1960), pp. 7, 10.
19. John Carey, '*The House in Paris*,' in *Pure Pleasure: A Guide to the Twentieth Century's Most Enjoyable Books* (London: Faber, 2000), p. 87.
20. Bowen, *The Little Girls*: notes, handwritten in spiral notebook, HRHRC. In the scene where the secret objects are ceremonially buried, Bowen rarely refers to the little girls by name: they become, in their own words, 'the Buriers of This Box' (*LG* 116–18).
21. Forster, *A Passage to India* (London: Everyman's Library, 1991), p. 120.
22. Mary Ellmann, 'Words, Words,' p. 126. See also Hermione Lee, *Elizabeth Bowen*, p. 196.
23. Ritchie, *The Siren Years*, p. 117.
24. *The Little Girls*, notes, HRHRC.
25. *The Little Girls*, notes, HRHRC.
26. *The Little Girls*, notes, HRHRC.
27. Glendinning, *Elizabeth Bowen*, p. 192.
28. See Bennett and Royle, *Elizabeth Bowen and the Dissolution of the Novel*, pp. 127–8.
29. See Glendinning, *Elizabeth Bowen*, p. 218.
30. *The Little Girls*, notes, HRHRC.
31. Bowen, 'The Gift that Speaks,' *The Tatler* 218 (7 December 1955) p. 660; 'Millionaire Queen of New York,' review of *The Vanderbilt Feud* by Grace Wilson Vanderbilt and *A Father and His Fate* by I. Compton-Burnett, *The Tatler* 225 (28 August 1957) p. 383; 'An English Master of the Novella,' review of *Death of a Huntsman* by H. E. Bates, *James Joyce's World* by Patricia Hutchins, and *From Russia with Love* by Ian Fleming, *The Tatler* 224 (8 May 1957) p. 329.
32. Bowen, 'Genius of the Deep South,' review of *The Ponder Heart* by Eudora Welty, *A History of Courtship* by E. S. Turner, *Bella North* by Diana Marr-Johnson, *The Tatler* 214 (13 October 1954) p. 108.
33. Bowen, 'Oxford Seen Darkly,' review of *A Cup of Tea for Mr Thorgell* by Storm Jameson, *The Blitz* by Constantine FitzGibbon, *Village Diary* by Miss Read, *The Main Chance* by Peter Wildeblood, *The Tatler* 226 (11 December 1957) pp. 652–3.
34. See Bennett and Royle's handy 'Novel Shopping-List' to cut out and keep, which lists all the lists (and then some!) in *The Little Girls* (*Elizabeth Bowen and the Dissolution of the Novel*, p. 131; see also pp. 129–33 for a provocative discussion of the use of such inventories in Bowen's fiction).
35. *LG* 17, 9, 76–7, 100, 108.

36. See Walter Benjamin, 'The Work of Art in an Age of Mechanical Reproduction,' pp. 219–53.
37. Another letter in the 'Unknown Language' was apparently written by Clare to her father but arrived too late, after his death (*LG* 115, 156).
38. The term 'hierarchy of significance' comes from Lukàcs's famous attack on modernism in *Realism in Our Time: Literature and the Class Struggle*, trans. John and Necke Mander (New York: Harper and Row, 1964).
39. Dinah regards *Macbeth* as a play 'full of particles of sadness which are seldom noticed' (*LG* 209). Bennett and Royle make the interesting point that *The Little Girls*, which has often been accused of being dated, is exploring the datedness endemic to consumer capitalism. The 'ephemeral bric-à-brac collected in the novel' alludes to 'the sheer transience of the objects of mass culture to which it refers. The novel as novelty – and like the contents of novelty gift shops, the contents of such novels carry with them a weight of pathos generated by their built-in redundancy, or designed obsolescence' (*Elizabeth Bowen and the Dissolution of the Novel*, pp. 123–4).
40. See Abraham and Torok, *The Shell and the Kernel*, pp. 128–9.
41. Sokolsky, 'The Melancholy Persuasion,' p. 130.
42. Derrida, '*Fors*: The Anglish Words of Nicolas Abraham and Maria Torok,' p. xix.
43. Lee, *Elizabeth Bowen*, p. 194.
44. *The Little Girls*, notes, HRHRC.

7

Folly: Eva Trout

Bowen's postwar fiction has received a cool response from many of her critics. The general consensus is that the novelist failed to update herself convincingly, lingering on like Major Brutt in *The Death of the Heart* as a relic of a former age: 'Makes of men date, like makes of cars; Major Brutt was a 1914–18 model . . .' (*DH* 90). If makes of men date, so do makes of novelists, and Bowen's critics have tended to regard her as a 1929–49 model, doomed to crash in the fast lane of postmodernism. *Eva Trout*, in particular, has disconcerted critics with its outsize heroine, implausible plot, inconsistent characters, dizzying scene changes, contrived set-pieces, farcical coincidences, and melodramatic finale. Patricia Craig's verdict is that 'Elizabeth Bowen ended by parodying herself,' letting her 'mannered manner run away with her.' Hermione Lee describes *Eva Trout* as a 'bizarre conclusion to her work':

> This last fiction, in its uneasy struggle with its own language and structure, and in its distressing account of alienation, describes an almost unbearable present, with which the traditional novel of order and feeling can no longer deal.[1]

On the other hand, the poststructuralist critics Bennett and Royle celebrate the shock tactics that other critics have condemned in *Eva Trout*. In an ingenious analysis of the formal and thematic 'convulsions' of the text, they argue that *Eva Trout* undermines the epistemological foundations of the novel, necessitating 'a new kind of literary critical writing': an immanent critique in which the text itself provides the terms of its interpretation, eluding all externally imposed vocabularies.[2] Yet as John Coates has pointed out, critics pro and contra *Eva Trout* concur in emphasising its disjunctions at the expense of its ethical dimension. According to Coates, Bowen never turns away from the moral concerns of her earlier fiction. For this reason *Eva Trout* should be read not as a roller-coaster ride through groundless fantasies, but as an anatomy of 'a disturbing moral problem, that of the injuries done by the injured, and the complicity of the "innocent" in their own destruction.'[3] My own view is that this critical controversy is battled out in *Eva Trout* itself. In the figure of its colossal heroine, with her vast wealth and unbridled imagination, Bowen asks how far fiction can go without ethics, or without forsaking any aspiration for the truth.

Rather than resolving this dilemma, the novel swings between its tantalising possibilities. At one level *Eva Trout* tells the story of a sentimental education, the belated initiation of a savage into language and sexuality. Described as 'an astray moose,' Eva is the most untamed of Bowen's innocents, an infant (in-fans) in the sense that she can scarcely speak (*ET* 14). The 'monstrous heiress,' raised by governesses in hotels while her father pursued his worldwide business interests, might have expected to be polyglot – instead she has lost her mother tongue (*ET* 63). At least she has lost all sense of colloquial English, so that rather than asking, 'Aren't you feeling well?' Eva says, 'Are you deteriorating?' (*ET* 100). Estranged from language, Eva also lacks a determinate sex: 'Trout, are you a hermaphrodite?' she is questioned at school (*ET* 51). Educating Eva is a matter of taming her imagination: the novel suggests that the fiction-making impulse is 'an astray moose' unless it is reined in by love.

Yet at another level, Bowen clearly colludes in her heroine's 'passion for the fictitious for its own sake,' although in the author's case this passion finds its outlet in verbal exuberance (*ET* 242). Where Eva is tongue-tied to the point of autism, the novel is 'abandoned to eloquence.' Mary Ellmann comments in a contemporary review:

> there is a chilly and quite exhilarating supremacy of words to people in *Eva Trout* . . . One moves through elaborate syntactical mazes, to arrive repeatedly at the solid, blatant, ludicrous bulk of Eva . . . Perhaps one should think of *Eva Trout* as a linguistic "folly," a structure as entertaining as it is inutile.'[4]

If Bowen's folly takes the form of verbal wizardry, Eva's takes the form of 'changing scenes,' the subtitle of the novel. Eva begets scenes, much as Maud Danby begets fights, stage-managing the squabbles of her entourage; but she also insists on constant scene changes, setting up one mise-en-scène after another. The phrase 'changing scenes' derives from the well-known hymn, 'Through All the Changing Scenes of Life,' familiar to Bowen as a church-goer.[5] But the scenes that Eva strives to conjure up are dumbshows, in which pictures take the place of words. Eva's mind could be compared to Dinah's cave, that sealed-off world where words have been displaced by things. In different ways, both Dinah and Eva seem to be testing the hypothesis, proposed in Swift's famous satire of the academicians of Lagado, that words should be replaced by the objects that they name.

> A Scheme for entirely abolishing all Words whatsoever . . . was urged as a great Advantage in Point of Health as well as Brevity . . . An Expedient was therefore offered, that since Words are only Names for *Things*, it would be more convenient for all Men to carry about them, such *Things* as were necessary to express the particular Business they are to discourse on . . . However, many of the most Learned and Wise adhere to the New Scheme of expressing themselves by *Things*, which hath only this Inconvenience attending it; that if a Man's Business be very great, and of various Kinds, he must be obliged in Proportion to carry a greater Bundle of *Things* upon his Back, unless he can afford one or two strong Servants to attend him. I have often beheld two of those Sages almost sinking under Weight of their Packs . . .[6]

When Eva describes herself as 'very heavy,' it is tempting to attribute her great weight to the things she lugs around instead of words (*ET* 65).

Where Eva differs from Dinah, however, is that she is magnetised to pictures rather than to objects; Dinah, by contrast, dreads the power of the picture to belie the authenticity of things. In the middle of *Eva Trout* Eva gives up language altogether, retreating with her deaf-mute adopted son into a 'cinematographic existence, with no sound-track.'

> They came to distinguish little between what went on inside and what went on outside the diurnal movies, or what was or was not contained in the television flickering them to sleep. From large or small screens, illusion overspilled on to all beheld. Society revolved at a distance from them like a ferris wheel dangling buckets of people. They were their own. Wasted, civilization extended round them as might acres of cannibalized cars. Only they moved.
>
> (*ET* 188–9)

Spurning the talkies, Eva tries to script her retinue into a silent movie, casting herself in the title role. Meanwhile her son Jeremy resorts to drawing, patterning, and sculpting, reminding us that Bowen herself set out to become an artist before she realised that her talent lay in writing. After a lifetime of story-telling, Bowen considers what she may have lost by abandoning the silence of pictures for the noise of words. *Eva Trout* sets up a contest between 'pictures and conversations': the charming phrase from *Alice in Wonderland* that provided Bowen with the title of her unfinished autobiography. Are pictures superior to conversations? What can words achieve that images cannot? The answer to the second question is interiority: Bowen makes it clear that only language can endow us with an inner life. Yet is this innerness merely a delusion concocted out of words? In *The Little Girls*, Bowen had experimented with presenting her characters 'entirely from the outside'; but in *Eva Trout*, she submits the novel to a further 'emotional hysterectomy' by questioning the very notion of an inner life.[7]

In her teaching notes for a course on the short story, given at Vassar in 1960, Bowen's discussion of the 'Simple Soul' provides an illuminating gloss on *Eva Trout*:[8]

> III By the Innocent – in my sense of the Simple Soul – we mean
>   (a) the *young* child
>   (b) the 'arrested' character
>   (c) the defective (idiot)
>   (3) the simpleton
>   (4) the abnormally *submissive* [. . .]
> *One regards Simplicity* – of the kind which handicaps a character in his or her ordinary traffic with the world
> as either
>   a deformity
>   or, a beauty.
> *Such a character tends also to be A CATALYST*

According to Bowen, the short story is better suited than the novel to the presentation of the simple soul:

> The Short Story – with its non-explanatory nature – deals well with non-rational behaviour – or – (better) with the non-self-explanatory character It can show the character in which calculation (in the sense of ordinary calculation) is suspended.

The novel, on the other hand, 'requires – for interest – *rational* character.'

> In novels, the centralizing around the 'innocent' character requires a prolonged *tour de force*
> e.g. *The Sound & the Fury*
> & *The Idiot*
> These are works of genius.

Bowen emphasises to her students that the presentation of the Simple Soul 'requires Art':

> most of all, Art in the sense of *VISION*
> *without* vision on the part of the writer, the depiction of the 'simple' is flat and pointless [. . .]

Some balance, Bowen proposes, must be found between the inner and the outer perspective: Eudora Welty's 'The Shower of Gold' presents the innocent from the outside, whereas Gertrude Stein's 'The Gentle Lena' offers both an inside and an outside view. Bowen concludes her class by raising the question:

> What, one might ask, is the point of the Simple Soul story
> Is it to be regarded – simply – as 'a curiosity'?
> *No.*
> It introduces the subject of 'The Kingdom of Heaven'
> Purity.

These notes suggest that Bowen's ambition in *Eva Trout* was to rival Faulkner and Dostoevsky in the *tour de force* of centring the novel on a simple soul. Eva, arrested on the brink of language, conforms most closely to Bowen's third category of simplicity: 'the "arrested" character.' As Mary Ellmann wittily observes, Eva is 'still gauche and untried at thirty-three, an age at which heroines normally expect to be retired rather than deflowered.'[9] Bowen presents this lunatic giant from the outside, the author's fluency posing a sharp contrast to the heroine's aphasia, but she also uses Eva to cast doubt on the very notion of interiority. In the last part of the novel, a visit to the National Portrait Gallery convinces Eva that human beings are as two-dimensional as paintings: 'every soul Eva knew became no longer anything but a Portrait. There was no "real life"; no life was more real than this. This she had long suspected. She now was certain' (*ET* 196). From Eva's point of view, only words create the illusion of an inner life; pictures, on the other hand, establish beyond doubt that there is nothing underneath the surface. Is her simplicity a form of madness or divinest sense? Is Eva an unfallen Eve, innocent of the deceits of language, her dumbness holding the keys to 'the kingdom of heaven'? Mischievously, Bowen leaves these questions dangling.

The details of the plot are scarcely plausible. At the beginning of the novel, twenty-four-year-old Eva Trout is staying as a paying guest with Iseult, her former teacher, and Iseult's husband Eric Arble at Larkins, the house attached to their failed fruit farm. On her twenty-fifth birthday Eva is due to inherit a vast fortune from her father, Willy Trout, who died by suicide some years before. Her mother, Cissie, bolted with a lover two months after her daughter's birth, but was killed immediately in a plane crash. Motherless from infancy, Eva was brought up under the shadow of Willy's 'total attachment' to his lover Constantine Ormeau, who became her legal guardian after her father's death (*ET* 17). A flashback recounts Eva's abortive education at a progressive school, housed in a pseudo-Bavarian castle, where she shared a room with Elsinore, a 'fairylike little near-albino' who was whisked away after an attempt to drown herself (*ET* 52). When the school was subsequently forced to close, Eva demanded to be sent to an English boarding-school for girls, where she fell in love with Iseult Smith, the gifted English teacher who began to fish her out of the deep waters of her inarticulacy.

Hermione Lee has pointed out that *Eva Trout* is 'full of guardians,' and most of the scene changes are propelled by Eva's efforts to escape their vigilance.[10] When the novel opens Eva feels betrayed by Iseult, having mistaken her 'vivisectional interest' for love, and turns for comfort to the local vicarage, where the Danceys, 'ridden with hay fever and fecundity,' provide her first glimpse of family life.[11] With the help of twelve-year-old Henry Dancey, Eva runs away to Broadstairs in Kent, where she rents a dilapidated villa called Cathay. Conducted round the house by an ingratiating estate agent called Mr Denge, Eva throws him out for demonstrating that the toilets flush – too loudly for her frazzled nerves. Later she fills Cathay with state-of-the-art audiovisual equipment, as if these mechanical prostheses could make up for the shortcomings of a simple soul.

Eva's minders lose no time in pursuing her to this retreat: within hours of her getaway, Eric has arrived on her doorstep, closely followed by Constantine, who jumps to the conclusion that Eric and Eva must be lovers. In fact, no sexual contact takes place between them, but they do come together in a strange embrace, unseen by Constantine, when Eric shakes Eva like a rag-doll:

> Eric got hold of Eva by the pouchy front of her anorak and shook her. The easy articulation of her joints made this rewarding – her head rolled on her shoulders, her arms swung from them. Her teeth did not rattle, being firm in her gums, but coins and keys all over her clinked and jingled. Her hair flumped all ways like a fiddled-about-with mop. The crisis became an experiment: he ended by keeping her rocking, at slowing tempo, left-right, right-left, off one heel on to the other, meanwhile pursing his lips, as though whistling, and frowning speculatively.

The experiment interested Eva also. Did it gratify her too much? – he let go abruptly.

(ET 88)

One of the oddities of this vignette is that Eva is usually presented as a monolith – vast, featureless, petrified – the very opposite of this loose-limbed marionette. Here her body seems devoid of will, helpless as the coins and keys that jingle in her pockets; rolling, rocking, clinking, and flumping in a macabre parody of orgasm. Her teeth are the only part of her anatomy that does not rattle. But if Eva has two bodies, one stony and the other floppy, both could be seen as modes of death: rigor mortis in the first case, decomposition in the second. Her joints, like her thoughts, 'don't connect,' and the disarticulation of her limbs mirrors the inarticulacy of her speech, as well as the disjointedness of the narrative (*ET* 62). Eva watches the experiment, as Eric does, with vivisectional interest, and nothing comes of it. But later, in an equivocation worthy of the witches in *Macbeth*, Eva announces she is going to have 'a little child' nine months after Eric's visit. This is all the ammunition Iseult needs to leave her husband (*ET* 121).

The next place Eva fishes up is in Chicago, where she purchases an infant from a baby-snatching racket. When Jeremy turns out to be deaf and dumb, Eva takes the opportunity to give up language altogether, communicating with her child through telepathy. Eight years after the adoption Eva returns to England with her young charge, ostensibly to seek treatment for his disability, but also to find refuge from her own. In the meantime the Arbles have separated, Iseult having escaped to Paris to write novels, and Eric having fathered two children on a Scandinavian au pair, a nameless incubator who never appears. Eva meets up again with Henry Dancey, now a handsome Cambridge undergraduate, and falls in love with him. He turns down her proposal of marriage, but under pressure he agrees to her bizarre request to fake a wedding journey for the benefit of her assembled relatives and minders. Once the train leaves the station Henry will be free to disembark, leaving Eva to ride into the sunset. The final scene takes place at Victoria Station, where to Eva's astonishment – and ours – Henry reveals that he means to elope with her in earnest: 'I'm not going to get off this train' (*ET* 266). For the first time in her life, Eva weeps. Through her tears she catches sight of Jeremy, waving a revolver that Iseult had planted in Eva's luggage. In the most outrageous scene of Bowen's fiction, Jeremy shoots Eva dead.

Ultimately *Eva Trout* defies paraphrase, for any summary of its events is bound to underplay its humour and demonic energy. To describe the novel as 'picaresque' would be an understatement: no sooner has a scene been set than another barges in, and the effect is one of channel-hopping or fast-forwarding. Iseult, the novelist man-qué of *Eva Trout*, declares that 'life is an anti-novel'; and Bowen attempts to capture the anti-novelistic element of life by disrupting the continuity of plot and character (*ET* 206). The narrative proceeds 'disjectedly,' like Eva's memory:

> Time, inside Eva's mind, lay about like various pieces of a fragmented picture. She remembered, that is to say, disjectedly. To reassemble the picture was impossible; too many of the pieces were lost, lacking. Yet, some of the pieces there were would group into patterns – patterns at least. Each pattern had a predominant colour . . .
>
> (*ET* 46)

Similarly, the novel consists of a mosaic of scenes, presented as autonomous set-pieces, such as the scene where Iseult and Eva meet at Bleak House where Dickens did not write *Bleak House*. Each chapter lights out into new territory. Yet the gusto of the narrative somehow overrides its fits and starts. Despite the jerky rhythm, Shandian digressions, and blatant unreality of the events, we still want to know what happens next.

Bowen also breaks the rules of consistency of character, particularly in her portrayal of Constantine, the fickle and manipulative lover whom Eva blames for her father's suicide. Hermione Lee accuses Bowen of dealing 'very unsympathetically with homosexuals' in *Eva Trout*, and it is true that Constantine – frigid, precious, devious – conforms to homophobic stereotypes.[12] Yet although he calls himself 'the Wicked Guardian,' it is difficult to tell if Constantine's malevo-lence is genuine or merely a reflection of the hostility of others (*ET* 100). His smoothness, both of physiognomy and manner, provides an ideal surface for projections: Iseult, for example, endows his 'sha-dowless face' with the 'power to haunt.' Constantine owes something to Uncle Silas in Sheridan Le Fanu's novel of that name: the enigmatic guardian whose wickedness was masked by beauty in his youth, and by overdone politeness in old age. Uncle Silas is suspected of a murder officially glossed over as a suicide; Eva harbours similar suspicions about Constantine. In a perceptive Preface to Le Fanu's novel, which Bowen described as one of the first 'psychological thrillers,' she points out that Uncle Silas is presented only through the eyes of his overwrought ward, Maud Ruthyn. Similarly, Constantine is presented only through the eyes of Eva and Iseult, neither of whom shows any commitment to objectivity. Like Eva, Maud is legated by her father to her wicked guardian, and her sense of alienation corresponds both to Eva and to Bowen's conception of the Anglo-Irish. 'Temperamentally, and because of her upbringing,' Maud 'moves about in a world of strangers. She is alternately blind and unnecessarily suspicious.'[13] Much of the terror of Le Fanu's novel derives from the inconsistencies of Uncle Silas, silky one moment and fiendish the next, and mostly occluded from the narrative. Similarly Constantine, despite his name, is wildly inconstant in his character: by the end of the novel he has undergone a moral transformation by falling in love with a charismatic priest, Father Clavering-Haight, who acts as confessor for the major characters (Uncle Silas also feigns or falls for religion in old age). Although Constantine is 'not quite opaque,' there is little evidence of a continuous inner life beneath the 'alabaster' of his blond, massaged, immobile face (*ET* 36–7).

If the characters are unpredictable, the narrator is equally volatile. For the whole of chapter 11, when Eva flies off to Chicago, the narrator also plays truant, leaving the story in the hands of a monstrous American philosophy professor called Portman C. Holman of Wyana University: a forerunner of David Lodge's Morris Zapp. Sitting near Eva in the plane, Professor Holman rescues her fallen apple from the floor – an otiose allusion to her biblical prototype – and makes a hilarious attempt to chat her up. He records the whole encounter in a self-regarding letter that returns to sender, Eva having wisely changed hotels. 'Am I to atrophy, have I in part done so? Already do I enact what I fail to feel? Emotionally, am I parasitic? Could that have been otherwise, could it still? I have it in me to sorrow? – or have I not? Tell me' (*ET* 127). In its rococo display of empty verbiage, this letter demonstrates how eloquence can turn into a folly under the baleful influence of academic narcissism. Iseult also flaunts her eloquence in a cascade of adjectives on Dickens' house: 'So gimcrack, so ghastlily cheerful, so hand-to-mouth, so desperately inordinate, so unscrupulous, so tawdry – so formidable.' Eva replies, 'What a lot you have thought' (*ET* 114). So much for Iseult.

Holman's is the most conspicuous of many letters in the novel that fail to reach their addressees, often boomeranging on their senders. Unfinished, unsent, misdirected, unreceived, these dead letters obviously indicate a breakdown of communication. Less obviously, they reflect the chanciness of Bowen's narrative, where causes, motivations, and desires go astray, rarely arriving at their destinations. In *The Little Girls*, Clare reflects that 'chance is better than choice; it is more lordly.' Accordingly, Bowen allows the lordliness of chance to overcome the petit bourgeois calculations of the plot in *Eva Trout*. Chance, rather than choice, determines the sequence of events, mocking the teleology of narrative. Iseult says that Eva's thoughts 'don't connect,' and the same could be said of the self-contained tableaux of which the novel is composed. It is telling that Eva's last words are 'what is "concatenation"?' (*ET* 268).

Critics tend to overlook the chanciness of *Eva Trout*, supplying motivation where Bowen deliberately leaves it out. If Eva 'begets trouble,' she does not premeditate it; trouble leaks from her, like fallout from an atomic bomb (*ET* 44). 'Ethically . . . you're a Typhoid Mary,' Henry tells her (*ET* 179). Does Eva mean to compromise Eric? Does she set out to ruin Iseult's marriage? Or does she hope to liberate her guru from domestic suffocation? Most baffling of all, does Jeremy mean to murder Eva? It is impossible to tell if such events are accidental or intentional. To criticise the action as 'haphazard,' in Lee's words, is to miss the point: Bowen is devising a new kind of novel for an age in which intention is irrelevant, an age in which the world can be destroyed by accident.[14] In these circumstances the novel can no longer rely on plot and character, for both imply a logic of cause-and-effect in which events proceed according to intelligible laws to a predictable conclusion. In *Eva Trout*, by contrast, the debacle is determined only by the arbitrary acquisition of a gun – like so many massacres in recent history. Closer to an earthquake than an individual, Eva *happens*. It remains to others, both inside and outside the book, to impose constructions on her sphinx-like impassivity.

The subtitle 'Changing Scenes' also draws attention to the way that Bowen experiments with one mode of scene-setting after another, creating a kaleidoscope of literary reminiscences. *Eva Trout* is an allegory of reading, as well as a sentimental education, and much of its wit arises from the clash between those modes. Eva confesses that she is 'frightened' of reading, but Iseult 'grew up in Reading,' where she later returns to take up residence in 'Roundabout Road' (*ET* 61, 38, 207). These puns on reading show Bowen playing with the notion of the self-reflexiveness of narrative. An avid reader, Iseult feels 'soiled by living more than a thousand lives' that she has 'lived through books' (*ET* 92–3). Her life-in-books is re-enacted in the prose itself, which races through pastiche after pastiche, enlisting

James, Dickens, Sterne, Swift, Ibsen, Browning, Lawrence, Woolf, along with Le Fanu and many other writers. Yet often these allusions deliberately mislead the reader: Eva is not Eve, Iseult is not Isolde, and Eva's schoolfriend Elsinore is not Ophelia, even though she almost drowns.

Of all these shades of former fictions, Virginia Woolf's *Orlando* is the antecedent that asserts itself most vigorously. In a 1960 Preface to *Orlando,* Bowen remembers the shock experienced by Woolf's admirers, 'still breathless' from *To the Lighthouse,* when *Orlando* shot into the world. Despite the 'wildness' of previous experiments, Woolf had always obeyed the 'musts' of the novel, defined by Bowen as 'a work of imagination fettered to earthly fact and subject to dire penalty if it break the chain.' But *Orlando* is 'a novelist's holiday, not a novel.' Here Woolf broke the fetters of fact and gave her fantasy free reign: 'Fantasy may juggle with time and space, and ignore, for instance, the law of gravity.'[15] Bowen herself distrusted fantasy, believing that it drove her forebears mad. 'Fantasy is toxic,' she wrote in *Bowen's Court,* 'the private cruelty and the world war both have their start in the heated brain' (*BC* 455). One reason why everyday things loom large in Bowen's fiction is to fasten her imagination to the earth, thus warding off her family's propensity to fantasy. Rereading *Orlando,* however, leads Bowen to re-evaluate the rival claims of fantasy and gravity. She wonders if this 'prank,' this gloriously 'foolish book' enabled Woolf 'to shatter some rigid, deadening, claustrophobic mould of so-called "actuality" which had been surrounding her' (*MT* 131, 133, 135).

The recklessness of *Eva Trout* reveals a similar impatience with the tyranny of actuality. Bowen never quite shatters the mould of realism, but she stretches it to bursting point, to the dismay of many of her erstwhile devotees. The terms she uses to describe *Orlando* – its 'bravura,' its 'rumbustious' narrative, and especially its 'splendid changing and shifting scenes' – apply with equal validity to *Eva Trout* (*MT* 133–5). The conflict between gravity and fantasy is embodied in the heroine herself: Eva describes herself as 'very heavy,' yet she is also constantly in flight, both physically and imaginatively. The suggestion that Eva is a hermaphrodite harks back to Orlando's ambiguity of gender, while the name Constantine evokes Constantinople, scene of Orlando's sex-change.[16] *Orlando* leapfrogs centuries, but Bowen also challenges the unity of time by reducing historical periods to stage sets, catapulting Eva from the atavistic castle of her schooldays to the futuristic world of audiovisual technology. On a sadder note, the constant references to drowning in *Eva Trout* suggest a preoccupation with Woolf's suicide, which had a devastating effect on Bowen and her contemporaries. 'She ended, as far as we know, in darkness, but – where is she now?' Bowen wondered. 'Nobody with that capacity for joy, I think, can be nowhere.'[17]

As a folly, *Eva Trout* owes much to the capacity for joy that Woolf displays in *Orlando*. Bowen also strives to keep the reader hooked: *Eva Trout* is an unexpected page-turner. This is largely due to one compelling theme that connects its autotelic scenes, which is Eva's failure to connect herself to other people. Curiously Bowen, despite her indefatigable socialising, seems to have identified with Eva's sense of alienation. In a 1948 collection called *Why Do I Write?* quoted in the first chapter of the present study, Bowen explains:

> Perhaps one emotional reason why one may write is the need to work off, out of the system, the sense of being solitary and farouche . . . My writing, I am prepared to think, may be a substitute for something I have been born without – a so-called normal relation to society. My books *are* my relation to society.

> (*MT* 223)

In her depiction of the Dancey family in *Eva Trout*, Bowen revisits her childhood in Kent, where her tutor, a vicar called Mr Salmon, tried to integrate the little Anglo-Irish refugee into his poor but happy family. The name 'Trout' is reminiscent of the Salmons' piscine surname. In *Pictures and Conversations*, written immediately after *Eva Trout*, Bowen remembers the Salmon household as her first view of 'genuinely idyllic family life.' Unfortunately it was too much for her. She responded by behaving 'like a yahoo,' with a 'belligerence' she blames in part on her Anglo-Irish ancestry (an ancestry she shares with Swift, inventor of the yahoos). Yet despite her efforts to wreak havoc, Elizabeth found she could not drive a wedge between the Salmon sisters, nor raise more than an eyebrow from the vicar, a twinkle from the eye of his sagacious wife. 'Possibly I was jealous of the whole family?' she wonders. In the oversized figure of Eva Trout, Bowen recaptures her early feelings of estrangement in this family, where she must have felt egregiously enlarged by her heredity: a mad father and a mountainous house. Bowen's stammer also resurfaces in Eva's mysterious linguistic handicap; and echoes of a scolding governess – who told Elizabeth to concentrate on one word at a time instead of trying to say everything at once – reverberate in Iseult's efforts to make Eva think sequentially.[18]

Like her author, Eva uses her imagination to overcome her sense of being solitary and farouche; but lacking Bowen's gift for words, Eva uses spectacle to construct her 'relation to society.' The novel begins with such a spectacle, when Eva takes the Dancey family on an outing to the crazy castle where she went to school. This edifice, rising straight up out a lake, appears neither ancient nor indigenous: 'the pile resembled some Bavarian fantasy.' Yet Eva announces to the disbelieving company: 'This is where we were to have spent the honeymoon.' Later we learn that this gigantic folly was the site of Eva's aborted education, not of her aborted honeymoon. Her supposed engagement turns out to be a castle in the air, but the castle on the 'wraithlike lake' looks no more convincing that her nuptial fantasies (*ET* 11, 52). 'Is that castle *bona fide?*' Henry Dancey wants to know. Evidently as prefabricated as the feelings it is fashioned to arouse, the façade seems to have been 'cut out, flat, from a sheet of cardboard,' and Catrina Dancey wonders if it has an 'inside.' At the same time the Danceys' mother, studying the monumental heroine, wonders if Eva has an inside: '*Is* she thinking? Mrs Dancey thought not. Monolithic, Eva's attitude was. It was not, somehow, the attitude of a thinking person' (*ET* 12–13). In *The Last September,* Lady Naylor complains that the English talk about their insides (perhaps they talk their insides into being?), but Eva seems to have no insides to divulge.

Thus *Eva Trout* both begins and ends by setting the scene for a make-believe marriage. Eva's first engagement never happened; her second is a piece of play-acting that unexpectedly turns into reality, only to be thwarted by the murder of the bride. By exposing Eva's betrothals as a hoax, Bowen mocks the traditional romantic novel, with its relentless impetus towards marriage. Until the final scene, Eva shows no sign of sexuality: 'her so-called sex bored and mortified her; she dragged it about after her like a ball and chain' (*ET* 243). In its indifference to sex, *Eva Trout* conforms to Bowen's conception of an Irish novel, as exemplified in *Uncle Silas*: 'it is sexless, and it shows a sublimated infantilism' (*MT* 101). Instead of sexual passion, Eva has 'a passion for the fictitious for its own sake.' While imposing her fantasies upon the world, however, Eva faces competition in the form of Iseult Smith, the gifted English teacher who initially attempts to rescue her from inarticulacy. When these characters first meet, Eva speaks like a 'displaced person,' having been posted round the globe throughout her childhood, like the many misaddressed and misdelivered letters in the novel. Coming from everywhere, she seems to

215

come from nowhere, alien as a creature from outer space: 'You roll round like some blind indeflectible planet,' Henry Dancey later tells her. Since she has no words to express herself, Eva has no self to express, no inside to 'press out.' In her dreams she is 'no one, nowhere.' It is significant that Bowen, often a painstaking physiognomist, never gives this heroine a face.[19]

In a BBC broadcast called 'Truth and Fiction,' Bowen considers whether the modern novel has finished with the 'study of the individualised character, the individual for his own sake, as a theme.' She poses the question: 'Are we going back to the symbolic, the masked speaker?'[20] I propose that Eva Trout is the masked speaker, an intruder from the novel of the future, cast adrift in a fictional world still premised on the notion of the individual. Desperate to become a character, Eva is searching for an author to provide her with an inner life. At first her teacher Iseult Smith, an admirer of Dickens' art of character, seems to answer Eva's needs. By coaxing Eva into language, Iseult offers her the prospect of a self: 'All that I know of me I have learned from you,' Eva cries. In this sense Iseult authors Eva, bringing her to life in words that 'sounded new-minted, unheard before' (*ET* 66, 58). But Iseult leaves her work unfinished, much as Frankenstein abandons his pre-linguistic monster and aborts the half-made Eve, his monster's bride.

Another antecedent is Pygmalion, the sculptor who falls in love with his own statue, Galatea, which is brought to life by Aphrodite. In Shaw's version of the story, Henry Higgins uses elocution lessons to animate his Galatea, transforming a Cockney flower-seller into a passable imitation of a duchess. Similarly Iseult teaches speech to Eva, who is often described as a statue, in order to release her soul from its prison of stone. But Iseult abandons the sculpture before it is completed, leaving Eva half-submerged in stone, like Michelangelo's slaves. Eva takes revenge by scripting Iseult into fictions of her own. A contest for authorship ensues, resembling the rivalry between the stylish Anna and the artless Portia of *The Death of the Heart*. Iseult is a would-be novelist, who uses language to make her dreams come true; but Eva is a would-be filmmaker, who uses her 'mountainous money' to cast herself as superstar in her own movie (*ET* 93). While Iseult tries to author Eva in language, Eva tries to script Iseult into a walk-on part in her last picture-show: the matrimonial extravaganza at Victoria. But Iseult's novel is 'born dead,' and Eva's silent movie is aborted by the bullet that kills off the leading lady and director in one shot (*ET* 228). Thus the contest between Iseult's words and Eva's pictures ends in mutual miscarriage: both authors find themselves outwitted by their own hijacked narratives.

If Eva is the masked speaker, the castle is the masked spectacle – neither seems to have an inside. But Bowen endows the castle with a temporary inner life by means of a satire of progressive education. In chapter 5 we learn that Willy Trout purchased this folly to get rid of Constantine's other lover, 'inspirational Kenneth of the unclouded brow and Parthenon torso,' by making him headmaster of the school. High-minded Kenneth's hopes of mixing races and classes were soon dashed: young proletarians were 'difficult to get hold of – the State was too fussy about them, a real old auntie,' and the 'wealthy little delinquents' whose parents could afford the fees were 'coloured only by having rushed about naked on private beaches.' Nonetheless, 'a wish to have such children kept off one's hands and deterred from out-and-out criminality, with few questions asked and at almost any price,' provided Kenneth with a haul of youngsters, who indulged in such high jinx as setting an 'Oedipus-trap' for a teacher by arranging an effigy of his mother in his bed (*ET* 48–51).

It was at this school that Eva was exposed for the first time 'to her own kind: juveniles – a species known to her so far only in parks in the distance or hotels fleetingly.' Like Miranda in *The Tempest* (a *locus classicus* for Bowen's simple souls), Eva marvelled at this brave new world that had such people in it: 'even the smallest seemed wondrously physically complete to Eva, who had been left unfinished. So these were humans, and this was what it was like being amongst them?' Yet nothing in this castle, including humans, ever seemed quite *bona fide.* The prose abounds with cinematic similes: winter was 'dark as the darkest celluloid,' and daffodils in spring reputed to be 'Yellow as Technicolor.' But Eva never saw these flowers, for the school survived less than a term. Her roommate Elsinore, who wept incessantly throughout the night, whereas Eva cannot weep at all, spent her waking hours rewriting an abusive letter to her mother. One day she walked into the lake, but instead of drowning like Ophelia, Elsinore was fished out of the water, only to fall into a coma that brought her to the brink of death. The giant Eva, keeping watch over the tiny child, 'destitute now of tears,' experienced what Freud would call the 'oceanic feeling' of symbiotic love.[21] 'This deathly yet living stillness, together, of two beings, this unapartness, came to be the requital of all longing.' Their wordless union was ruptured, however, when Elsinore's mother belatedly arrived to take the invalid away. Eva was never told if her tearful alter ego lived or died: 'down came oblivion – asbestos curtain' (*ET* 55–7).

Chronologically this is the first of Eva's relationships in which her urge for 'unapartness' with another being is disrupted by the intervention of a shadowy third. As we have seen, this triadic structure recurs in much of Bowen's fiction, and emerges in its clearest outlines in 'Look at All Those Roses,' the story discussed in the first chapter of the present study. 'Big Eva' and little Elsinore resemble the Mathers, mother and daughter, coffined together in their silent universe of two (*ET* 53). In *Eva Trout*, Elsinore's mother takes the role of Edward in 'Look at All Those Roses': that is, the agent of language and society who rescues the sleeping princess from the deathly stillness of dyadic love. But Elsinore does not die, and Eva gets a second chance for symbiosis when she improbably bumps into the pathetic creature in Chicago, amidst the phantasmagoria of Christmas shopping. Now a wretched housewife, Elsinore begins to weep as soon as she finds herself alone again with 'Trout.' But Eva disappears into the night, leaving Elsinore to drown in tears: 'You came back too late, Elsinore' (*ET* 143). By this point Trout has other fish to fry, having made nefarious arrangements to acquire Jeremy. When the baby turns out to be deaf and dumb, Eva recreates with him the unapartness she enjoyed with Elsinore – 'near as twins in a womb' – before a third term broke the silence of their coalescence (*ET* 188).

Iseult, on the other hand, refuses to be drowned in Eva's love. It is Iseult's 'vivisectional interest' that functions as the third term in this relationship, thwarting Eva's fantasy of mutual engulfment. In the last part of the novel, Iseult again performs the role of shadowy third by destroying the conspiracy of silence between Eva and her son. By this time Eva has already started to detach herself from Jeremy, having dreamed up her matrimonial charade, and has taken to depositing the child with a North London sculptress called Applethwaite. The creepiest of the novel's guardians, Applethwaite allows the little boy to be kidnapped by a mystery woman, eventually revealed as Iseult in disguise. A few hours later, Jeremy returns to Eva's hotel, safe but irrevocably altered: Iseult's intervention has shattered the hermetic world of mother and child. From now on, Eva and Jeremy 'were not alone together: an unbridgeable ignorance of each other, or each other's motives, was cleft between them, and out of the gulf rose a breath of ice' (*ET* 205). Vivisecting though it is, this gulf provides Jeremy with a means of entry into language. Iseult's intervention awakens Jeremy's desire for self-expression, freeing his spirit from its stone of silence, just as her earlier assault on Eva's 'cement-like' speech had opened up the possibility of inner life (*ET* 17).

Eva, terrified by the abduction, bundles Jeremy off to France, but instead of trying to restore her oceanic union with her son, she unexpectedly allows him to be treated for his handicap. It is as if her own vivisectional interest in what he might become had got the better of her desperate need for unapartness. Carrying Iseult's intervention further, she leaves her child in Fontainebleau with the Bonnards, the first doctors to make progress with his speech – apparently by freeing him from English into French. By contrast, Eva's inability to make a home, either in English or in England, reflects the position of the Anglo-Irish: an *unheimlich* enclave alien to its own abode. Jeremy and Eva's 'cinematographic existence, with no sound-track' also echoes Bowen's description of the Anglo-Irish: 'to most of the rest of the world we are semi-strangers, for whom existence has something of the trance-like quality of a spectacle.'[22] By learning to speak French, Jeremy follows the example of an Anglo-Irish writer very different from Bowen, Samuel Beckett, who extricated himself from both sides of his hyphenated nationality by recreating his identity in French. For Jeremy, the French language breaks his bell jar, shattering the 'trance-like quality' of his existence, while acting as the third term that separates the child from the mother.

It is Eva who masterminds the final vivisection by forcing Jeremy to witness her phoney elopement, but Jeremy pre-empts this rupture with a gun. At Victoria Station, where Henry and Eva are to stage their 'hymeneal fiction,' all the characters turn up to see the couple off, with the exception of the Danceys, who know nothing of this crowning folly, and Father Clavering-Haight, who disapproves of it.[23] Constantine, the newly reunited Arbles, the 'mist-like phantoms' of Eva's unknown uncles and aunts, even Mr Denge of the noisy toilets gather together in the train station, where the tear-jerking theatrics of departure, familiar from so many movies, are about to be replayed. In fact a movie seems to be in progress further down the platform, where Jeremy emerges with his gun: 'Film either being shot or they're televising a royalty or celebrity: cameras galore!' Mr Denge excitedly reports. The spectators, convinced that they are witnessing a 'shooting' in the cinematic sense, fail to circumvent the child's deadly 'shot.' ' "Leave him alone," said someone, "he's only acting!" ' The toy gun, like the fake betrothal, turns out to be real, while Eva herself – 'outsize, larger-than-life in every way' – turns out to be all too human (*ET* 264–5, 236).

Bowen may be playing on the term 'revolver' by revolving it around the cast of characters, like the blacksmith's file in *Great Expectations*, so that everyone who mentions it is implicated in the inevitable shoot-out. Just as Jeremy circulates between surrogate parents (purchased by Eva, lent to Applethwaite, kidnapped by Iseult, donated to the Bonnards), so the murder weapon circulates among Eva's guardians. Iseult, in her 'roundabout' way, originally took the gun from Eric, attempted to foist it onto Constantine, and finally left it in Eva's luggage, where it fell into Jeremy's hands. This heavy-handed build-up culminates in the wildly melodramatic scene where Jeremy murders his adoptive mother. This revolver resembles other circulating objects in Bowen's novels, such as the violets in *The House in Paris* or Guy's letters in *A World of Love*, in that it binds the characters together in collective culpability. But the gun in *Eva Trout* is also associated with the references to fish that reappear like chronic symptoms through the narrative. Iseult asks Constantine to 'fish' up the revolver – an expression that cannot be ignored in a novel so obsessed with fish (*ET* 226). The expression 'kettle of fish' turns up three times, along with a 'fish-kettle,' while people and situations are frequently described as 'fishy.'[24] In Chicago, a horrible old man figures out that Willy Trout was Eva's father because 'Trout's not a usual name except for a fish' (*ET* 138).

If the 'fish' is connected with the name of the father (Willy Trout), the revolver that 'fishes up' throughout the narrative, concatenating Eric, Iseult, Constantine, Eva, and Jeremy in a chain of guilt, suggests that Eva's suicidal father is the fountainhead of violence. But there is something fishy in this very fatalism: the gun changes hands so clumsily that one wonders if this melodramatic contrivance is a smokescreen. In this context, Eva's ignorance of 'concatenation' may be wiser than the reader's urge to join things up, for the recurrence of the signifier 'fish' cannot be rationalised as a determinism. The scattering of fish throughout the narrative draws attention to the play of chance, rather than the work of fate. Sometimes metaphorical, sometimes literal, and usually embedded in clichés, the term 'fish' loses meaning every time it surfaces, just as the word 'Trout' ceases to mean fish when the capital T transforms it from a common noun into a proper name.

While the fish is associated with the proper name, the signature of selfhood, it also implies the slipperiness of personal identity. 'What a slippery fish is identity; and what *is* it, besides a slippery fish?' This is the question Eva asks herself after receiving a surprise phone call from Iseult, whose vivacity seems so overacted that Eva wonders if the caller might be dead – 'a deceased person purporting to be a living one' (*ET* 193). We have seen how Bowen constantly associates the telephone with death – a phone booth is an upright coffin, a ringing telephone a death-knell – and it is therefore logical that Eva should mistake a phone call for a message from beyond the grave. The scene is reminiscent of Muriel Spark's black comedy *Memento Mori* (1959), in which each character in turn receives an anonymous phone call reminding them that they must die. 'Alone with a voice, shut up with it,' unable to identify its source with any certainty, Eva loses faith in the existence of a speaker prior to the voice (*ET* 193).

It is this loss of faith that provides the pretext for the flagrant set-piece where Eva visits the National Portrait Gallery to see how painters catch the slippery fish of identity. The scene harks back to the famous episode in the National Gallery in Henry James's *The Wings of the Dove*, where Milly Theale, overwhelmed by the Turners and Titians, turns her attention to the lady copyists instead, with their domesticated versions of the masterworks.[25] In *Eva Trout*, by contrast, Bowen takes us on a guided tour through centuries of patriarchal portraiture. As the faceless heroine wanders through the galleries of faces, none of them answers her question, 'What *is* a person? Is it true, there is not more than one of each?' In the end, 'they *were* all "pictures." Images.' These pictures have no insides: even 'the most penetrating artist' fails to plumb the depths of personal identity (*ET* 194–6). For this reason Eva leaps to the postmodernist conclusion that the depths do not exist: there is nothing hidden underneath the surface, no inner life behind the mask. Pictures are at least as real as people.

Does the novelist endorse this vision? It is difficult to tell, partly because Bowen turns off the voice-over, depriving the reader of the guidance of the narrator. In *Eva Trout*, her last completed novel, written at the end of her life, Bowen tries to imagine a 'cinemato-graphic existence, with no soundtrack' – a wordless universe opposed to everything the novel represents. Pictures often pose a threat to words, and even to reality, in Bowen's work. In *The Death of the Heart*, the 'bad portrait' of Anna, like a trick mirror at the circus, disconcerts the viewer by revealing difference precisely where identity should be confirmed. 'No drawing from life just fails: it establishes something more; it admits the unadmitted.' What is more, the picture en-croaches on reality, usurping the original: 'Any face, house, land-scape seen in a picture, however bad, remains subtly but strongly modified in so-called real life – and the worse the picture, the stronger this is' (*DH* 207). Bad or good, the picture falsifies merely by surviving the ravages of time – 'it's here when the street is not' (*LG* 169).

Eva, on the contrary, maintains that pictures are as real as the scenes that they replace; that portraits are as real as people. But the final episode belies her two-dimensional conception of the world. When Eva learns that Henry loves her, she weeps for the first time in her life, thus revealing the existence of an inner spring of tears.

> Something took place: a bewildering, brilliant, blurring filling up, swimming and brimming over; then, not a torrent from the eyes but one, two, three, four tears, each hesitating, surprised to be where it was, then wandering down. The speediest splashed on to the diamond brooch. 'Look what is *happening* to me!' exulted Eva.
>
> (*ET* 266–7)

Here Henry's words succeed, where Iseult's failed, in endowing Eva with an inside, which she literally ex-presses in the form of tears. As soon as they appear, these tears become the crowning Kodak moment, splashing on Eva's brooch like diamonds upon diamonds. The effect is reminiscent of Man Ray's famous photograph of a stylish woman weeping one fat pearl. But as Henry observes, 'an unreal act collects round it real-er emotion that a real act, sometimes' (*ET* 261). Corny though they are, Eva's tears elicit real emotion in the reader, just as the creakiest machinery of melodrama can move an audience more deeply than footage of the grisliest atrocities. (This is a lesson Bowen learned from Dickens, the master of melodrama, whose study in Bleak House provides a meeting-place for Iseult and Eva. 'It took Dickens to not be eclipsed by Eva' (*ET* 114).)[26] In any case, it is crucial that Eva's tears are summoned from the depths by words of love. Blurring her vision, these tears mark the limits of Eva's 'visual universe,' and open up a world of love beyond the world of spectacle (*ET* 189).

A fine photograph of Bowen, taken in 1953, shows the author reading in a deckchair; in her hands is James Baldwin's *Go Tell It on the Mountain*; on her lap is *The Second Sex*, the book in which Simone de Beauvoir argues that a woman is not born but made. Eva Trout tries to make herself into a woman, faking engagement, motherhood, elopement, as if the masquerade of femininity could make her female, and integrate her into human life. But the last scene shows that gender is more than a performance. Eva must be loved in order to become a woman, or even to become a human being – a woman can be made, but not self-made. It is the desire of another that endows her with a sex, the language of another that endows her with a self. Yet if Eva is a Galatea, brought to life by love and language, her author kills her off at the very moment she is born. Her baptism of tears is immediately followed by the fatal shot – not a snapshot of the surface, but a fatal penetration of the depths. When Jeremy shoots Eva, he also shatters the delusion that a person is nothing but a picture. Eva has – or had – an inside after all.

In an essay on the art of novel-writing called 'The Roving Eye' (1952), Bowen writes: 'Concentration on any one writer's work almost always ends by exposing a core of naïvety – a core which, once it has been laid bare, seems either infantile or august' (*MT* 64–5). A simple soul, Eva Trout embodies both the infantile and the august. By killing Eva, Bowen may be murdering her own august naivety; the infantile core of her own writing; the pictorial imagination before it has been taught to speak. In contrast to the Romantic tradition, which depicts the power of imagination in the form of light and air, Bowen depicts this power in the form of Eva: a weight to be hauled up to the surface, heavy as the stones that Virginia Woolf loaded in her pockets when she drowned herself. 'You are dragging me up from the bottom of a lake, Miss Smith?' asks Eva. 'I am very heavy . . .' 'Sometimes you cling to being in deep water,' Iseult replies (*ET* 64–5). In Nietzschean terms, Iseult represents the Apollonian principle of form that drags the Dionysian principle of force out of the deep; in Kristevan terms, she stands for the 'symbolic' that articulates the pre-linguistic mur-mur of the 'semiotic.'[27]

At the beginning of the novel, we are told that Iseult's 'powers . . . transcended her; they filled her with awe and wonder . . . such as one may see in a young artist.' 'There was something of Nature before the Fall' about her 'state of grace' (*ET* 61). When Iseult meets Eva, grace meets gravity: for the rest of the narrative, these forces wrestle with each other, unable either to separate or to unite. Yet the novel suggests that this struggle galvanises the creative process: at the moment that Iseult is ready to assume her powers as an artist, she confronts the gigantic resistance of the inarticulate. In the figure of Eva, Bowen incarnates the imagination as a 'monstrous heiress': mute, faceless, leviathanic, mountainously rich. The artist cannot do without this monster, but draws her genius from its lunatic bulk. In a review essay called '*The Shadow*

Across the Page' (1937), Bowen argues that 'every artist adds year by year to a major unwritten work' (*CI* 136).[28] Eva Trout embodies that unwritten work: she represents the silence of the worlds that Bowen never lived to rescue from the deep.

Notes

1. Craig, *Elizabeth Bowen*, p. 135; Lee, *Elizabeth Bowen*, pp. 198, 203.
2. Bennett and Royle, *Elizabeth Bowen and the Dissolution of the Novel*, ch. 8, pp. 140–57, xiv.
3. John Coates, 'The Misfortunes of Eva Trout,' p. 78.
4. Mary Ellmann, 'Words, Words,' pp. 125–6.
5. See Coates, 'The Misfortunes of Eva Trout,' p. 61.
6. Jonathan Swift, *Gulliver's Travels*, ed. Paul Turner (Oxford: Oxford University Press, 1986), pt. III, ch. 5, pp. 184–5.
7. Spencer Curtis Brown, Foreword to Elizabeth Bowen, *PC* xxxviii; *ET* 225.
8. 'The Simple Soul,' dated Thursday 26 April 1960, Notes for lectures at Vassar College on the short story, HRHRC.
9. Mary Ellmann, 'Words, Words,' p. 124.
10. Lee, *Elizabeth Bowen*, p. 201.
11. *ET* 33; Mary Ellmann, 'Words, Words,' p. 124.
12. Lee, *Elizabeth Bowen*, p. 200.
13. Bowen, Preface to *Uncle Silas* (1947), *MT* 103.
14. Ibid., p. 101.
15. Bowen, '*Orlando*' (1960), *MT* 131–6.
16. Bowen writes: 'The change of sex took place in Constantinople . . .' (*MT* 134).
17. Quoted in Glendinning, *Elizabeth Bowen*, p. 102.
18. *PC* 15–19; *MT* 272–4.
19. *ET* 17, 179, 53. Commenting on *The House in Paris*, Bowen admitted that she could not always see her characters in their entirety: 'I can see all Henrietta except her *features*; Karen's figure, movements and ways but I don't know what kind of nose she had' (letter to A. E. Coppard, 31 August [1935], HRHRC).
20. Bowen, 'Truth and Fiction' (1956), *A* 134.
21. *ET* 49–55; See Freud, *Civilisation and its Discontents* (1930), SE, vol. 21, pp. 64–5, where Freud proposes that 'oceanic feeling' is the basis of religion.
22. *PC* 23; *MT* 276.
23. Bennett and Royle, *Elizabeth Bowen and the Dissolution of the Novel*, p. 155.
24. *ET* 33, 105, 218, 29, 57, 171, 208. Bennett and Royle discuss these references to fish and their relation to the instability of personal identity in *Elizabeth Bowen and the Dissolution of the Novel*, pp. 152–3.

25. John Coates makes this connection in 'The Misfortunes of Eva Trout,' p. 77.
26. Asked in an interview which writers had most influenced her, Bowen replied: 'Well, the influence nobody ever spots are the Dickens novels . . . That sounds an exaggerated thing to say, but it isn't. Those novels were read to me before I was able to read at all, and that romantic feeling for haunted places and those obsessed characters and that burlesque comedy . . .' Interview with Elizabeth Bowen by John Bowen, William Craig, W. N. Ewer, 11 September 1959, HRHRC.
27. See Friedrich Nietzsche, *The Birth of Tragedy*, trans. Douglas Smith (Oxford: Oxford University Press, 2000); Julia Kristeva, *Revolution in Poetic Language*, trans. Margaret Waller (New York: Columbia, 1986).
28. Elizabeth Bowen, review of *The Shadow Across the Page* by G. W. Stonier (1937), *CI* 136.

Selected Bibliography

Works by Elizabeth Bowen

Manuscript collections

Elizabeth Bowen letters to Isaiah Berlin, Berlin Archive, Wolfson College Oxford.

Elizabeth Bowen Collection, Harry Ransom Humanities Research Center, University of Texas at Austin.

'Notes on Eire,' Report to the Secretary of State for Foreign Affairs, 9 November 1940, The Foreign Office Papers (FO 800/310), Public Records Office, Kew, London.

Books

Encounters (London: Sidgwick and Jackson, 1923).

Ann Lee's and Other Stories (London: Sidgwick and Jackson, 1926).

The Hotel (1927; Harmondsworth: Penguin, 1943).

Joining Charles and Other Stories (1929; London: Cape, 1952).

The Last September (1929; Harmondsworth: Penguin, 1942).

Friends and Relations (1931; Harmondsworth: Penguin, 1943).

To the North (1932; Harmondsworth: Penguin, 1945).

The Cat Jumps and Other Stories (1934; London: Cape, 1949).

The House in Paris (1935), intro. A. S. Byatt (Harmondsworth: Penguin, 1976).

The Death of the Heart (1938; Harmondsworth: Penguin, 1962).

Look at All Those Roses (1941; London: Cape, 1951).

Bowen's Court (1942; reissued in 1964 with revised Afterword); in *Bowen's Court and Seven Winters*, ed. Hermione Lee (London: Virago, 1984).

English Novelists (1942; London: William Collins, 1945).

Seven Winters: Memories of a Dublin Childhood (1942), in *Bowen's Court and Seven Winters*, ed. Hermione Lee (London: Virago, 1984).

The Demon Lover and Other Stories (1945; London: Cape, 1952); published in the USA as *Ivy Gripped the Steps and Other Stories* (New York: Knopf, 1946).

Anthony Trollope: A New Judgement (London: Oxford University Press, 1946).

Collected Impressions (London: Longmans, Green, 1950).

Why do I Write? An Exchange of Views Between Elizabeth Bowen, Graham Greene, and V. S. Pritchett (London: Percival Marshall, 1948); reprinted in part in *MT*.

The Heat of the Day (1949; Harmondsworth: Penguin, 1962).

The Shelbourne: A Centre for Dublin Life for More than a Century (1951; London: Vintage, 2001).

A World of Love (1955; Harmondsworth: Penguin, 1983).

A Time in Rome (London: Longmans, Green, 1960).

Afterthought: Pieces about Writing (London: Longmans, Green, 1962).

The Little Girls (1964; Harmondsworth: Penguin, 1982).

A Day in the Dark and Other Stories (London: Cape, 1965).

The Good Tiger (London: Cape, 1965).

Eva Trout, or Changing Scenes (1968; Harmondsworth: Penguin, 1982).

Pictures and Conversations, Foreword by Curtis Brown (London: Allen Lane, 1975); reprinted in part in *MT*.

The Collected Stories of Elizabeth Bowen, intro. Angus Wilson (Harmondsworth: Penguin, 1983).

The Mulberry Tree: Writings of Elizabeth Bowen, ed. Hermione Lee (London: Virago, 1986).

'Notes on Eire': *Espionage Reports to Winston Churchill, 1940–2*, ed. Jack Lane and Brendan Clifford (Aubane: Aubane Historical Society, 1999).

Essays, prefaces, introductions, and reviews

Many of Bowen's most important essays are collected in *CI*, *A*, and *MT*. Below are uncollected short pieces consulted in addition to those previously cited in the footnotes.

'Advance in Formation,' review of *New Writing in Europe*, ed. John Lehmann *Spectator* 166 (17 January 1941) p. 65.

'Flaubert Translated,' *Spectator* 167 (15 August 1941) p. 161.

'Meet Elizabeth Bowen,' Interview with *The Bell* 4 (September 1942) pp. 420–6.

Introduction to *Pride and Prejudice* by Jane Austen (London: Williams and Norgate, 1948), pp. vii–xv.

'On Writing *The Heat of the Day*,' *Now and Then* 79 (Autumn 1949) p. 11.

'The Cult of Nostalgia,' *Listener* 46 (August 1951) pp. 225–6.

Preface to *Frost in May* by Antonia White (London: Eyre and Spottiswoode, 1957), pp. v–x.

Preface to *Critics Who Have Influenced Taste*, ed. A. P. Ryan (London: Geoffrey Bles, 1965) pp. vii–x.

'Ecstacy of the Eye,' *Vogue* (December 1968) pp. 189–90.

Introduction to *The House by the Church-Yard* by Sheridan Le Fanu (London: Anthony Blond, 1968), pp. vii–xi.

'A Passage to E. M. Forster,' in John Arlott, Elizabeth Bowen et al., *Aspects of E. M. Forster: Essays and Recollections Written for his Ninetieth Birthday*, (London: Edward Arnold, 1969), pp. 1–12.

Other works consulted

Abraham, Nicolas and Maria Torok, *The Wolf Man's Magic Word*, trans. Nicholas Rand (Minneapolis: University of Minnesota Press, 1986).

Abraham, Nicolas and Maria Torok, *The Shell and the Kernel*, trans. Nicholas Rand (Chicago: University of Chicago Press, 1994).

Ashworth, Ann, ' "But Why Was She Called Portia?" Judgment and Feeling in Bowen's *The Death of the Heart*,' *Critique: Studies in Modern Fiction* 28: 3 (1987) pp. 159–66.

Austin, Allan E., *Elizabeth Bowen* (1971; Boston: Twayne, 1969).

Barbeito, Manuel (ed.), *Feminism, Aesthetics and Subjectivity: Women and Culture in Early Twentieth Century British Literature* (Santiago de Compostela: Universidade de Santiago de Compostela Press, 2001).

Barthes, Roland, *Writing Degree Zero*, trans. Annette Lavers and Colin Smith (London: Cape, 1971).

Bayley, John, *The Short Story: Henry James to Elizabeth Bowen* (Brighton: Harvester, 1988).

Beauvoir, Simone de, *The Second Sex*, trans. H. M. Parshley (Harmondsworth: Penguin, 1972).

Beckett, J. C, *The Anglo-Irish Tradition* (1976; Belfast: Blackstaff Press, 1982).

Bence-Jones, Mark, *Twilight of the Ascendancy* (London: Constable, 1987).

Benjamin, Walter, 'The Work of Art in the Age of Mechanical Reproduction,' in *Illuminations*, trans. Harry Zohn, ed. Hannah Arendt (London: Fontana, 1973), pp. 219–53.

Benjamin, Walter, *The Arcades Project*, trans. Howard Eiland and Kevin McLaughlin (Cambridge, MA: Harvard University Press, 1999).

Bennett, Andrew and Nicholas Royle, *The Bowen Newsletter* 1–3 (1992–6).

Bennett, Andrew and Nicholas Royle, *Elizabeth Bowen and the Dissolution of the Novel: Still Lives* (Basingstoke: Macmillan, 1995).

Blodgett, Harriet, *Patterns of Reality: Elizabeth Bowen's Novels* (The Hague: Mouton, 1975).

Bloom, Harold (ed.), *Elizabeth Bowen* (New York: Chelsea House, 1987).

Borch-Jacobsen, Mikkel, *The Freudian Subject*, trans. Catherine Porter (Stanford: Stanford University Press, 1988).

Brooke, Jocelyn, *Elizabeth Bowen* (London: Longmans, Green/British Council, 1952).

Terence Brown, *Ireland: A Social and Cultural History, 1922–79* (London: Fontana, 1981).

Burkart, A. J. and S. Medlick, *Tourism Past, Present and Future* (1974; London: Heinemann, 1981).

Calder, Angus, *The People's War: Britain 1939–1945* (1969; London: Pimlico, 1992).

Caserio, Robert L, '*The Heat of the Day*: Modernism and Narrative in Paul de Man and Elizabeth Bowen,' *Modern Language Quarterly* 54: 2 (1993) pp. 263–84.

Chessman, Harriet S., 'Women and Language in the Fiction of Elizabeth Bowen,' *Twentieth Century Literature* 29 (Spring 1983) pp. 69–85; reprinted without footnotes in Harold Bloom (ed.), *Elizabeth Bowen*, pp. 123–38.

Coates, John, 'The Misfortunes of Eva Trout,' *Essays in Criticism* 47: 1 (1998) pp. 59–79.

Connolly, Claire. '(Be)longing – The Strange Place of Elizabeth Bowen's *Eva Trout*,' in Monika Reif-Hülser (ed.), *Borderlands: Negotiating Boundaries in Post-Colonial Writing* (Amsterdam: Rodopi, 1999), pp. 135–43.

Coughlan, Patricia, 'Women and Desire in the Work of Elizabeth Bowen,' in Éibhear Walshe (ed.), *Sex, Nation and Dissent in Irish Writing* (Cork: Cork University Press, 1997), pp. 103–34.

Craig, Patricia, *Elizabeth Bowen* (Harmondsworth: Penguin, 1986).

Cunningham, Valentine, 'The Age of Anxiety and Influence; or, Tradition and the Thirties Talent,' in Keith Williams and Steven Matthews (eds) *Rewriting the Thirties: Modernism and After* (London: Longman, 1997), pp. 5–22.

Czitrom, Daniel J, *Media and the American Mind: From Morse to McLuhan* (Chapel Hill: University of Carolina Press, 1982).

Deane, Seamus, *Celtic Revivals: Essays in Modern Irish Literature 1880–1980* (London: Faber, 1985).

Deane, Seamus, *A Short History of Irish Literature* (London: Hutchinson, 1986).

Deane, Seamus (ed.), *The Field Day Anthology of Irish Writing* (Derry: Field Day Publications, 1991).

Derrida, Jacques, *Spurs: Nietzsche's Styles*, trans. Barbara Harlow (Chicago: University of Chicago Press, 1979).

Derrida, Jacques, '*Fors*: The Anglish Words of Nicolas Abraham and Maria Torok,' trans. Barbara Johnson, Foreword to Nicolas Abraham and Maria Torok, *The Wolf Man's Magic Word*.

Derrida, Jacques, *Acts of Literature*, ed. Derek Attridge (New York: Routledge, 1992).

Douie, Vera, *Daughters of Britain: An Account of the Work of British Women during the Second World War* (Oxford: George Ronald, 1950).

Ellmann, Mary, *Thinking about Women* (New York: Harcourt, Brace and World, 1968).

Ellmann, Mary, 'Words, Words,' Review of *Eva Trout*, *Atlantic* 222 (November 1968) pp. 124–6.

Ellmann, Maud (ed.), *Psychoanalytic Literary Criticism* (London: Longman, 1994).

Fisk, Robert, *In Time of War: Ireland, Ulster and the Price of Neutrality 1939–45* (London: Andre Deutsch, 1983).

Foster, R. F., *Paddy and Mr Punch: Connections in Irish and English History* (Harmondsworth: Penguin, 1993).

Foster, R. F., *The Irish Story: Telling Tales and Making It Up in Ireland* (London: Allen Lane, 2001).

Freud, Sigmund, *The Complete Psychological Works of Sigmund Freud*, Standard Edition, trans. James Strachey, 24 vols (London: Hogarth, 1953–74).

Gauthier, Dominique, *L'Image du réel dans les romans d'Elizabeth Bowen* (Paris: Didier Erudidian, 1985).

Gibbons, Luke, *Transformations in Irish Culture* (Cork: Cork University Press, 1996).

Gibbs-Smith, Charles H., *Aviation: An Historical Survey from its Origins to the End of World War II* (London: Science Museum, 1985).

Girard, René, *Deceit, Desire, and the Novel: Self and Other in Literary Structure*, trans. Yvonne Freccero (Baltimore: Johns Hopkins University Press, 1972).

Girard, René, *Violence and the Sacred* (Baltimore: Johns Hopkins University Press, 1979).

Glendinning, Victoria, *Elizabeth Bowen: Portrait of a Writer* (1977; London: Orion, 1993).

Greene, Graham, Review of *The Death of the Heart*, *Spectator* 161 (7 October 1936) p. 578.

Grubgeld, Elizabeth, 'Cultural Autobiography and the Female Subject: The Genre of Patrilineal History and the Lifewriting of Elizabeth Bowen,' *Genre: Forms of Discourse and Culture* 27: 3 (Fall 1994) pp. 209–26.

Hall, James, *The Lunatic Giant in the Drawing Room: The British and American Novel Since 1930* (Bloomington: Indiana University Press, 1968).

Hanson, Clare, 'Little Girls and Large Women: Representations of the Female Body in Bowen's Later Fiction,' in Avril Horner and Angela Keane (eds), *Body Matters: Feminism, Textuality, Corporeality* (Manchester: Manchester University Press, 2000), pp. 185–98.

Harrisson, Tom, *Living through the Blitz* (1976; Harmondsworth: Penguin, 1978).

Heath, William, *Elizabeth Bowen: An Introduction to her Novels* (Madison: University of Wisconsin Press, 1961).

Henn, T. R., 'The Big House' (1967), in *Last Essays: Mainly on Anglo-Irish Literature* (New York: Harper and Row, 1976), pp. 207–20.

Hildebidle, John, *Five Irish Writers: The Errand of Keeping Alive* (Cambridge, MA: Harvard University Press, 1989).

Hoogland, Renée C., *Elizabeth Bowen: A Reputation in Writing* (New York: New York University Press, 1994).

Hopkins, Chris, 'Elizabeth Bowen,' *The Review of Contemporary Fiction* 21: 2 (Summer 2001) pp. 115–51.

Hughes, Douglas A., 'Cracks in the Psyche: Elizabeth Bowen's "Demon Lover,"' *Studies in Short Fiction* 10 (Fall 1973) pp. 411–13.

Jones, Ernest, 'The Psychology of Quislingism,' *International Journal of Psycho-Analysis* 22: 1 (January 1941) pp. 1–6.

Jones, Hester, 'Triumphant Obstination: Reading Adrienne Rich and Elizabeth Bowen,' in Philip Davis (ed.), *Real Voices: On Reading* (New York: St Martin's, 1997), pp. 103–21.

Jordan, Heather Bryant, 'The Territory of Elizabeth Bowen's Wartime Short Stories,' *The Library Chronicle of the University of Texas at Austin* 48 (1989) pp. 69–85.

Jordan, Heather Bryant, *How Will the Heart Endure: Elizabeth Bowen and the Landscape of War* (Ann Arbor: University of Michigan Press, 1992).

Kenney, Edwin J., *Elizabeth Bowen*, Irish Writers Series (Buckness: Bucknell University Press, 1975).

Kern, Stephen, *The Culture of Time and Space, 1880–1918* (Cambridge: Harvard University Press, 1983).

Kershner, R. B., Jr., 'Bowen's Oneiric *House in Paris*,' *Texas Studies in Literature and Language* 28: 4 (1986) pp. 407–23.

Kiberd, Declan. *Inventing Ireland: The Literature of the Modern Nation* (London: Jonathan Cape, 1995).

Kirby, Lynn, *Parallel Tracks: The Railroad and Silent Cinema* (Durham: Duke University Press, 1997).

Klein, Melanie, *Love, Guilt and Reparation and Other Works 1921–1945* (New York: Delta, 1977).

Klein, Melanie, *Envy and Gratitude and Other Works 1946–1963* (London: Virago, 1988).

Kreilkamp, Vera, *The Anglo-Irish Novel and the Big House* (Syracuse: Syracuse University Press, 1998).

Kristeva, Julia, *Revolution in Poetic Language*, trans. Margaret Waller (New York: Columbia, 1986).

Lacan, Jacques, *Ecrits: A Selection*, trans. Alan Sheridan (London: Tavistock, 1977).

Lacan, Jacques, 'Of Structure as an Inmixing of an Otherness Prerequisite to Any Subject Whatever,' in Richard Macksey and Eugenio Donato (eds), *The Languages of Criticism and the Sciences of Man: The Structuralist Controversy* (Baltimore: Johns Hopkins University Press, 1970), pp. 180–201.

Lacan, Jacques, *Feminine Sexuality: Jacques Lacan and the École Freudienne*, ed. Juliet Mitchell and Jacqueline Rose (London: Macmillan, 1982).

Lassner, Phyllis, *Elizabeth Bowen* (Basingstoke: Macmillan, 1990).

Lassner, Phyllis, *Elizabeth Bowen: A Study of the Short Fiction* (New York: Twayne Publishers, 1991).

Lassner, Phyllis, 'Resisting Romance: Popular Fiction of the Second World War,' *Women: A Cultural Review* 8: 1 (1997) pp. 12–32.

Lassner, Phyllis, *British Women Writers of World War II: Battlegrounds of Their Own* (London: Macmillan, 1998).

Lee, Hermione, *Virginia Woolf* (London: Vintage, 1997).

Lee, Hermoine, *Elizabeth Bowen*, revised edition (London: Vintage, 1999); originally published as *Elizabeth Bowen: An Estimation* (London: Vision Press; Totowa, NJ: Barnes and Noble, 1981).

Lenoir, Timothy (ed.), *Inscribing Science: Scientific Texts and the Materiality of Communication* (Stanford: Stanford University Press, 1998).

Levinas, Emmanuel, *Otherwise than Being or Beyond Essence*, trans. Alphonso Lingis (Dordrecht: Kluwer Academic Publishers, 1991).

Levinas, Emmanuel, *Entre Nous/on thinking-of-the-other*, trans. Michael B. Smith and Barbara Harshav (London: Athlone, 1998).

McCormack, W. J., *Dissolute Characters: Irish Literary History through Balzac, Sheridan Le Fanu, Yeats and Bowen* (Manchester: Manchester University Press, 1993).

McCormack, W. J., *From Burke to Beckett: Ascendancy, Tradition and Betrayal in Literary History*, revised edition (Cork: Cork University Press, 1994).

Mengham, Rod and N. H. Reeve (eds), *The Fiction of the 1940s: Stories of Survival* (Basingstoke: Palgrave, 2001).

Merleau-Ponty, Maurice, *The Visible and the Invisible*, trans. Alphonso Lingis (Evanston, IL: Northwestern University Press, 1968).

Miller, Kristine A., ' "Even a Shelter's Not Safe": The Blitz on Homes in Elizabeth Bowen's Wartime Writing,' *Twentieth-Century Literature* 45: 2 (Summer 1999) pp. 138–58.

Moynahan, Julian, 'Elizabeth Bowen: Anglo-Irish Postmortem,' *Raritan* 9: 2 (1989) pp. 68–97.

Moynahan, Julian, *Anglo-Irish: The Literary Imagination in a Hyphenated Culture* (Princeton: Princeton University Press, 1995).

Muller, John P. and William J. Richardson (eds), *The Purloined Poe: Lacan, Derrida, and Psychoanalytic Reading* (Baltimore: Johns Hopkins University Press, 1988).

O'Faolain, Sean, *The Vanishing Hero: Studies in Novelists of the Twenties* (London: Eyre and Spottiswoode, 1956).

Parsons, Deborah L., 'Souls Astray: Elizabeth Bowen's Landscape of War.' *Women: A Cultural Review* 8: 1 (Spring 1997) pp. 24–32.

Phillips, Adam, 'Bombs Away,' *History Workshop Journal* 45 (1998) pp. 183–98.

Piette, Adam, *Imagination at War: British Fiction and Poetry 1939–1945* (London: Macmillan, 1995).

Plain, Gill, *Women's Fiction of the Second World War: Gender, Power and Resistance* (Edinburgh: Edinburgh University Press, 1996).

Pool, Ithiel de Sola (ed.), *The Social Impact of the Telephone* (Cambridge, MA and London: MIT Press, 1977).

Radford, Jean, 'Late Modernism and the Politics of History,' in Maroula Joannou (ed.), *Women Writers of the 1930s: Gender, Politics and History* (Edinburgh: Edinburgh University Press, 1999), pp. 33–45.

Rau, Petra-Utta, *Moving Dangerously: Desire and Narrative Structure in the Fiction of Elizabeth Bowen, Rosamond Lehmann and Sylvia Townsend Warner*, PhD thesis, University of East Anglia, 2000.

Rauschbauer, Otto (ed.), *Ancestral Voices: The Big House in Anglo-Irish Literature* (Hildesheim: Olms, 1992).

Ritchie, Charles, *The Siren Years: Undiplomatic Diaries 1937–1945* (London: Macmillan, 1974).

Rose, Jacqueline, 'Daddy,' in Maud Ellmann (ed.), *Psychoanalytic Literary Criticism*, pp. 221–59.

Rose, Jacqueline, 'Bizarre Objects: Mary Butts and Elizabeth Bowen,' *Critical Quarterly* 42: 1 (2000) pp. 75–85.

Rossen, Janice, 'Running Away from Home: Perpetual Transit in Elizabeth Bowen's Novels,' in Rosemary M. Colt and Janice Rossen (eds), *Writers of the Old School: British Novelists of the 1930s* (London: Macmillan, 1992), pp. 103–19.

Royle, Nicholas, *E. M. Forster* (Plymouth: Northcote House/ British Council, 1999).

Schivelbusch, Wolfgang, *The Railway Journey: The Industrialization of Time and Space in the Nineteenth Century* (1977; Leamington Spa: Berg Publishers, 1986).

Schneider, Karen, *Loving Arms: British Women Writing the Second World War* (Lexington: University Press of Kentucky, 1997).

Sedgwick, Eve Kosofsky, *Between Men: English Literature and Male Homosocial Desire* (New York: Columbia, 1985).

Sekine, Masaru (ed.), *Irish Writers and Society at Large* (Gerrards Cross: Colin Smythe, 1985).

Sellery, Jonathan and William O. Harris, *Elizabeth Bowen: A Descriptive Bibliography* (1977; Austin: The University of Texas at Austin Press, 1981).

Sheridan, Dorothy (ed.), *Wartime Women: An Anthology of Women's Wartime Writing for Mass-Observation 1937–45* (London: Heinemann, 1990).

Siegert, Bernhard, 'Switchboards and Sex: The Nut(t) Case,' in Timothy Lenoir (ed.), *Inscribing Science: Scientific Texts and the Materiality of Communication*, pp. 78–90.

Siegert, Bernhard, *Relays: Literature as an Epoch of the Postal System*, trans. Kevin Repp (Stanford: Stanford University Press, 1999).

Sinfield, Alan, *Literature Politics and Culture in Postwar Britain* (London: Athlone Press, 1997).

233

Smith, Patricia Juliana, *Lesbian Panic: Homoeroticism in Modern British Women's Fiction* (Oxford: Oxford University Press, 2000).

Sokolsky, Anita, 'The Melancholy Persuasion,' in Maud Ellmann (ed.), *Psychoanalytic Literary Criticism*, pp. 128–42.

Stewart, Susan, *On Longing: Narratives of the Miniature, the Gigantic, the Souvenir, the Collection* (Baltimore: Johns Hopkins University Press, 1984).

Stonebridge, Lyndsey, 'Anxiety at a Time of Crisis,' *History Workshop Journal* 45 (1998) pp. 171–82.

Stonebridge, Lyndsey, 'Bombs and Roses: The Writing of Anxiety in Henry Green's *Caught*,' in Rod Mengham and N. H. Reeve, *The Fiction of the 1940s: Stories of Survival*, pp. 46–69.

Tillinghast, Richard, 'Elizabeth Bowen: the House, the Hotel and the Child,' *The New Criterion* 13: 4 (December 1994) pp. 24–33.

Trotter, David, *Cooking with Mud: The Idea of Mess in Nineteenth-Century Art and Fiction* (Oxford: Oxford University Press, 2000).

White, Terence de Vere, *The Anglo-Irish* (London: Gollancz, 1972).

Wyatt-Brown, Anne M., 'The Liberation of Mourning in Elizabeth Bowen's *The Little Girls* and *Eva Trout*,' in Anne M. Wyatt-Brown and Janice Rossen (eds), *Aging and Gender in Literature: Studies in Creativity* (Charlottesville and London: University of Virginia Press, 1993).

Young, Robert J. C., *Postcolonialism: An Historical Introduction* (Malden, MA: Blackwell, 2001).

Index